张小红博士1983年开始从事基础教育外语教学工作，曾获市外语优秀课大赛第一名、省外语优秀课大赛一等奖，荣获"市教书育人能手"、"市十大杰出青年"、"省优秀青年教师"、"全国中（小）学外语教师园丁奖"和"英语国家级骨干教师"等各种荣誉称号。2002年，她获得教育部国家公派留学资格，于2004-2005年在澳大利亚巴拉瑞特大学做访问学者，主要从事英语教育研究并获得了该大学颁发的"特别海外留学博士奖学金"。2006年底，赴澳攻读博士学位，经过几年的寒窗苦读，于2009年12月获得澳大利亚巴拉瑞特大学颁发的哲学博士学位。曾多次应邀参加西班牙、新加坡、马来西亚等地的国际学术会议，在国内外期刊上发表了数篇论文。2010年3月，作为高层次人才被福建工程学院引进，开始从事英语教学工作，主持并参与了部、厅社科类课题研究。2010年6月应邀注册了澳大利亚巴拉瑞特大学的博士生导师，曾数次被外刊邀请为论文评审专家，现为中国英语教学研究会会员。

全球化语境下的英语课程改革

张小红　著

EFL Curriculum Reform in the Context of Globalization

武汉大学出版社

图书在版编目(CIP)数据

全球化语境下的英语课程改革/张小红著.—武汉：武汉大学出版社，
2013.1

　ISBN 978-7-307-10259-0

　Ⅰ.全…　Ⅱ.张…　Ⅲ.英语课—课程改革—研究—中学
Ⅳ.G633.412

中国版本图书馆 CIP 数据核字(2012)第 264459 号

责任编辑:罗晓华　　　　责任校对:黄添生　　　　版式设计:韩闻锦

出版发行:**武汉大学出版社**　　(430072　武昌　珞珈山)
　　　　　(电子邮件:cbs22@whu.edu.cn　网址:www.wdp.com.cn)
印刷:武汉中远印务有限公司
开本:720×1000　　1/16　　印张:19.5　字数:357 千字　　插页:2
版次:2013 年 1 月第 1 版　　　2013 年 1 月第 1 次印刷
ISBN 978-7-307-10259-0/G·2637　　　定价:36.00 元

序

  本书以现象学和重构主义为方法论，通过一项个案研究，探索了英语课程改革与全球化之间的内在联系。以我国加入 WTO 和成功举办北京 2008 年奥运会这两个重大事件作为切入点，展现了我国政治、经济、文化、教育等方面的巨大变化和发展，探究了英语课程目标、大纲、教材与教学方法在课程发展过程中的重要作用。

  本书采用现象学的研究方法，选择东北地区城市和农村的 42 名中学英语教师为研究对象，开展了相关的实证研究，主要探究英语教师对国家相关政策、新课程改革的理解及其在具体贯彻实施新课程过程中的认知和实践。在分析方法上，引入了 van Manen（1990）的教育生活体验中的 four existentials，即 lived space，lived time，lived body 和 lived other，从人的心理的四个维度尝试性地描述和解读了英语教师的内心世界。

  该研究揭示了全球化背景下政治、经济、文化与教育之间的新型关系和现行英语课程改革的突出特色，探讨了影响教师贯彻实施课程改革的教育观念和教学态度，以及他们职业生活体验和专业化发展的重要因素。同时，该研究也分析了我国现行英语课程改革在实施过程中教师专业发展、教育资源分布等方面存在的问题与不足，为我国的英语教育改革研究，特别是英语课程改革方面的研究提供了基础研究资料和文献积累。

北京师范大学

王蔷教授

2012 年 11 月 7 日

Preface

In this book, Dr Zhang Xiaohong tells a remarkably detailed story of teachers working with a nationally significant curriculum reform inChina, that of English as a Foreign Language (EFL). In doing this, she has positioned the work of teachers within a larger context of national and international economic imperatives and social implications, basing her considerations on two important events: China's becoming a member of the World Trade Organization (WTO) in 2001and hosting the 2008 Olympic Games in Beijing. These events are in themselves evidence of challenges for English language education to improve English competence in Chinese secondary school students.

Working with classroom teachers, she has examined ways that their school, their town, their region and indeed their country is placed in relation to world events and issues. Eschewing broad brushstrokes in her telling of their stories, she has provided a fine-grained and detailed account of their lives as professionals engaging one of the biggest education reforms implemented in their country. The original idea to depict a unique English language teacher experience based on teacher knowledge of language and understandings of what it means to be knowledgeable Chinese citizens has been an inspired one.

The conversations that she has engaged have revolved around the more obvious features of day-to-day demands of the classroom: the resources available; the cohorts of students; advantaged or disadvantaged circumstances; and the development of important professional knowledge and understandings in teachers in relation to achieving what is demanded of them by the new curriculum. Through their words, Dr Zhang has enabled us to see how they have enthusiastically taken up the program for themselves, and the effectiveness of their endeavours. What she has also done, though, is made visible dimensions of the inequitable with which teachers are confronted.

We have not had a complete understanding of what underpins education successes or otherwise in relation to ways in which teachers have on individual professional levels worked through such issues. We encounter teachers who find themselves conflicted, and we see that they have had to resolve the problems for themselves, often with limited resources. With this research, we have been able to find out about the impact onthe teachers themselves of the EFL curriculum reform being implemented. We now have more to go on than our own assumptions about differences in school locations in a country, and even in a region, with careful and detailed research to confirm what we might have thought, but could not actually prove, about the program's educational success or otherwise. Dr Zhang's research has provided insights to participants' experiences that have deepened our own understandings of what it means for teachers to implement curriculum reform of this magnitude.

Dr Zhang is a well respected scholar with a strong track record of rigorous research publications and extensive and intensive foci on her specialist area. With this book she continues to build on that record, capitalizing on the important research that is reported in her PhD thesis to contribute to the world's store of knowledge in her field. This book has the potential for having a powerful influence, as it shows that a detailed consideration of ways in which curriculum reform impacts on teachers' experiences of it adds something very special to curriculum debates. It shows the importance of rich learning experiences for language teachers that goes beyond an administrative or management view of it. It shows the importance of an active and productive leadership in the implementation of curriculum reform that engages the details of teacher professional life. Readers of this book are presented with the opportunity to view curriculum positioned within a larger view of education informed by social and economic national and international developments, and with this research, will be able to engage the unique aspects of this curriculum reform as underpinning the success that is anticipated in China.

Margaret Zeegers (PhD)

Associate Professor

School of Education and Arts

University of Ballarat

Victoria

Australia

Foreword

I have used the name "EFL Curriculum Refom in the Context of Globalization" in relation to my study of English as a Foreign Language (EFL) curriculum reform as I have linked economic, political and social developments of the late 20th and early 21st centuries in China with education developments that have occurred at the same time as the reform has been implemented. The EFL curriculum reform that I have researched is based on a program of considerable investigation and preparation designed on the basis of a balance between English language teaching and learning, curriculum, economic development and globalization. I have argued that implementing the current EFL curriculum reform is both a necessary process and a challenge for this country in the context of globalization, evidenced by China's becoming a member of the World Trade Organization (WTO) in 2001 and hosting the 2008 Olympic Games. Such phenomena have posed challenges for English language education as it has shifted its focus from traditional to modern EFL curriculum design to improve English competence in the current cohort of Chinese secondary school students.

My focus is on current EFL curriculum reform in secondary schools in a single province—Liaoning Province, in Northeast China. I have explored ways in which the current EFL curriculum reform in China has played out in a number of secondary schools as China seeks a new balance between the curriculum and the country's social, economic, political and cultural development. Shortcomings in EFL curriculum identified by Chinese political and education authorities in 1993 have been addressed in relation to pressures exerted on its economy under globalization forces since it opened its doors to a globalizing world, which has in turn influenced English language education. Since the goal of the latest EFL curriculum reform is in line with moves towards quality rather than quantity in schools' approach to teaching and learning, this reform embraces concepts and strategies of quality education, enhancing students' comprehensive English language competence. I have discussed these concepts and strategies from a Reconstructionist perspective.

In this book I have drawn on a number of works, particularly as those relate to Phenomenology, to which I have turned as a theoretical perspective to underpin my research. Phenomenology has allowed me to enter participant EFL teachers' inner worlds to gain an in-depth understanding of their lived experience, enabling me to understand its meaning for teachers as they implement the reform under study. This is of some importance as I have been able to approach my research questions by means of these EFL teachers' perspectives, attitudes, feelings, and reflections on their professional experience in relation to the reform. My research has focused on an investigation of EFL teachers' experiences as part of generating an understanding of the relationship between the reform and globalization.

I anticipate that this book will contribute to the research literature on English language education in general. I further anticipate that it will contribute to the research literature on the possibilities suggested by influences of globalization as part of major EFL curriculum reform in China. Part of this contribution may be anticipated as feeding into education debates and professional discussions on the implementation of the current EFL curriculum reform in Chinese secondary schools, in Northeast China in particular, as I have identified changes that have occurred in secondary schools by examining processes of EFL curriculum reform and EFL teachers' perception and attitudes towards change. The implications of this sort of debate are not inconsiderable given the enormous nature of the task of implementation of the reform of such dimensions.

Contents

Chapter 1
Setting the Scene

1.1 Introduction

My research is a study of English as a Foreign Language (EFL) curriculum reform in an area of Northeast China, given its magnitude in the face of influences within a globalizing world and China's increasingly prominent positioning of itself in the world economy. I am interested in studying the current EFL curriculum reform in secondary schools because of my lengthy personal experience in this field, firstly as a secondary school teacher of English in Northeast China, secondly as a teacher ranked at the top of the Chinese national teacher levels, and then as a visiting scholar in Australia. These experiences have brought me into contact with related curricula in different areas and in different countries, which have prompted me to reflect in systematic and orchestrated ways on the current EFL curriculum reform in China. As van Manen (1990) argues, a researcher's own experience may accommodate the research with hints for linking oneself to the research problem as well as to all the other stages of the research (p. 40).

In 2001, I became more aware of issues concerning the reform and its relationship with globalization. It was the time that I, ranked as a top EFL teacher in a secondary school in Northeast China, undertook a national level teacher training program in Fujian Normal University. This national training program aims to equip leading EFL teachers with contemporary education ideas and enable them to understand the significance of this reform. Further, the expectation is that these EFL teachers will sow the seeds of the reform and spread new education ideas to guide others in implementing the new curriculum reform in their respective provinces, cities and counties (Ministry of Education, 2000).

Experiencing the three-month national training as well as engaging in one year's research into practice in Northeast China, I gradually became aware of the purpose of the current EFL curriculum reform in secondary schools, the ways in which it has been implemented and what changes it has brought about. There were still some issues which I considered to be problematic in relation to teaching practice. Implementation of the reform under study has given rise to a growing concern about it, reported in the research literature (Hu, 2002b, 2005b; Jin & Cortazzi, 2002; Lam, 2002; Wang, 2007), a growing concern which I have addressed in my research.

Modernizing curricula to meet challenges of globalization has featured prominently in recent education reforms in a number of countries (Moyles & Hargreaves, 1998; Wang, 2007; Yonezawa, 2003; Zhong, 2006). Modernization of curricula is an issue that has become a focus of China's education system, particularly in English language education (Zhang & Zhong, 2003). I have proceeded on the basis of innovation in curriculum signaling new relationships between politics, economics, education and language teaching in the context of globalization. These are issues that I have explored in my research.

1.2   Research Questions

My research project has been designed to explore ways in which the current EFL curriculum reform in Chinese secondary schools is linked to globalization, and this has become the main question of my research:

In what ways is the current EFL curriculum reform in Chinese secondary schools linked to globalization?

In order to investigate the research question in detail and keep the research process focused, I have determined the necessity of identifying teacher understandings of policy, curriculum and their own professional practice in relation to these. To this end, I have developed subsidiary questions, one of which is:

In what ways has the current EFL curriculum reform in Chinese secondary schools developed?

According to Huang (2004), curriculum is dynamic; the current curriculum reform is an on-going process as China seeks a new balance between the curriculum and the country's social, economic, political and cultural development. China's increasingly important status on the global stage has highlighted the significant role of English in this country in this context (Fong, 2009). I have suggested that the processes involved in developing the role of English in China may be indicators of effects of globalization, taking the position that this needs to be established by investigation.

Consideration of such issues has enabled me to engage in an evaluation of ways in which the reform under study has contributed to English language education in the area of China under investigation.

I have developed these questions to focus on considerations of the most significant factors related to my research. My key question regarding ways in which the current EFL curriculum reform in Chinese secondary schools may be seen as a response to globalization has guided my research. The subsidiary questions have also provided guidance regarding ways in which the reform has developed and ways in which it may be constructed.

The reform under study has become the subject of increasing interest for researchers and educators (Zhang & Zhong, 2003). I have considered that one issue that needs to be clarified in this research is that of the different terms used in the literature to describe English language teaching and learning. English as a Foreign Language (EFL), for example, is "the English that people learn for eventual social, educational or professional gain, not necessarily widely used in the community in which it is being studied" (Brandt, 2000, p. 10). English as a Second Language (ESL) is the English learned when people who come from non-native English speaking countries find themselves having mostly to use English (Lock, 1986). English Language Teaching (ELT) focuses on studying ways in which to teach the English language to EFL or ESL learners. I have drawn upon the term EFL as it accords with the curriculum offered to English language learners in the Chinese context. Nevertheless, aspects of ESL and ELT are included in the English language education programs in China, as Hu (2005b) argues. These are issues that I have explored in the following sections.

1.3 Traditional Approaches

Since English language has become a global language (Nunan, 2003), this has influenced English Language teaching and learning (Warschauer, 2000). This influence has occurred more impressively in China than in other parts of the world as a result of "integrating with the world economy at a breath-taking pace" (Xu & Warschauer, 2004, p. 301). Increasing industrial, economic and multicultural development has spurred language educators in China to question the EFL curricula on which their work has been based, particularly those in secondary schools, which my research has highlighted.

English language teaching and learning in secondary schools has traditionally pursued examination-oriented education, which has been designed to cater for the demands of college entrance examinations in China (Hu, 2002b). College entrance examinations have traditionally tested students' textbook knowledge, largely ignoring the testing of students' abilities in using and creating language knowledge (He, 2002; Lam, 2002). Research into this sort of testing indicates that the students taking college entrance examinations and similar tests in English language are required to have more competence in Reading and Writing than in Speaking and Listening (Wang & Robertson, 2004). The literature indicates that knowledge of grammar and language points in relation to college entrance examinations have been addressed in detail in curricula and by English teachers in their classroom teaching, while students have been concerned with completing grammar and translation exercises as well as keeping notes (Zheng & Adamson, 2003). The literature further points to a lack of meaningful or interactive activities having taken place between teachers and students (Zheng & Adamson, 2003). What has happened is that students have not developed sufficiently competent or proficient levels of English language use and usage to meet the emerging challenges of globalization, a situation which has given rise to the project of modernizing the EFL curriculum across the country (Hu, 2002b; Zhu, 2003). At this point it is necessary to give some consideration to more detailed historical features that provide important contextual aspects for my research.

1.4   Background to the Research

Although China has experienced a number of reforms in EFL teaching and learning since the late 1970s, and considerable efforts have been made in regard to improving outcomes of college entrance examinations, research indicates that examination-oriented education programs still figure in major ways in EFL curricula (Hu, 2002b, 2005b). Traditional teacher-centred methods emphasize the role of teachers in class while grammar-translation method promotes "rote memorising, heavy grammar instruction and vocabulary explanation", the very things that Confucian educational ideas advocate (Jin & Cortazzi, 2002, p. 136). These sorts of traditional teaching methods do not position students as the main stakeholders of education, and they also ignore improving students' comprehensive language competence (Zhan, 2008). Teacher-centred approaches and grammar-translation methods are now considered outmoded approaches, approaches which restrict students' development in using language to the extent that they are unable to meet the emerging demands of China's rapid economic and social development (Wang, 2007).

Having experienced this form of teaching and learning in EFL, Chinese students have found it difficult to communicate with native English speakers, even though they hold College English Test Band 4 (CET-4) certificates which represent higher levels of English proficiency in China than those of secondary school graduates (Jin & Cortazzi, 2002). These same students are dissatisfied with their current levels of competence in using the English language, having expected to have had greater English proficiency at these levels of accreditation than they indeed have (Zhu, 2003). According to Mak and White (1996), an increasing number of Chinese students who have traveled abroad for further studies at secondary or tertiary levels have limited proficiency in English. These students have found it more difficult to accustom themselves to the norms of overseas classrooms, especially in relation to interactions between staff and students in the English language in Reading, Writing, Speaking and Listening (the four macro skills of any basic EFL course) (Hu, 2005c). English proficiency skills have not been as well developed in China as they could have been.

This situation was identified as a shortcoming by Chinese political and education authorities in 1993 as far as that EFL curriculum was concerned, a shortcoming to be addressed by EFL curriculum reform in secondary schools in 2001 (Adamson & Morris, 1997; Hu, 2005b; Wang, 2007). While the reform of 1993 had an appropriate focus on English language communication as part of independent student learning to deliver "quality education" (Adamson & Morris, 1997; Hu, 2005b; Jin & Cortazzi, 2002), the programs that it put in place did not achieve the expected goals. The reform lacked effective policies, sufficient resources and corresponding training in appropriate teaching and learning approaches (Adamson & Morris, 1997; Hu, 2005a), so that it had little chance of achieving what it had set out to do. It was evident by the turn of the 20th century that EFL curriculum reform needed to be developed further than in 1993 in order to enhance students' competences in using the English language in the 21st century (Hu, 2002b, 2005b; Li, 2007; Smith, 2007; Wang, 2007).

Such issues have prompted academics and government education officials to question EFL curriculum in China further, particularly in relation to secondary schools (Hu, 2005b; Wu, 2001). As Zhong (2006) argues, the curriculum had lost its significance and function: the teaching and learning designed around the curriculum had come to seem meaningless, and the existing EFL curriculum had not been able to meet the needs of the country's rapid economic, social, scientific and technologic developments (Qin, 1999, cited in Wu, 2001), driving a demand for further reform of EFL curriculum in secondary schools. It has been argued that such reform should be designed to respond to increased demand for improved English language teaching and learning in the context of globalization (Hu, 2005c), a point which I will address in more detail in Chapter 2.

The pressures of globalization means that English language teaching and learning continues to play a significant role in China (He, 2002; Jin & Cortazzi, 2002). Hu (2003) argues that English has increasingly gained priority over other subjects and disciplines in China in the last two decades, and that this has occurred because English is seen as a valuable resource for promoting modernization for the country as a whole, while students perceive it as integral to ensuring their personal well-being in their own futures. There has been an unprecedented demand for English language competence development and this has influenced education reform in this area (Hu, 2002b, 2005c; Wang & Robertson, 2004). EFL curriculum reform in China has been focused on making basic changes to support new institutions and systems, rather than hold on to traditional ones and rely on adjustments and amendments as suggested by Klein (1994). Contemporary EFL education reform efforts have been associated with new ways of thinking about reconstruction of curricula in the context of demands of globalization on the country (Xu & Warschauer, 2004). The aim has been to cater for new demands emerging from international education markets which China now confronts. Two significant events in China's economic history have been its entry into the World Trade Organization (WTO) in 2001 and its hosting of the 2008 Beijing Olympic Games, both of which have drawn world attention (Adamson, 2004; He, 2002; Lam, 2005). I have argued that these two events have become catalysts for accelerating the implementation of this latest EFL curriculum reform, which I will discuss in more detail in the following section.

WTO and Beijing 2008 Olympic Games

The WTO is the largest economic organization in the world, which integrates trade and business among its members as the single authorized and institutional infrastructure of global economic systems (Wang & Robertson, 2004). China's entry into the WTO has been designed to result in "openness, competitiveness and innovativeness in the business, legal, and other sectors of the People's Republic of China (PRC) developing economy" (Pang, Zhou & Fu, 2002, p. 201). Entry into the WTO is instrumental, as far as China is concerned, in meeting the challenges of and assuring success in the global marketplace (Wang & Robertson, 2004).

Since the late 1970s, China has become a major player in economic competition within a globalizing world (Asia Society Business Roundtable Council of Chief State School Officers, 2005). Entry into the WTO has produced a more open market for more foreign technology, services and materials, including education services. As Wang and Robertson (2004) put it, this integration spurs education in China to accommodate more human resources needs in order to establish fundamental commercial capacities. Being a member of the WTO has posed challenges for English language education, with particular focus on modernizing EFL curriculum to improve English proficiency.

Since English is an essential and prominent factor influencing processes of reform and modernization on a global stage (Gil, 2005), the Chinese have turned to

English proficiency in its people as an indispensable instrument for interaction with foreign countries in business and economics in the context of globalization (Hu, 2007; Wang & Robertson, 2004). English proficiency has, accordingly, become the focus of education reform. The 2008 Olympic Games were held in Beijing, a stimulus to the concept of general English proficiency among Chinese people (Hu, 2005b). As Jin and Cortazzi (2002) argue, English would be pivotal in 2008 in welcoming foreign visitors. English proficiency is not only of importance to students and young adults, it is a desirable proficiency that has been extended to all ages and occupations (Jin & Cortazzi, 2002). As Kang (1999) suggests, English has never before had such a significant status in China, arguing that this language will continue to play a paramount role in China because of 21st century globalization pressures. It is a significant factor of the background of the EFL curriculum reform currently being implemented.

China has demonstrated its capacity to participate successfully in international affairs, particularly shown in the entry into the WTO and hosting the Beijing 2008 Olympic Games, with its successes in here providing new challenges for the country to confront. A reformed EFL curriculum has emerged (Xu & Warschauer, 2004), linking English language education with world contexts (Wang & Robertson, 2004). This is also in line with Hargreaves' (1997) statement:

> More than ever today, schools cannot shut their gates and leave the troubles of the outside world on the doorstep. Schools can no longer pretend that their walls will keep the outside world at bay (p.5).

Drawing on this perspective, I have positioned EFL curriculum reform in the context of globalization; I have not examined it as an education phenomenon isolated and disconnected from its wider social context.

1.5 Purpose of the Research

My research focuses on the implementation of the current EFL curriculum reform which was introduced to secondary schools in China in 2001. Curriculum reform is concerned with "an updating of content, the selection of a new text, or a revised curriculum emphasizing new or additional skills and knowledge" (Klein, 1994, p. 19). Reformed and reforming curricula is a common way of improving student skills, as well as developing intelligence and creativity (Demidenko, 2007). Curriculum is expected to engage challenges of social and economic development, and to develop students' present and future intellectual and academic competence as it provides the necessary cultural foundations for this to occur (Zhong, 2006). According to Klein (1994), curriculum reform specifies what has to be changed. This may be done as follows:

> First, some possible reasons are suggested why the status quo is so persistent, then some alternatives in curriculum design are identified from the curriculum literature which would change the status quo, and finally, some fundamental changes are identified which must occur if curriculum reform is to become a reality (Klein, 1994, p. 20).

I have examined the current situation of EFL curriculum in secondary schools in Northeast China as it presents in the teaching and learning conducted in these schools. I have also investigated the rationale for modernizing EFL curricula as response to issues that have emerged in the context of globalization. To this end, I have examined relationships between politics, economics, and education in general and English language education in particular by analysing relevant documents such as government policies, curriculum statements, and EFL teachers' perceptions and attitudes.

In doing so, I have foregrounded processes involved in the reconstruction of EFL curriculum. I have also surveyed EFL teachers' understandings and evaluations of this reform in relation to their professional practice. I have done this through an analysis of a completed questionnaire and transcripts of taped interviews with teachers, which have enabled me to focus on EFL teachers' beliefs, perceptions and attitudes as they pertain to this reform. In particular, given the ascendancy of English language, I have examined teacher perceptions of the potential of the EFL curriculum reform to position Chinese EFL curriculum reform in the context of globalization as it presents in China.

1.6　The Significance of the Research

Although political and economic development in China has increasingly attracted international attention over the last two decades, a review of the research literature suggests that little of that attention has been directed to studies of education reform, particularly as this relates to English language education (Xu & Warschauer, 2004). Research that has been conducted in this area has focused on overviews of EFL curriculum reform, and not addressed in detail (He, 2002; Hu, 2003, 2005b, 2005c; Jin & Cortazzi, 2002). The research literature indicates little empirical research on this reform as it has been carried out in regional contexts, such as that of Northeast China. Even less has focused on the current EFL reform in Chinese secondary schools from a perspective of Reconstructionism. The research that I have examined focus on new and constantly evolving and developing relationships between globalization and this curriculum reform. My research has taken up such issues on a number of levels of significance which will be detailed below.

Firstly, my research explores the influences of globalization as part of major EFL curriculum reform in China. My work provides a timely analysis of new relationships between politics, economics, culture and education that include this shift in EFL curriculum, given China's entry into the WTO as it embraces processes of globalization and what this entails. Traditional language education ideas are deeply rooted in educational practitioners' consciousness in China (Modiano, 2000), and my research investigates ways in which these practitioners accept new education ideas.

Secondly, my research may influence the implementation of the current EFL curriculum reform in Chinese secondary schools, in Northeast China in particular. I have identified changes that have occurred in secondary schools by examining processes of EFL curriculum reform and EFL teachers' perceptions and attitudes towards change. In doing so, I have discovered fertile grounds for further scholarly research. My research, then, may feed into current debates and professional conversations at government, bureaucratic and school levels on particularly salient features and intent of the EFL curriculum reform as it applies in the schools themselves.

1.7　The Structure of the Book

In Chapter 1, I have first explained the reasons for taking up this research with a brief description of my personal experience. I have then introduced the research questions and the purpose of the research, discussing the significance of the research and its potential as contributing to knowledge, and giving a brief outline of my research project.

I will present a review of the research literature on globalization, economic and political as well as education development in the Chinese context, and the role of English and English language education in China in Chapter 2. I will review the literature on research undertaken on the issues that I will outline to date, and this enables me to position my research within the existing body of research literature.

In Chapter 3, I will discuss curriculum and curriculum reform to include concepts of curriculum, curriculum development and curriculum implementation. I will also explore language pedagogy in relation to EFL curriculum reform, including an examination of teaching and learning approaches based on sociocultural perspectives and task-based learning.

I will describe my methodological approach in Chapter 4, outlining my theoretical stance and my rationale for adopting a qualitative approach. I will particularly highlight Phenomenology as a theoretical perspective to inform the conduct of my research, and Reconstructionism as a theoretical perspective to underpin my considerations of curriculum and EFL curriculum reform in China. I will also discuss issues of trustworthiness in that chapter.

In Chapter 5, I will illustrate the research method that I have used, that of case study method. In that chapter I will discuss my rationale for case selection, my strategies for data collection, and the conceptual tools used for data analysis as well as ethics considerations.

I will engage data analysis from Chapters 6 to 9, that data having been collected from school sites in two contrasting regions in Northeast China, and from relevant policy and curriculum documents. A number of themes have emerged from the data, and I will discuss them under the headings of lived space, lived other and lived time, based on van Manen's (1990) concept of lifeworld existentials. I will do this as part of Phenomenological constructs that have informed the conduct of my research.

In Chapter 6, I will present the analysis of the data from policy statements and curriculum documents, teasing out the features and intent of the new EFL curriculum. In Chapter 7, I will present the data from a questionnaire which addresses participant EFL teachers' lived experience. From Chapters 8 to 10, I will present the analysis of data from interviews with participant EFL teachers. In Chapter 8, I will discuss the data in relation to the theme of lived space. In Chapter 9, I will discuss the data in relation to the theme of lived other discussing stakeholders in this reform as students, parents, principals and governments. In relation to the theme of lived time presented in Chapter 10, I will focus on temporal ways of teachers' lived experience of the reform under study.

In the final chapter of this book, Chapter 11, I will discuss my research outcomes and issues to be faced as well as suggestions for further study within Fullan's (2007) ten elements of successful change in relation to my research questions from Reconstructionist perspectives. In the following chapter I will present my review of the research literature.

Chapter 2
Globalization and China's Development

2.1 Introduction

My research focuses on ways in which the EFL curriculum reform currently being implemented in Chinese secondary schools is linked to globalization. In this chapter I will present a review of literature which pertains to the development of that reform. To this end, I have reviewed the literature on globalization and extended my discussion of it to economic, political, cultural and education domains, particularly in relation to the influences of globalization on these in the Chinese context. I have also examined the literature in relation to the role of English and English language teaching and learning in China in the context of globalization.

A review of the literature shows an increasing emphasis on research into English language teaching and learning in China the 1990s (He, 2002; Hu, 2005b; Luo, 2007; Mak & White, 1996). Common issues that have been raised in such studies are policy changes (Hu, 2005b; Lam, 2002, 2005; Wang, 2007); the status of English in China (Adamson, Bolton, Lam, & Tong, 2002; Jin & Cortazzi, 2002; Kang, 1999; Nunan, 2003); professional development of EFL teachers (Lamie, 2006; Ran, 2001; Zhan, 2008; Zheng & Adamson, 2003); and pedagogy and strategies of EFL teaching and learning (Hu, 2005a; Savignon, Savignon, & Wang, 2003; Wang & Bergquist, 2003; Zheng & Adamson, 2003; Zheng & Davison, 2008). Despite this sort of mounting interest, my review of the literature indicates that there is little scholarly research on ongoing EFL curriculum reform in Chinese secondary schools, particularly in Northeast China. There is also a lack of attention in the literature in relation to this reform from a Reconstructionist perspective, with a similar lack of empirical studies of possible relationships between globalization and the development of the reform under study. While a number of scholars have referred to the importance of China's entry into the WTO and hosting the Beijing 2008 Olympic Games (Luo, 2007; Zheng & Adamson, 2003; Zheng & Davison, 2008), the literature shows a lack of research that would specifically link these two events and the major EFL curriculum reform that I have studied. I will detail these issues below.

2.2　Globalization

The concept of globalization has drawn scholars' attention since 1990s (Altman, 1999; Block & Cameron, 2002; Giddens, 1990; Held, Anthony, Goldblatt, & Jonathan, 1999; Kubota, 2002; Robertson, 1992; Robertson & Scholte, 2007), with no real agreement on its meaning (Cheng, 2004; Robertson & Scholte, 2007), but globalization can be generally comprehended as reworking space and time in the face of increasing international flows in goods, business and human resources (Stromquist, 2002). The literature does make the point that the processes of globalization are ongoing and not yet complete (Giddens, 1990; Harris, Leung, & Rampton, 2002; Held, et al., 1999; Robertson, 1992), as these processes forge interdependence and interconnection across national boundaries, at the same time as local changes are wrought (Altman, 1999; Block & Cameron, 2002; Giddens, 1990; Held, et al., 1999; Kubota, 2002; Robertson, 1992). Robertson (1995) contends that globalization is the integration or interconnection between the global and the local. Globalization "has infused the ever-present need to learn about each other with an urgency and emphasis like no other in history" (Arnove, 1999, cited in Crossley, 2000, p.319).

　　Globalization, then, is a complex phenomenon which has been linked in the literature to a number of profound social, political, cultural and economic changes (Altman, 1999; Ngok & Kwong, 2003; Okano, 2006; Robert, 2005; Waylen, 2004). Held (1995) points out that globalization challenges not only development within the world's economies but also a range of developments in law, political decision-making and cultural traditions. In similar vein, Okano (2006) contends that globalization is responsible for increasing and improving movements between nations with regard to culture, economy, education, and a number of other domains. The literature suggests these as key factors to be considered in relation to globalization (Altman, 1999; Lo Bianco, 2000; Robert, 2005; Robertson, 1992; Waters, 1995), and these are the factors on which I have concentrated.

A number of scholars see globalization as a trend (Chase-Dunn, 1999; Chase-Dunn & Babones, 2006; Enderwick, 2006); others see it as a transformation (Bartelson, 2000; Held & McGrew, 2002; Mittelman, 2000). Still others see it as a movement (Rondinelli & Heffron, 2007), and similar such phenomena (Carnoy, 2000; Robertson, 1992, 1995; Robertson & Scholte, 2007). Enderwick's (2006) view of globalization is that it is a trend moving the world's countries towards a single, integrated and interdependent unit. Rondinelli and Cheema (2003, cited in Rondinelli & Heffron, 2007) state that globalization is "the movement toward greater interaction, integration, and interdependence among people and organizations across national borders" (p. 1). Although there is no agreement in the literature on the concept of globalization itself (Bartelson, 2000), there is a common perception that globalization is a phenomenon that allows interrelation and association across national boundaries resulting in local transformation through cooperation or communication (Carnoy, 2000; Robertson, 1992, 1995; Robertson & Scholte, 2007). The literature tells me that globalization is an intense form of international relationships forged between countries and their governments, as well as those countries' and governments' ecological, social, political, cultural and education movements, be they official or unofficial in status. The literature suggests that the complexities of the sorts of interrelationships forged under the umbrella concept of globalization has generated a number of tensions out of expectations raised by the possibilities that globalization offers to governments and government agencies as they negotiate its parameters. I have drawn on such common perceptions of globalization to inform my research.

I have approached the idea of globalization in my research as a phenomenon which has spread throughout the world in a number of domains, including education, influencing international, national and local configurations, with changes such as Chinese EFL curriculum reforms initiated to cope with its requirements. As Dale (1999, cited in Ngok & Kwong, 2003) argues, globalization is "a set of new ideas, rules and practices that may affect education policy-making" (p. 162), as educational adaptations are made to new contexts. According to Scholte (2003), the concept of globalization provides researchers with an analytical tool for obtaining an understanding of relevant social, political, economic or cultural changes as they occur in the contemporary world, and education changes in particular. Such is the context for my research.

As a number of scholars (Angus, 2004; Chang, 2006; Giddens, 1990; Khan, 2004) argue, globalization is an irresistible force that researchers may explore as a contemporary phenomenon on a world stage. I have drawn on this work to develop a better understanding of the EFL curriculum reform, which my research has focused on, by situating it in broader, indeed global, political and economic as well as cultural and education contexts than a study isolated from such considerations allows for, so that globalization and the reform under study are assumed in my research to be closely related. I will discuss the interrelatedness of these aspects below.

2.2.1 Economics

The literature shows economists representing globalization as a new type of world economic system through the activities of corporations and organizations across the world (Chase-Dunn, 1999; Kellner, 2002; Turner, 2000; Waters, 1995). Warschauer (2000) argues that globalization is a new economic order that has taken the place of past ones, based on global manufacturing, management, and production and consumption. Enderwick (2006) states that globalization is "a process of growing internationalization of economic activity resulting in high levels of interdependency between countries and markets" (p. 6). Both of these scholars acknowledge the significant role of economics in relation to globalization.

In Waters' (1995) view, countries' economies are dominated by international cooperation and organizational practices that have turned the world into "a single market for commodities, labor and capital" (p. 51). Economics encompasses a number of dimensions such as those of the market, of capital, of labor, of production, and of commodities. Labor is one of main components of these (Enderwick, 2006; Lee, 1997), being the activities engaged by workers in relation to the process of promoting "economic growth and accumulation" (Benería, 1981, p. 25). Labor forces have conventionally been defined as workers who engage in these activities in relation to that process (Beneria, 1981), but who, under the influence of globalization, have become more commodified. My research is in relation to the current EFL curriculum reform in Chinese secondary schools which focuses on promoting student development. Students are represented as future labor forces, as suggested by Steinberg, Greenberger, Garduque and McAuliffe (1982). I have taken up the education and training of labor forces that are becoming increasingly commodified in relation to economic demands within globalization as one of the issues in discussing economics in globalization to inform my research.

Within constructs of globalization in the literature, labor forces are themselves commodities (Beneria, 1981), and play such a role in the economic systems that operate in a globalizing world as far as a country's economic growth or development is concerned (Hanushek & Kimko, 2000). In the context of globalization, labor forces are no longer only devoted to the production of material commodities but have been turned to in new ways in the development of commodities services (Waters, 1995). Such shifts require labor forces to have relevant applicable skills for engaging challenges associated with the sorts of changes faced with globalization pressures. As Rees, Fevre, Furlong and Gorard (2006) argue, "Economic competitiveness ... is dependent on a highly skilled labor force"(p. 927). Castells (1996) argues that new requirements for the quality of labor forces in relation to their skills as workers play a vital role in helping globalizing economies succeed. Such requirements have also posed challenges for education (Furlong, 2005; Ilon, 2000; Waters, 1995). As Hanushek and Kimko (2000) argue, the quality of labor forces is based on quality of education as education is "a direct input into production" (Hanushek & Kimko, 2000, p. 1187). It is a view that adds a particular dimension to education, that of "input" to production processes, that further guides me to focus on issues of labor forces and their quality as part of the reform under study.

My research addresses developing students' comprehensive English language competence for the demands that are placed on the 21st century citizens in China through learning English as a school subject, which indicates that this extra dimension of quality labor forces has meant that the role of such competence has been extended to one that is to be considered in relation to citizenship. EFL curriculum reform then takes on a feature of a means to enhance the quality of labor forces, based on students as China's future quality labor force and good citizens. According to Ke, Chermack, Lee and Lin(Ke, Chermack, Lee & Lin, 2006), China's history as a semifeudal and semicolonial society, and its agrarian economy, within an uneven political context, provided a context for the production of a labor force of low skills, particularly where there was no formal education for workers (Ke, et al. , 2006).

Since 1949, and the late 1970s in particular, China has experienced a remarkable economic development, implementing economic reform and an openness to the rest of the world policy, both of which have called for different sorts of highly skilled labor forces which would serve the purposes of "diversification of enterprise ownership" such as state- and collectively-owned enterprises and multinational corporations (Ke, et al., 2006, p. 42). This sort of shift has posed challenges for new education systems, a major part of which positions curriculum reform as working towards the development of a corresponding quality of China's labor force.

As Warschauer (2000) argues, the sorts of multinational corporations now operating in China require relevant, practical and applicable skills appropriate to the needs of a high level of international communication, and one of these relates to English language competence. I have considered the need for highly skilled labor forces in the context of globalization in relation to English as a subject, in particular the emphasis in the new EFL curriculum on addressing students' comprehensive English language competence. As Hanushek and Kimko (2000) argue, the quality of a labor force can be measured from one of two sources: "measures of schooling inputs (such as expenditure or teacher salaries) or direct measures of cognitive skills of individuals" (p. 1186). According to the Ministry of Education (2001a), students' comprehensive language competence includes developing students' cognitive skills, as I will discuss in Chapter 6. Students are expected to use their comprehensive English language competence to help China to be competent in international communication systems as part of a globalizing movement. The country's entry into the WTO is a salient example of this, as is hosting the Beijing 2008 Olympic Games. The literature has enabled me to position my research as directly linked with issues of the quality of China's labor force as it participates more fully in the economic activities of a major player in a globalizing world.

The literature suggests that the market is another main economic component in discussing globalization, being the place where interactive operations occur in the context of globalization (Altman, 1999; Cohn, 2005; Enderwick, 2006). Economists use the evidence of an increasing interaction between markets in different countries to explain globalization (Robertson & Scholte, 2007). According to Wong (2004), markets in China have experienced a series of reforms since the country implemented its open door programs in the late 1970s, reforms which range from rural reforms to transformations in urban economies, from reforming welfare to reforming labor markets, enterprise and price, and a shift in focus from domestic to global markets. In the course of these reforms, China has gradually shaken off its hallmark features of economic shortages, turning this into economic surpluses, and in doing so has been able to focus on what it has perceived as inevitable global economic competition, actively preparing itself for its entry into the WTO (Wong, 2004). This sort of change indicates the scope and range of influences of globalization on China's markets, as they have been driven towards global markets. As I have discussed above, such shifts call for different qualities in the country's labor forces to cope with challenges that all of this has posed. As I have discussed in Chapter 1, China's entry into the WTO is one of the main events which has driven the EFL curriculum reform, as the country needs labor forces with competent English language competence to support its competitiveness in international commerce. The reform under study is in such ways positioned as part of developing current students' comprehensive language competence in using English before they become members of labor forces that are to engage the demands that entry into the WTO present. I have taken up markets as another issue related to EFL curriculum reform in relation to globalization as informing my research.

The literature also treats information technology as playing an increasingly significant role in globalization, pointing to the remarkable development in this field as intruding on everyday life, including those of teachers and students (Chase-Dunn, 1999; Mok, 2003). Without the electronic technological capacities of the Internet to accommodate commercial enterprise needs for fast and efficient capital flows across national borders, that is, the fast capitalism that is the hallmark of globalization (Robertson & Scholte, 2007), current configurations of corporate enterprise could not exist. The possibilities of these same technologies intrude on education activities, as this is integral to the education of the next generation of labor which is expected to be skilled in technology as it applies to commercial activities. Education programs incorporate the development of such skills in students, generally with television, computers and various forms of Internet facilities, singly or in combination, playing their part in the development of technology literacy as well as English language skills (Chase-Dunn, 1999; Mok, 2003). Schools, for example, are urged to employ a multimedia approach in classroom teaching and learning, using computers with CD-ROM drives, videodisc and video players and recorders, iPods, blackberries, and so on (Adair-Hauck, Willingham-McLain & Youngs, 1999), on the understanding that such multimedia facilitate meaningful collaboration and cooperation in Listening, Speaking, Reading and Writing at the same time as they provide vivid and dynamic visual and audial engagement with language (Pusack & Otto, 1997). Multimedia can provide learners with a rich virtual cultural context to engage in relevant oral and written discourse in order to communicate in virtual contexts (Garrett, 2001).

The literature looks to the Internet used around the world and its concentration on telephones and videos as having enlarged opportunities for more teachers and their students to approach English on a daily basis as they formally and informally engage the language through material to be found there (Warschauer, 2000). The literature has investigated a variety of successful trials in the use of handheld devices, such as mobile telephones, iPods, MP3 players and other such items, to assist in language learning (Chinnery, 2006, cited in Wishart, 2008). The reported successes of such trials indicate that using such devices can support English language teaching and learning in positive ways (Wishart, 2008). As Meunier (1994, cited in Adair-Hauck, et al., 1999) says, "Multimedia thus has the capability to stretch our curriculum beyond the traditional walls of the classroom and to integrate much needed sociolinguistic authenticity into our programs" (p. 271). My explorations of teacher implementation of EFL curriculum reform is consistent with the sorts of benefits of multimedia to be used in classroom teaching identified in the literature. What is not considered in the literature, though, is the ways in which such features of the new curriculum reform as described in the curriculum documents and policy statements cannot be applied as local variations in a globalizing world have come into effect, to the detriment of the capacities of remote and rural regions of Northeast China that lack the necessary infrastructure, and even the funds, to carry out this feature of the new curriculum. It is an issue that has emerged in my research.

Services are another important issue to be considered in relation to globalization. As Dossani and Kenney (2007) argue, services are "the next great wave of globalization" (p. 4). Services provision includes various aspects of infrastructure, health, education, and transportation (Dunleavy, 1994). According to Ho and Lo (1987), services play a significant role in promoting economic development, influencing other parts of the economy. The literature on services in the context of globalization emphasize an international type of provision (McLaughlin & Fitzsimmons, 1996), and they are ascribed as requiring high standards in rapid economic development, emphasizing a concern with service quality (Rondinelli,

2007). Services developed to such levels require the underpinning of an education and training infrastructure that will produce well-educated labor forces in service delivery as they engage increasingly high standards that are part of economic development in the context of globalization (Dossani & Kenney, 2007). Such labor forces need to possess relevant competence to engage such requirements (Dossani & Kenney, 2007), an issue, which has emerged out of my research, as discussed below.

According to Ho and Lo (1987), services in China were regarded as "a non-productive remnant of capitalism", ignored in the last thirty years as far as Chinese economic development was concerned (p. 29). Until the mid-1980s when China opened its door to the world, service delivery had been only gradually addressed in an economic development that moved away from depending solely on production (Hu & Lo, 1987). Hosting the Beijing 2008 Olympic Games foregrounded services as an important feature in China (Zhang & Zhao, 2007). As Ren (2008) argues, the Beijing 2008 Olympic Games posed challenges for various infrastructures in China during its bidding and hosting processes, which included services. Such a shift in the role of services in China indicates the country's perception of this as linked to the global world, engaging international standards. Such a change has applied pressures on education in China, on EFL teaching and learning in particular, as part of demonstrating China's capacity to deliver the quality of services, particularly in relation to service provision to international types and standards. More intellectual foci by labor forces are then required for this aspect of economic development, particularly for workers' comprehensive competence in what is now a global language. Labor forces with such English language competence have played no small part in ensuring the international success of the Games in 2008. It is a feature of economic development in China that has figured prominently in informing my research.

International communication, as an important requirement for modern labor skills, has been a major factor influencing economic development in the context of globalization (Block & Cameron, 2002). In the literature, English is represented as a component of human capital as a valuable commodity on the labor market (Adamson, 2001; Block, 2004; Block & Cameron, 2002; Grin, 2003; Imam, 2005). English in China is represented as an indispensable skill for the betterment of personal well-being in the context of globalization (Adamson, 2004; Jin & Cortazzi, 2002), but it has wider implications for a skilled labor force. The literature suggests that improving English language competence will produce competence in international communication, and that it cannot be underestimated (Chan, 1999). It is an indication of the commercial dimensions of English language study suggested by globalization, where English language is no longer a practical skill to be developed or not, but a commodity upon which competent English language users may trade in a globalizing world. The benefits for the country as a whole with a commodified student cohort in English language studies, then, takes on even greater significance in a globalizing world. I have drawn on such concepts as they pertain to globalization and English language study as it manifests in policy and curriculum statements regarding the overall goal of the current curriculum reform in Chinese secondary schools. The stated aims are to develop students' comprehensive language competence. I have argued that the national benefits of achieving such aims are tied to globalization issues.

2.2.2　Politics

The literature refers to politics as "a highly territorial activity" (Waters, p.122), pursued by the power or government in a given state (Cohn, 2005). Politics is:

> The most powerful form of globalization, because it is a process whereby the autonomy of the nation-state is being radically reduced and its sovereignty eroded. In some ways it is a consequential effect of other forms of globalization (Olssen, Codd, & O'Neill, 2004, p.8).

This perspective indicates the salient role of politics in any discussion of globalization. According to Kelly (1999), politics is linked to the state, policies and social process as well as economic development, so that the state and policies are two central elements to be considered in relation to politics and globalization. The current EFL curriculum reform in China is based on policies designed to enable EFL teachers and other stakeholders to take up this curriculum implementation throughout secondary schools in China. I have, then, taken up such issues to discuss politics as they play out in relation to globalization to inform this research.

The state is an entity that engages "economic regulation, political power and culture formation", central issues to a discussion of politics in relation to globalization "when national political boundaries are increasingly porous to flows of capital, commodities, people and information" (Kelly, 1999, p. 389). As Held and McGrew (2002) argue, the state is a significant feature in relation to politics and globalization. Waters (1995) argues that the state is most important when it comes to establishing activities in the areas of international relations and political culture, indicating the interrelationship of the state and international relations, and linking this to considerations of politics in relation to globalization. As Held and McGrew (2002) suggest, relations between states have played a key role in political issues as they pertain to international relations which have increasingly become part of the politics to be engaged in relation to globalization (Held, et al. , 1999; Turner, 2000; Waters, 1995). According to Woodward (2003), international interactions form the main focus of activities between states, playing dominant roles in a global system (Robertson & Scholte, 2007; Waters, 1995). The literature suggests a number of issues to be pursued in relation to the political body that is contemporary China, and the state's role in international relations in a globalizing world. A political focus on China has enabled me to emphasize the influences of globalization on economic, political and education development, the context of the reform under study. Such investigation has helped me to address issues of China's international relations, the significant role that China may play in a globalizing world and particularly its entry into the WTO and hosting the Beijing 2008 Olympic Games. I have raised these issues in Chapter 1 and will detail them further below.

Policies, as strategies of governments, play another important part in considering politics in globalization. As Kettl (2000) argues, globalization challenges government decision-making in relation to policies. National policies are required to move a state at international levels at the same time as they need to be tailored to local conditions and the demands of diversity that this implies (Kettl, 2000). It is a key issue regarding the formulation of policies in the context of globalization which I have taken up to inform my research. According to Hutschenreiter and Zhang (2007), China adopted a policy of reform and openness in the late 1970s, driving it to engage in foreign trade and investment and eventually to its entry into the WTO. Such a shift has turned China's economy into the most open, large, and developing one now in the global world (Hutschenreiter & Zhang, 2007).

Since China embraced the rest of the world in the late 1970s, it has turned to policy contexts of decentralization (Mok, 2002). As Jun and Wright (1996) argue:

Linkages of local and national actions to global changes require institutional changes that take into account the decentralization of intergovernmental relations. In the centralized system of governance, the national government may not be very responsive to the needs and ideas of subnational governments. It is necessary to reform governing structures and processes in order to allow more autonomy at the local level so that local administrators can learn to become effective in solving local problems and active in promoting international activities. Centralized governments, in general, respond slowly not only to domestic but also to international problems (p.4).

According to Mok (2002), the state has offered local governments and education departments more flexibility and autonomy, providing a framework to promote its development, at the same time allowing other non-state organizations and individuals to be involved. This is an issue that I have taken up in my research in the two different regions within Northeast China that I have selected for focus. The policies regarding the curriculum reform have been initiated by the Central Government, but they have also been tailored by the provincial and local governments to engage the diversity in their individual context, which I will discuss further in Chapter 9.

The literature also suggests that tensions are inherent features of policies at international, national and local levels in various fields. As Cichowski (1998) argues, tensions between international, national and local policies have been evident in a globalizing world. I have drawn on this idea in conducting my research, where policy statements have played significant roles in establishing a new EFL curriculum system, thereby influencing the professional activities of the teachers who are to implement it. I have examined such tensions that have emerged as national policy statements, as big picture proposals, that have been unable to deal with the complexities of local requirements and attention to details of implementation that this implies, in particular in the Chinese context. I will discuss this further in Chapter 9.

2.2.3 Culture

In the literature, culture is represented as "a product of social interaction" (Robertson, 1992, p. 35), generated from human interaction in a given society.

Culture emphasizes relevant exchanges ·of symbols which include culturally constructed values as these relate to knowledge, tastes, and values (Robertson & Scholte, 2007; Waters, 1995). The concept of culture provides a real, feasible and grounded stance for a given society to display its languages, customs and practices (Hall, 1986). Robertson and Scholte (2007) consider culture as:

> The ways in which people give meaning to their lives. More concretely, it consists of many types of symbols that human beings can learn from each other. Among these are the knowledge, tastes, and values that communities share (p. 258).

The literature suggests that culture is influenced by globalization in ways similar to those in relation to economics and politics, but it is a field which is different from that of economics and politics. As Waters (1995) points out:

> It is clearly not the case that culture, as an arena differentiated from economics and politics, has ever been totally globalized, it has nevertheless shown a greater tendency towards globalization than either of the other two arenas (pp. 124-125).

Culture in relation to globalization may be seen as the ways in which people engage symbolic forms to interpret social experience, a process of being that is increasingly salient in contemporary times with the spread of symbolic products and related ideas on a global scale (Robertson & Scholte, 2007). That spread focuses on promoting the exchange of cultural symbols among people in the world, influencing changes in local cultures and identities (Green, 1999; Nijman, 1999; Robertson, 1995). Such views as presented in the literature have provided important insights for me to pursue in my research in relation to exploring ways in which culture in China has been influenced by globalization, and particularly, the role of English as a cultural symbol in a globalizing world, and in the Chinese context. As Olssen, et al. (2004) argue, globalization, at the cultural level, " involves the expansion of Western (especially American and British) culture to all corners of the globe, promoting particular values that are supportive of consumerism and capital accumulation" (p. 6). According to Bush and Qiang (2002), Confucian ideas as traditional features of Chinese culture have a long history of influencing various aspects of life in China, particularly in education domains. Confucian ideals address "the virtues of benevolence, propriety, respect for social hierarchy, and commitment to collective interests" (Egri & Ralston, 2004, p. 213). As Tweed and Lehman (2002, cited in Han, 2008) state, Confucians consider education as a means to enable people towards the development of virtuous behaviours so that they may achieve individual success and social harmony. Confucianism stems from 551 BC, the time that Confucius was born more than 2,500 years ago, and his education ideas constitute the core of education that dominates Chinese society (Cleverley, 1991, cited in Bush and Qiang, 2002). In its long distinctive history and in the last 50 years in particular since it was established, China has engaged an isolated system resistant to external influence of such things as Western culture (Bush & Qiang, 2002). Until it had engaged the policies of reform and openness in the late 1970s, which inspired "individual achievement, materialism, economic efficiency, and entrepreneurship" (Egri & Ralston, 2004, p. 214) and led to its unprecedented economic development, China had allowed Western ideas to have more influence in various fields, including that of education. Bush and Qiang (2002) suggest that the national context plays a significant role in considering Chinese education changes as it is important in measuring education policies and their implementation. Such policies are to be considered in an examination of issues of culture, specifically in the context of globalization. I have drawn upon such perspectives to gain an understanding of tensions between innovations and traditions experienced by participant EFL teachers in implementing the reform under study, which I have discussed further from Chapters 6 to 10.

As Lee (2005b) argues, globalization as a complex phenomenon where the contemporary world is linked to "the past movements of people and ideas around the world", which position globalization "within a certain historical context" (p. xv). At the same time I have considered that such influences have posed challenges for EFL teachers and students in China in relation to developing intercultural knowledge and learning English so that they can take up responsibilities in engaging challenges for China posed by globalization.

According to Nijmam (1999), economic development, particularly that of information technologies in the context of globalization, allows the acceleration of rapid development of cultural features, which influences local cultural development as well. The literature, then, suggests another issue to be considered in discussing globalization: glocalization. Glocalization is the term used to describe the local application of features of globalization (Harris & Chou, 2001), where a global perspective is adapted to local contexts (Mok & Lee, 2003). As Robertson (1991, cited in Lim & Renshaw, 2001) argues, glocalization is "interpenetration of the universalisation of particularism and the particularization of universalism" (p. 12). Lingard (2000) defines glocalization as, "the interactions and interconnections between local, national and global levels that are mediated by the local and national history and also by relevant political factors" (p. 81). Such discussions in the literature represent glocalization as the interconnections between global and local cultures that foreground a complex interaction within a globalizing world (Lim & Renshaw, 2001).

The literature is not consistent in its defining of glocalization as it applies in different areas for consideration. Socially speaking, glocalization may be seen as ways in which social actors construct meanings, characteristics and institutional structures (Giulianotti & Robertson, 2006). In relation to culture, glocalization may be seen as cultural differentiation in a global world (Giulianotti & Robertson, 2007). In economic terms, it is concerned with "the creation of products or services intended for the global market, but customized to suit the local cultures" (Wordspy, cited in Khondker, 2004, p. 15). The literature indicates that glocalization as a multidimensional term where distinctive localism is recognized in a global context (Lim & Renshaw, 2001). I have highlighted the issue of glocalization in relation to cultural fields as this is the focus of my research. China actively promotes processes of globalization as it ascribes a significant role of the English language as a cultural symbol in its own response to what it sees as a salient feature of a developing new culture in globalization. My research has examined ways in which the reform under study has been implemented by EFL teachers in Chinese secondary schools, particularly by those in schools located in Northeast China. Taking up issues of glocalization has allowed me to gain understanding of a particular aspect of the reform under study, and that is how this has played out in local applications in the region of Northeast China in which I have conducted my research. This has allowed me to investigate ways in which constructing "specific 'local' forms of identity" may be identified in the context of globalization, as suggested by Giulianotti and Robertson (2006, p. 172). In the following section I will discuss education in relation to globalization.

2.2.4 Education

The literature suggests that it is not sufficient to explain a country's development in relation to global trends in economics and politics (Cheng, 2004; Green, 1999), implying that systems of education not only cannot be ignored, but are to be stressed in relation to globalization (Demidenko, 2007; Green, 1999). According to Carnoy (2000):

> Two of the main bases of globalization are information and innovation, and they, in turn, are highly knowledge intensive. Internationalized and fast-growing information industries produce knowledge goods and services. Today massive movements of capital depend on information, communication, and knowledge in global markets. And because knowledge is highly portable, it lends itself easily to globalization (p. 43).

As Bottery (2006) argues, "The new economy, then, is a 'knowledge economy', the new capitalism is 'knowledge capitalism', and such a knowledge economy, however, will bring more flexibility in career and more movement between jobs" (p. 104). The literature suggests the significant role that knowledge has to play in globalization (Bottery, 2006), such as in relation to the structure and the quality of labor forces around the world (Lyotard, 2006). Education is the means used by a society to assist children, who are the learners, to survive in the world (Durkheim, 2006). Durkheim (2006) defines the concept of education as:

> The influence exercised by adult generations on those that are not yet ready for social life. Its object is to arouse and to develop in the child a certain number of physical, intellectual and moral states which are demanded of him [sic] by both the political society as a whole and the special milieu for which he [sic] is specifically destined (p. 80).

The literature also represents education as a commodity in relation to economic, politic and cultural issues in considerations of globalization (Rizvi, 2005), describing it as "one of the most globalized of all social institutions" (Robertson & Scholte, 2007, p. 366). According to Tsang (2000), education plays a key role in developing human contribution to production and supporting scientific and technological development of markets in a globalizing world. Education is to engage "knowledge audits", determining what to learn and what to know in relation to labor, and such education allows the transfer of such knowledge and understanding (Bottery, 2006, p. 104), particularly in the context of globalization.

The literature represents changes that have occurred in education throughout the world as being influenced by globalization, particularly as they appear in pedagogy used to promote knowledge transmission (Carnoy, 1999, 2000; Carnoy & Rhoten, 2002; Green, 1999; Lim & Renshaw, 2001; Stromquist, 2002). As Lim and Renshaw (2001) argue, globalization has shifted emphases in pedagogy in relation to "learning to build new knowledge and new possibilities, learning to deal with change, learning with others" (p. 13), all of which the literature emphasises that people are required to be equipped with to engage challenges of globalization (Lim & Renshaw, 2001). The literature highlights the interrelationship between education and knowledge in the context of globalization, which has drawn me to such issues in my research on the current EFL curriculum reform as part of the field of education. Within traditional pedagogical perspectives in China, teachers are positioned as "knowledge holders", embracing "teacher-centred, book-centred, grammar-translation methods" and addressing "deep understanding and repetitive learning" (Anderson, 1993 cited in Zheng and Davison, 2008, p. 5). The literature suggests that such traditional pedagogical perspectives cannot engage challenges of globalization (Hu, 2005a, 2005b). EFL teachers are then encouraged to shift from traditional pedagogical perspectives towards modern ones that embrace student-centred and task-based teaching approaches in the reform under study, which I will discuss in detail in Chapter 3.

Global transformations of education have increasingly required children to develop new skills to prepare them as highly qualified 21st century citizens (Suárez-Orozco & Qin-Hilliard, 2004). Children's lives and experiences are linked in the literature to various aspects of a global world as being influenced by economic, political and cultural development (Suárez-Orozco & Qin-Hilliard, 2004). The literature represents the role of education as being to develop children's comprehensive competence as successful learners in relation to their "cognitive skills, interpersonal sensibilities, and cultural sophistication", being responsive to processes of transformation in their local contexts as these have been affected by globalization

(Suárez-Orozco & Qin-Hilliard, 2004, p. 2). As Cheng (2004) states, education in a global world aims to develop a person with global knowledge and wisdom, one who will be able to compete locally as well as globally. I have drawn upon such perspectives to inform my research in relation to public articulations of what the reform under study has been intended to achieve. This reform aims to develop students' comprehensive language competence, rather than just knowledge and skills in EFL, with a focus on improving the quality of labor forces and 21st century citizens, which I have detailed in the foregoing.

According to Demidenko (2007), economic development in the context of globalization calls for the improvement of the quality of education. Such considerations have attracted increasing attention to education policy-making and reconstructions of curriculum (Carnoy, 1999, 2000). As Burbules and Torres (2003) say, a growing understanding of globalization has posed challenges for relevant policies in relation to "evaluation, financing, standards, teacher training, curriculum, instruction, and testing" (p. 17). Education changes in China, including the reform under study, are designed to engage the country's rapid economic, political, cultural development, and with that certain implications for preparing students for being qualified citizens in a globalizing world as suggested by Rizvi (2005), which I will discuss below. My review of the literature on globalization in relation to economics, politics, culture and education has allowed me to engage an investigation of globalization and its influences on education in particular—of ways in which the current EFL curriculum reform is linked to globalization—on the basis of participant EFL teachers' experience. I will discuss this further from Chapters 6 to 10.

To sum up, the literature indicates that education plays one of the most significant roles in social and economic development within nation-state contexts (Carnoy, 1999; Demidenko, 2007; Henry, Lingard, Rizvi, & Taylor, 1999; Rizvi, 2005). As Armstrong (2005) argues, a nation's economic, political and social development is strongly influenced by the quality of its education. Torres (2002) argues that education in nation-state contexts has been "shaped by the demands of preparing labor for participation in its economy and to prepare citizens to participate in the polity" (p. 363). Each nation or local community has its distinguishing features (Cheng, 2004). Such views have allowed me to turn to an examination of the literature on the Chinese context in relation to its economic, political, cultural and education development, and to foreground these as the context for the reform under study.

2.3 Economic-political Development

My review of the literature has identified a number of scholars who have approached issues of economic and political development in China (Dietrich, 1986; Hunnum, 1999; Jacobs, Guopei, & Herbig, 1996; Roseman, 2005; Wang & Robertson, 2004; Zhou, 2008; Zhu & Dowling, 1998). My review of the literature, has identified an absence in the published research that would specifically link economic and political development in China in the past ten years with curriculum development, EFL curriculum development in particular. The literature does, though, present an overview of relevant economic and political contexts in which the EFL curriculum reform that is the focus of my study has been initiated and implemented.

China is a country which occupies two-thirds of the population of all developing nations, having a history of civilization of thousands of years (Lin, Cai, & Li, 2003; Qi & Tang, 2004). In the following section, I will highlight the rapid economic and political development since the late 1970s, when China opened its door to the rest of the world. Such consideration has enabled me to foreground economic and political contexts in which the reform under study has occurred in early 21st century in China.

The literature shows that before the late 1970s, China had focused on the development of a self-sufficient, small-scale economy, accompanied by a closed-door policy, a course of action which limited the growth of the domestic market and prevented the establishment of international markets (Jacobs, et al. , 1996). Since the late 1970s, China has engaged reform, having instigated a policy of opening up as it has implemented a series of economic reforms designed to drive it towards what it has called "The Four Modernizations Program" (Li, 2007, p. 150). The program is based on a number of features, "industrialization and maketization of economic life, development of science and technology, and social reconstruction" (Qi & Tang, 2004, pp. 465-466). China has seen extraordinary success in this shift from a centrally-planned economy to a market-oriented one (Lin, et al. , 2003; Qi & Tang, 2004; Vidovich, Yang, & Currie, 2007). The literature indicates that China has achieved remarkable transformation in economic development, particularly in its domestic economy, and it is this transformation in relation to EFL curriculum reform that I have explored as part of my research.

China has also achieved rapid growth in commercial domains on a world stage (Adamson, 1995; Dewen, Cai, & Gao, 2007), having established a number of successful multinational corporations that enjoy both global and local market success (Sham, 2007). According to Hale and Hale (2008), China has become "a far more important economic player now than Russia then" ("Then" here refers to the late 1990s) (p. 6). The literature explores the economy of China as having developed dramatically in the 1990s playing a key and influential role in the early 21st century global economy (Hale & Hale, 2008). According to the reports of the Asia Society Business Roundtable Council of Chief State School Officers (2005), China's economy has consistently been on the rise: "Between 1990 and 2004 China's economy grew at an average rate of 10 percent per year, three times the world average, and in recent years (2001-2004) China has accounted for one-third of global economic growth." (p. 8) The China Daily Online (2007) reports that the Chinese economy remained in good shape in the first half of 2007, as China's gross domestic product (GDP) grew 11. 9 percent in the second quarter and 11. 5 percent in the first six months of 2007. These points highlight China's economic position, "Few other countries have been able to match the pace of China's sustained economic growth and China has become a major player in the global economy" (Mathew, 2005, p. 1).

China's successes in economic development have both contributed to and been the outcome of its economic reform and opening. This is a transformation from its previous position as the greatest opponent of globalization into the most powerful advocate of it (Overholt, 2005), a transformation made possible by China taking advantage of globalization. With its economic success through more active and more positive diplomacy, China has attained a greater status on the international stage than previously (Economy, 2005). As Zhou (2008) states, "In the globalized economy, China and the United States are increasingly interdependent, with the stability and growth of their economies holding the balance of the world economy" (p. 112), a view that emphasizes the significant global role of China. China's entry into the WTO and successfully hosting Beijing 2008 Olympic Games has further emphasised that significant role in the world, which I have described in more detail in Chapter 1.

According to Ehrich (2003), any phenomenon is to be understood within its specific context, an idea which I have drawn upon to position the reform under study in a Chinese context characterized by rapid economic and political development. My literature review has guided me to explore ways in which curriculum in China, including the reform under study, has developed to engage China's rapid economic development and its own increasingly significant role in a globalizing world. As Tsang (2000) points out, education development is inevitably linked with economic and political development in the larger Chinese social context. In the following section I will turn to a discussion of education development in China.

2.4 Education Development

My review of the literature shows that China administers the largest education system in the world as it serves 26 percent of the world's students (Asia Society Business Roundtable Council of Chief State School Officers, 2005; Bush, Coleman, & Xi, 1998; Rastall, 2006; Yang, 2002). Although China's education has a long history, 80 percent of the population in the 1940s was estimated to be illiterate, and in the 1980s, people over the age of 15 had received only 7.8 years of education (Asia Society Business Roundtable Council of Chief State School Officers, 2005). In all that long history, China's education system had not been accessible to large sections of the population, and the estimated 20% literacy rate suggests a focus on a Chinese elite. The literacy rate in 2005 was above 96 percent of the population, with 93 percent having received a nine year basic education (Asia Society Business Roundtable Council of Chief State School Officers, 2005). Education in China has rapidly developed since the late 1970s, not only in relation to literacy rates but also in overall terms, including EFL curriculum reform (Chan, 1999; Wang & Bergquist, 2003). I will give a brief consideration of education development in China below, specifically addressing the current curriculum reform. Such literature has provided me with a basis from which to explore ways in which the current curriculum reform has developed.

Since the late 1970s, education in China has increasingly played a pivotal role in promoting social and economic development, particularly in engaging challenges of globalization (Adamson, 2004; Hu, 2002b, 2005b). According to Tsang (2000), education in China is the key to the "human input to production" and to "the development of science and technology", represented in developing students' skills, knowledge and well-being (p. 4). To this end, the Chinese education system has been reformed, starting with the first nine years of compulsory education, and decentralization and diversification in education administration and education provision (Hu, 2005b; Tsang, 2000, 2001). The major goal of education since 1978 has, then, constantly and successfully turned to the ideals of cultivating skilled people for the promotion of economic development (Adamson, 2004; Boyle, 2000; Gil, 2005; Lam, 2002, 2005).

The literature suggests that the education system in China has had phenomenal progress since it was established, particularly since the late 1970s (Hawkins, 2000; Lan, 2006; Tsang, 2000). Its scale has been considerably enlarged to create more learning opportunities for all sorts of people in a range of education programs in a number of institutions to produce the best people for this country (Tsang, 2000). This emphasises a successful element in the current EFL curriculum reform which I will discuss in Chapter 10. Since 1978, China has successfully followed the former general designer of China's development, Deng Xiaoping's, thinking along such lines, with education policy-making that has incorporated the reform of the education system in 1985, and the later *Outline of Educational Reform and Development* in 1993 (Tsang, 2000, p.9). While the literature has canvassed such developments, it has also explored education in China as still not engaging requirements of the greater economic reform that would be required to meet the needs of rapid economic development in relation to quality education at the end of 1990s (Hawkins, 2000; Huang, 2004; Yang, 2002). China wished to establish a new education system to prepare people for better interaction with a global society even at the end of the 1990s (Hawkins, 2000; Xu & Warschauer, 2004). China also sought a new balance between the design of curricula and the needs of Chinese society, individuals, culture, and national development (Huang, 2004). Such requirements have posed challenges for curriculum reform (Bush, et al. , 1998; Yang, 2002).

The current curriculum reform is an extension of the previous reform of the 1990s (Liu & Teddlie, 2003, p. 253). As Wang (2004) argues, it is the biggest reform in scale and depth of secondary curriculum since 1949. It was initiated to accomplish China's transformation of its economic and political system and carried out to engage challenges of globalization in relation to economic, social and education development. More specifically, it was to match the requirements of modern scientific technology for teaching and learning and quality education (Guan & Meng, 2007; Hu, 2005b). The current curriculum reform has been designed to promote the implementation of what China conceives as being quality education, a conception which incorporates the implementation of a new curriculum and the cultivation of well-rounded students (Guan & Meng, 2007; Qing & Meng, 2007; Zhong, 2006). It shifts a focus from a knowledge-oriented one to one on individual development, addressing individual comprehensive competence, particularly the creative competence of students (Sun, 1998, cited in Huang, 2004). This is a thorough reform of initiation and implementation, and content, teaching methods and evaluation, as well as teachers' professional development, all based around a new curriculum (Hu, 2005b; Huang, 2004; Wang, 2007).

In this reform, a set of curriculum standards and sets of relevant materials have been produced one after the other (Wei & Thomas, 2005). All the relevant publishers are permitted to publish textbooks required to engage the requirements of the new curriculum standards (Guan & Meng, 2007). Curriculum standards were designed to be implemented through pilot experiments and then carried out in senior secondary schools throughout China in 2007 (Chen, 2003). The current curriculum reform has been implemented at three levels of curriculum management: national, local and school (Guan & Meng, 2007). I have considered such strategies as they have been used to engage diverse requirements of social, economic and cultural development in different regions in China (Guan & Meng, 2007).

The literature suggests that education in China has been developed alongside economic and political development. As Ngok and Kwong (2003) argue, China's increasingly rapid economic and political development, particularly its integration with the global economy, has posed new challenges for education. I have argued that the current curriculum reform can be seen as a response to challenges of Chinese economic and political development in the context of globalization, and I have explored this response in relation to the reform under study. The literature on education development in the Chinese context has provided a basis from which I have explored ways in which EFL curriculum reform has developed in relation to the role of English in a global and a Chinese context, considering this part of developments in English language education discussed below.

2.5　The Role of English

The literature suggests that the role of English as an international language had expanded rapidly and prominently between the 19th and mid-20th centuries, particularly after the 1950s, when a greater mobility of people was facilitated by the growth of air travel and international tourism (Richards, 2001). At the same time, English established its importance as the language to be used in international trade and commerce, an importance which was supported by the growth of service and entertainment industries such as radio, film, and television (Richards, 2001), so that English may be seen as having become a global language in the late 20th and early 21st centuries (Crystal, 1997; Nunan, 2003), "A language achieves a genuinely global status when it develops a special role that is recognized in every country" (Crystal, 2003, p. 3), a role that English has come to play in a globalizing world (Waters, 1995), seen with the growing number of speakers who regard English as their second or foreign language (McKay, 2003).

The role of English has been highlighted in economic and scientific exchange since the 1950s (Warschauer, 2000; Waters, 1995). It is estimated that there are 350 million native speakers of English, with 1, 900 million competent speakers around the world, which would mean that almost a third of the world's population is already fluent or competent in English (Crystal, 1997; Wardhaugh, Phillipson, & Crystal, 2003). Crystal (1997) notes that 85 percent of international organizations in the world employ English as an official language, and that at least 85 percent of the world's film market is in English. More than 50 percent of the millions of academic papers published are written in English, with the percentage growing every year (Swales, 1987). As Crystal (1997) claims, "English is the global language" (p. 1); no other language can match this growth.

According to Pennycook (1995), English, based on the history of its development and use, carries worldwide ideologies, values, and norms. Imam (2005) contends that in developing countries, English is widely seen as a tool for promoting economic and social development. As Warschauer (2000) points out:

There will be a growing basis for learners around the world to view English as their own language of additional communication rather than as a foreign language controlled by the "other" (p. 515).

English in China is used in various fields of culture, education, history, and linguistics (Adamson, et al. , 2002; Kang, 1999; Lam, 2002; Zhao & Campbell, 1995) Not since 1949 has English occupied such an impressive role as it does in the early 21st century in China; it has become increasingly relevant to the life of the Chinese people (Kang, 1999). The literature indicates that English has come to be seen as a personal asset, demonstrated by its being a compulsory subject from Grade 3 onwards in school, one of the main subjects for national college entrance examination, and essential for students in obtaining their first degrees at universities, colleges, as well as being considered a necessary skill for personal well-being (He; 2002; Hu, 2002b, 2005b; Jin & Cortazzi, 2002; Kang, 1999; Qiang & Woff, 2005; Zheng & Davison, 2008).

The literature also suggests that English has a significant role to play in Chinese national modernization and economic, social and education development (Adamson & Morris, 1997; . Hu, 2005b, 2005c; Nunan, 2003). The following point of view emphasizes this:

> The Chinese view English primarily as a necessary tool which can facilitate access to modern scientific and technological advances, and secondarily as a vehicle to promote commerce and understanding between the People's Republic of China and countries where English is a major language (Cowan, Light, Mathews, & Tucker, 1979, p. 465).

English in the 21st century has developed as a significant language in the Chinese context and gained a much higher status than before (Gil, 2005; Hu, 2002a). This has grown out of China's growing stability (Zheng & Davison, 2008). More specifically, China's entering into the WTO in 2001 and hosting the Beijing 2008 Olympic Games have provided further opportunities to make closer contact with the outside world, emphasizing English and its growing new importance in China as a global language (Nunan, 2003; Zhan, 2008; Zheng & Davison, 2008). According to Jin and Cortazzi (2002), taxi companies in Shanghai in 2001 began to offer their drivers English classes and provide them with learning materials and facilities in order to practise English when picking up their customers. The national newspapers in

China such as *The People's Daily* were published in English, and delivered throughout the country, in small towns and fishing villages, as part of preparations for the Beijing 2008 Olympic Games (Jin & Cortazzi, 2002). English has been seen and heard in every corner of China since the early 21st century (Jin & Cortazzi, 2002; Kang, 1999; Lam, 2002, 2005; Zhu, 2003).

My review of the literature on the role of English has allowed me to gain an understanding of its increasingly significant status in a globalizing world, and its priority role in the Chinese context. The literature suggests that globalization has greatly influenced culture around the world, including China, and that influence is embodied in the changing role of English in China. The literature has offered me an understanding of ways in which the current EFL curriculum reform may be identified as an area of priority in the current general curriculum reform in China. In the following section, I will address the development of English language education in China in relation to the current EFL curriculum reform as it pertains to the literature.

2.6   The Development of English Language Education

As discussed in the literature, the status of English in China has experienced rises and falls because of shifts in political and economic contexts from the 1950s onwards. The same may be said of English language education in China (Adamson, 2001; Adamson, 2004; Adamson & Morris, 1997; Jin & Cortazzi, 2002; Ng & Tang, 1997; Zheng & Davison, 2008). As Crotazzi and Jin (1996, cited in Ng & Tang, 1997) argue, social, economic and political contexts are key factors influencing the development of English language education in China. At this point, it is necessary briefly to canvass some of the literature on the history of the development of English language education in China.

In the late 1950s, English took over from Russian as the main foreign language, with influences of audio-lingual methods and drill practices and substitution tables popular in EFL teaching and learning (Jin & Cortazzi, 2002). In the early 1960s, a political focus on economic modernization saw education policies shifting from "politics to the fore" (Adamson & Morris, 1997, p. 10), to "expertise" (Adamson & Morris, 1997, p. 6). The curriculum, pedagogical approaches and textbooks produced in the early 1960s also shifted in focus from strongly reflecting political elements in their contents at the expense of pedagogical issues, to a focus on not only ideology, but also linguistics and pedagogy (Adamson & Morris, 1997).

During the "Cultural Revolution" (1966-1976), the far-reaching and chaotic political movement disrupted economic and cultural development in the country, as well as the education system, including English language education (Hu, 2002b; Jin & Cortazzi, 2002). Education institutions were disrupted and closed down for years (Adamson & Morris, 1997; Jin & Cortazzi, 2002). English was considered as pursuing foreign thinking, and most schools were not allowed to teach English for years. Even when English began reappearing in the curriculum, EFL curriculum development was conducted by subordinate agencies (Adamson & Morris, 1997), where provincial and municipal governments were commissioned to produce English textbooks (Tang and Gao, 2000, cited in Hu, 2002b). Such institutions lacked experience, and had had little exposure to pedagogical approaches (Adamson & Morris, 1997). Politically-oriented texts and contents were presented in almost all the textbooks, and teacher-centred, grammar-translation methods dominated in teaching and learning (Hu, 2002b).

In the late 1970s, though people still had occasional fears in relation to being seen as accepting Western culture, English was seen as having an important role in the economic reform and modernization of the nation (Adamson, 2004; Adamson & Morris, 1997; Jin & Cortazzi, 2002; Ng & Tang, 1997). The EFL curriculum focused on English skills and reading passages on the cultures of foreign countries, and the pedagogical approaches were audio-linguist and grammar-translation method (Adamson, 2004; Adamson & Morris, 1997; Jin & Cortazzi, 2002). By the 1980s, new English curricula were introduced and the communicative aspects of language learning were emphasized, while learning English became a popular activity (Jin & Cortazzi, 2002).

Since the 1990s, China has further integrated with the economy, education, science and technology of a globalizing world, emphasizing its pivotal status in international competition (The Ministration of Education, 1998, cited in Ngok & Kwong, 2003). English is seen as an important means and valuable resource to assist national development in the context of globalization. At the same time it has been identified as a key factor to make opportunities for people's higher levels of professional development or further education, either at home or abroad (Hu, 2002b; Kang, 1999).

Establishing a new EFL curriculum in China is pivotal to adapting to new global orientations and the promotion of international understanding and empathy; it focuses on a basic English language knowledge, communication skills and practical abilities (Chen, Wang, & Cheng, 2002; Hu, 2002b; Rizvi & Walsh, 1998). EFL curriculum reform, presents its own distinguishing characteristics as changes have proceeded (Hu, 2002b, 2005b; Huang, 2004; Ministry of Education, 2001a). The changes include a shift from a focus on teaching the knowledge of language to a focus on developing students' comprehensive competence in using the language; a shift from teacher-centred and grammar-translation method to a student-centred and task-based teaching method; and a shift from a singular focus on summative assessment to an incorporation of formative assessment practice (Ministry of Education, 2001a; Wang, 2007; Zhong, Cui, & Zhang, 2001).

My review of the literature has allowed me to gain an understanding of ways in which EFL curriculum reform has developed in China. The literature suggests that such development has been on the basis of economic and political development in the Chinese context, providing a basis for me to explore further ways in which the reform under study may be constructed. The literature shows that a number of researchers have started to take up studies of the current EFL curriculum reform (Adamson, 2001; Hu, 2002a, 2002b, 2003; Hu, 2005a; Hu, 2005b, 2005c; Wang, 2007; Zheng & Adamson, 2003; Zheng & Davison, 2008). They have conducted their studies from Constructivist perspectives, with little or no attention being given from a Reconstructionist perspective. The studies have addressed the reform as illustrating a general picture taken from the whole China, rather than specific empirical studies on particular cases, and none has been undertaken in Northeast China in particular, let alone engaged in detail ways in which it is linked to responsive or proactive challenges emerging from rapid economic, political, and cultural development in the context of globalization in this region. The literature has helped me to take up these issues to foreground in my research.

2.7 Conclusion

In this chapter, I have reviewed the literature on globalization, positioned in relation to its influences on economics, politics, culture and education. I have drawn on the relevant literature on globalization as serving to explain a number of phenomena emerging in language teaching, particularly in English language teaching and learning as it relates to the reform under study. I have also investigated economic, political and education development in the Chinese context, and discussed the possibilities of the role of English and the development of English language education. I have approached these issues in relation to the reform under study, reviewing relevant contributions from the literature in this field. I will give consideration to curriculum in the following chapter.

Chapter 3
Consideration of Curriculum

3.1 Introduction

In the previous chapter I have reviewed the literature in relation to my research. My research questions listed in Chapter 1 are rooted in concepts of globalization, socio-political and economic considerations in Chinese contexts, and the role of English and English language teaching and learning in China. This context represents a broad review of social, cultural, economic and political aspects of the current EFL curriculum reform that I have studied as it provides an historical context for examining the development of EFL curriculum in Chinese secondary schools. As Lawton (1980) argues, it would be meaningless to study curriculum if researchers ignored considerations of relevant social, cultural, and historical contexts. In this chapter, I will further explore such issues in my consideration of curriculum.

My main research question is: In what ways is the current EFL curriculum reform in Chinese secondary schools linked to globalization? To address this question, I have considered implications of curriculum reform in general and EFL curriculum reform in particular. In this chapter, I will focus on issues related to curriculum as it informs language pedagogy. My approach in doing this is consistent with Kelly's (2004) argument that theoretical constructions and practices are to be taken into consideration when exploring a curriculum. In this chapter, firstly, I will examine the notion of curriculum and curriculum reform as I have used the terms in my study. Secondly, I will examine a framework for language pedagogy which is related to EFL teaching and learning as far as this relates to my research. My examination includes considerations of theoretical bases for EFL pedagogy as well as teaching and learning methods used in the implementation of the EFL curriculum reform.

At its most simple level, curriculum may be seen as planning for learning (March & Willis, 2007). Such a definition fails to take into account those wider social, political, cultural, economic and historical contexts of the sorts that I have focused on in my research. Such a definition, for example, does not take into account what may underpin a given curriculum in relation to wider community concerns. In Chapter 4, I will discuss in detail the importance of Reconstructionism as underpinning the current EFL curriculum reform in China, but I wish to make the point here that this is the sort of consideration that such a simple definition does not allow for. While curriculum is a systematic field of study closely related to institutions such as schools, colleges and universities, it is also at a deeper level the reconstruction of knowledge and experience which promotes learners to develop their abilities to engage knowledge and experience (Tanner & Tanner, 2007). When one includes considerations of Reconstructionism as an informing principle of China's EFL curriculum reform, a more complex definition emerges for discussion.

3.2 The Notion of Curriculum Used in the Research

More complex definitions of curriculum are given by a number of scholars. Henson (2001) says that curriculum is the totality of educational experiences which are planned for a school or students. Marsh and Willis (2007) state that curriculum is the organized plans and experiences that students are to undertake within arrangements made by schools. Richards (2001) says that a curriculum employed in a school context is "...the whole body of knowledge that children acquire in schools" (p. 39). Drawing on the foregoing, I have taken the position that curriculum is a school plan involving specified and unspecified experiences that guide learners to obtain what a particular education institution considers to be required knowledge, skills and abilities as suggested by Tanner and Tanner (2007) and Henson (2001). I will go further to give consideration to China's national concerns regarding EFL curriculum reform, and have situated my study of this particular curriculum reform in the context of Reconstructionism, globalization, and Phenomenology, considered in further detail in Chapter 4.

In doing so, I acknowledge that considerations of different definitions can provide researchers with diverse insights to emphases and characteristics of curriculum (Marsh & Willis, 2007). The curriculum I have investigated is a national curriculum delivered for students in secondary schools, implemented according to administrative arrangements of regional governments, schools and teachers. This is in line with Moon's (1994) and Scott's (2008) statements on a national curriculum as one that involves the intentions of governments, engaged not only in setting goals for students that are designed to match students' needs, revising textbooks' contents, methods of teaching and assessments, but also underpinned by government concerns for the programs that they fund and support.

I have found that considerations of curriculum relate to established goals of government at national, regional and local levels as part of China's EFL education program. Such features of curriculum manifest in the EFL curriculum reform now being implemented in Chinese secondary schools, and this provides a basis for further analysis of two particular cases of EFL curriculum reform in China. I have selected these two cases for the focus of my research as they may be considered to be representative of EFL curriculum reform in China in general. As Hewitt (2006) argues, "Reform movements are never about just one issue; they birth a range of issues, some that disappear, others that survive and may become the focus of change later in the life of a movement" (p. 354).

3.3　Curriculum Development

Curriculum development itself occurs in the context of political, social, economic and technological change in cultures. It is the means used by institutions to address the educational experiences of learners (Mckernan, 2008). It is not a finite process, for curricula are subject to reform as those political, social, economic and technological situations change. Curriculum development is, then, a process of making decisions for matching stakeholders' needs and those that develop out of wider community aims or goals. This is as well as being a process of determining the contents and methods of teaching and learning, and assessments (Behar, 1994; Brady, 1995; Richards, 2001; Uys, 2005b). As McKernan (2008) proposes, curriculum development is a systematic and decisive process within which a program plan for teaching and learning is made, and which is expected to achieve certain specified education goals.   Mckernan (2008) further argues that curriculum development implies:

> Deliberately planned activities involving the design of courses: their aims, content, methods and modes of evaluation and styles of organizing students in courses of study and patterns of educational activity, which have been offered as proposals for improvement (p.32).

I have drawn on this sort of conceptualization of curriculum development to examine the concept of curriculum reform, as this sort of systematic and decisive processes is currently in play in China.   Curriculum development in language teaching, as Richards (2001) argues, is a process which includes producing an appropriate syllabus, course structure, teaching methods and relevant materials, as well as evaluation.   I have drawn on this idea when describing the reform under study.   In doing so, I have focused on an investigation of curriculum and associated goals, syllabus, teaching methods and textbooks, as suggested by Hewitt (2006).   I have also given consideration to issues of assessment as part of curriculum implementation.

3.3.1   Goals

Goals, aims, objectives and purposes are terms that indicate educational intentions of nations, institutes, schools and teachers (Brady, 1995; Brandt, 2007; Richards, 2001; Tanner & Tanner, 2007; Uys, 2005a, 2005b).   I have used the term "goal" as a general statement of a society's intention for learners (Brady, 1995).   Brandt (2007) argues that it is necessary to establish goals for any curriculum because they determine what learners can learn within valuable and limited instruction time.   In general, the establishment of educational goals in curriculum takes three key factors into account: the nature of knowledge; the nature of society; and the nature of learners (Brandt, 2007).   In an ideal situation, these factors are equally balanced, with none overemphasized (Brandt, 2007). Knowledge, society and individuals are three significant factors to be considered in a new curriculum such as in the reform of EFL curriculum in Chinese secondary schools.   Such considerations have been evident in the statements of goals for the reform under study.

Chinese authorities' policy statements stress the need to enhance students' competence in using the English language, including students' language knowledge, skills, concerns, learning strategies and cultural understandings (Ministry of Education, 2001a; Wang, 2007). Articulating goals for the reformed EFL curriculum in relation to these has been underpinned by the recognition of the role of English as a global language, especially in the Chinese context. China is confronted with challenges of rapid economic development and its increasingly significant role in the world, as indicated by its entry into the WTO and its successful hosting of the Beijing 2008 Olympic Games. This has positioned the role of English in China as being of particular importance, as it requires the Chinese people in general and young students in particular to cope with the global language that is English in the face of challenges posed by globalization, as discussed in Chapter 2.

English is not only a subject required for students in Chinese secondary schools (Adamson, 2001; Ministry of Education, 2001a); it is also regarded as a means by which students may achieve individual success in relation to job prospects (Ministry of Education, 2001a; Wang, 2007). The goals set for previous EFL curriculum reform in the 1950s ignored equally balancing the three factors of knowledge, society, and individuals (Adamson, 2004). The goals set for the reform under study, while it is still part of a movement to address issues identified as national concerns of the Chinese government and Chinese society, incorporate concerns for students as stakeholders in need of individual development as well (Hu, 2002b). Wang (2007) quotes the *Standards for EFL Curriculum* document:

> English, in particular, has become an important means of carrying out the Open Policy and communication with other countries. Learning a foreign language is one of the basic requirements for 21st century citizens (p. 94).

This further indicates the significant role of English in Chinese contexts of the 21st century as a means by which the country may develop the skills of upcoming workforce members to engage a wider world than China itself in relation to political and economic concerns.

A new term has come into use in China's approach to EFL: "competence". It has been employed in relation to this reform, a departure from older curriculum document statements. The idea of competence represents a particular and new type of goal setting for EFL curriculum in China. Competence is the ability and readiness of learners to carry out a task or series of tasks. It can also be interpreted as the application of skills or abilities in a workable context (Moore, 2002). The goals established for the reform under study which focus on students' competence in using the English language indicate that students are expected to have the abilities to use the English language effectively and flexibly in intercultural communication (Ministry of Education, 2001a). These specified abilities, while they are important for helping individual student development, are also pivotal in assisting China as a nation to meet the demands of its rapid economic development in relation to its own and other nations' globalizing economies across the world.

3.3.2　Syllabus

In considering such developments in EFL curriculum reform, I have turned to a consideration of syllabus as an important factor. A syllabus outlines processes and procedures for instruction and lists what is to be taught and what is to be tested (Richards, 2001), which suggests that while the foci of syllabi are much narrower than those of curriculum, they are nonetheless within the domain of a curriculum. The curriculum may be seen as part of big picture deliberations and documentation of what is to be taught and learned; the syllabus deals with the finer day-to-day details of how a curriculum is put into practice in education contexts. Marsh and Willis (2007) say that curriculum includes syllabus, which refers to the content to be taught in one course, sometimes used to supplement curriculum statements with statements of general goals and student activities. Given this, I have accepted the distinction between curriculum and syllabus as two separate and distinguishable terms as Green (2003) suggests. I have not focused on syllabus beyond these terms, as my research is concerned with the reform of the EFL curriculum in relation to the larger issues of globalization and Reconstruction as far as China is concerned. The minutiae of syllabus have not featured in my research.

I have taken up considerations of the official *Curriculum Standards* (Huang, 2004) documents in relation to my research. The *Curriculum Standards* documents are a description of what should take place programmatically in the process of formal schooling in general and EFL curriculum in particular in China. They offer a guide to new EFL curriculum and goals that are expected to be achieved as suggested by the National Council for the Social Studies (1994). The *Curriculum Standards* go beyond what might be expected to be contained in a syllabus, including as they do suggestions for teaching and learning as well as considerations of all planned teaching and learning experiences that may be expected in formal schooling contexts. As Chen (2006) argues, curriculum standards are the basis for textbooks designed for the reformed EFL curriculum, guiding teaching and learning as well as relevant evaluation and assessment processes and procedures. I have investigated the published *Curriculum Standards* as providing more information for teaching and learning than syllabi in school contexts. According to Vinson, in countries where national curriculum standards have been developed and published for a general use in national school systems, they have figured as an important component of any significant educational reform. What is more, he argues that where such standards exist, there has been an increase in curriculum research as such documents provide a mine of information to be explored by education researchers. Such an increase in education research has occurred in China, where since the publication of the *English Curriculum Standards* (*ECS*) that sit alongside the reform under study, a growing attention by educators and researchers has occurred (Chen, 2006).

ECS for Chinese secondary schools are the official education documents of instruction to be used nationally in China, specifying the content for English teaching and learning (Ministry of Education, 2001a). They are, as Vinson (1998) says:

> Authoritative policies seeking to prescribe curriculum or content to determine and limit what teachers can and should teach and what students can and should learn, for the entire country (p.4).

The *ECS* provide significant guidelines for English language teaching and learning in Chinese secondary schools. According to Chen (2006), curriculum standards are more flexible for teachers in relation to creative dimensions of their teaching than a syllabus. Embedding EFL curriculum reform in *ECS* indicates a progressive stance towards curriculum, which, as Vinson (1998) says, is also one of today's most heated topics in research in education.

3.3.3 Textbooks

A discussion about textbooks is central to understanding the process of the development of EFL curriculum reform in Chinese secondary schools. Textbooks are one of the most influential factors in a study of curriculum development (Richards, 2001). Textbooks, as a part of curriculum materials, play a key role in everyday activities of teaching and learning (Marsh, 1992, 2004). Textbooks are used as tools by teachers to work with students to enable them to understand topics or problems (Marsh, 1992, 2004). Textbooks are also resources that can provide students with comprehensive and reasonable course content (Uys, 2005a), the hub which links the processes of both obtaining and transmitting knowledge.

According to Hewitt (2006), a textbook is a product of curriculum development designed to match the requirement of a particular curriculum. Richards (2001) argues that a textbook can ideally only be used in one situation as it has to match the requirements of that situation perfectly, and if the situation has changed, the same textbook may be considered unsuitable. This indicates that a textbook should be constantly revised in line with situational contexts, in similar vein as curriculum development discussed above. In processes of EFL curriculum development, the textbooks that are created aim to match learners' needs and goals of that EFL curriculum, reflecting learners' utilizing EFL in present or future practices (Cunningsworth, 1995, cited in Richards, 2001). Textbook improvement is a mark of the development of curriculum (Bloom, 2007). Such considerations underpin textbook improvement undertaken in the development of EFL curriculum reform in Chinese secondary schools, on the understanding that they need to be revised and reformulated to meet the demands of 21st century political, economic, cultural and social contexts. These considerations correspond with the perspectives derived from a Reconstructionist perspective as part of my research. I will discuss this aspect in further detail in Chapter 4.

EFL textbooks in China have undergone significant changes since 1949. According to Adamson (2004), in the early 1950s there were no English textbooks produced in China, which banned the importation of books from English-speaking countries. Such policies were influenced first of all by the USSR, at a time when Russian was identified as the main foreign language in China (Adamson, 2004).

This situation lasted until 1956, when the first of three series of English textbooks were published between that year and 1960, two of which textbooks attempted to maintain an alignment with concepts of the "red" and "expert" with teaching and learning grounded in reading-based, teacher-centred pedagogy with strong political contents: "politics to the fore" with political tracts written by or about national leaders (Adamson & Morris, 1997, p. 10). When applied to the consideration of textbooks, the political needs of the state and the demands of the economy were both foregrounded in textbook contents in ways suggested by Paine (1995).

With an emphasis on economic modernization in the early 1960s, another two series of English textbooks were produced. They were designed with a view towards politicization of students and attempted to improve pedagogical quality in Chinese education (Adamson, 2004). During the "Cultural Revolution" (1966-1976), EFL curriculum development was conducted by subordinate agencies (Adamson & Morris, 1997), when provincial and municipal governments were commissioned to produce English textbooks (Tang and Gao, 2000, cited in Hu, 2002b). The textbooks produced at that time were full of politically charged texts which were used to serve the then political requirements of the nation (Hu, 2002b). Hu (2002b) further points out that these textbooks were not designed with a basis of relevant theories of language teaching and learning as they had an ulterior political purpose.

According to Adamson and Morris (1997), in the pre-reform and the reform era of the late 1970s, with the softening of political rhetoric and the Open Door Policy supporting the "Four Modernizations Program", another two series of new textbooks were produced. They were considerably revised in the 1980s in response to changes in the Chinese context, including changes in curriculum (Adamson & Morris, 1997). These new textbooks began to focus on English skills and reading passages on the culture of foreign countries (Adamson & Morris, 1997). Diversity of regional needs and developments also began to emerge as areas of concern with accompanying political moves to decentralise decision making and regional autonomy in relation to the production of textbooks. Since 1993, a new series of EFL textbooks has been produced for the nine years' compulsory education (the primary and junior schools) with a new series of textbooks for senior high schools in 1999 (Huang, 2004). They were issued by the State Education Committee and the Ministry of Education respectively and distributed throughout China (Huang, 2004). The new textbooks are of good quality production and show traces of Western pedagogical trends, as well as a synthesis of traditional approaches associated with the four macro skills of Listening, Reading, Speaking and Writing and new approaches such as Communicative Language Teaching (Adamson, 2001).

The textbooks have incorporated more current EFL language teaching and learning principles, increasing the amount of EFL language input and emphasizing learner independence (Hu, 2002b). Hu (2002b) also states that the textbooks in the new EFL curriculum provide teachers with more flexible intellectual space to conduct a more creative form of teaching in accordance with students' diverse abilities and needs. These changes embodied in the new textbooks signify a remarkable progress in curriculum materials in EFL curriculum development in China.

The new EFL textbooks employed in the reform under study have addressed modern pedagogical concerns in their content and approaches as they have been designed to address the requirements of Chinese economic, political, cultural and social as well as individual development (Ministry of Education, 1998). Their designs have also taken into account diverse areas in the broad context that is China, suggesting that they can meet different students' requirements and promote student development. The new EFL textbooks designed for this reform are comparatively progressive in the development of EFL curriculum reform in Chinese secondary schools.

3.3.4 Teaching Methods

According to Brady (1995), teaching methods are the ways in which teachers employ pedagogical content to meet students' needs in their classroom teaching, being a set of organized teaching practices guided by specific perspectives (Richards, 2001). Choice of effective method or methods is based on the objectives and content in curriculum (Brady, 1995). A shift from a focus on teacher-centred to a focus on student-centred method is a significant change which the EFL curriculum reform in Chinese secondary schools has presented EFL teachers (Wang, 2007). It is a shift towards helping students to become more independently and more intelligently engaged in the challenges of being the 21st century citizens required by China.

Teacher-centred methods, which are officially gradually being got rid of as part of the EFL curriculum reform in Chinese secondary schools, are traditional illustrative approaches which focus on explanation and narration, based on the idea that they strengthen learning through practice and revision (Brady, 1995). Marsh (1992) argues that teacher-centred methods have their advantages in giving students an introduction related to a topic. Even so, they have their disadvantages where students are treated as passive listeners, assumed to be interested in the topic and required to have a certain concentration span (Brady, 1995). Teacher-centred methods tend to give prominence to the role of a teacher, constraining student individual development. EFL teachers in China, though, have appreciated and engaged teacher-centred methods for a long time (Hu, 2005c; Wighting, Nisbet, & Tindall, 2005). Traditional relationships between teachers and students in China have been strongly influenced by Confucian ideas, where students rarely show their opinions and generally attempt to hide their abilities (Zhu, 2003). Students seldom challenge their teachers or their parents, who are regarded as the authorities that govern their lives, and it is the exertion of this authoritative role that turns students into obedient listeners (Zhu, 2003). This sort of powerful relationship between teachers and students is a major underpinning of teacher-centred methods employed in the context of Chinese EFL teaching and learning (Burnaby & Sun, 1989). Teacher-centred methods are not consistent with what the current EFL curriculum reform advocates in its focus on promoting individual student development. There is a tension between social conventions and language teaching and learning reform to be considered in the successful implementation of the new EFL curriculum.

Student-centred methods require that teachers promote students' independence in learning and assist them to develop intelligently (Walker & Soltis, 1992). As Brady (1995) points out, student-centred methods involve "...range of teacher structuring in which the predominantly self-directed learner interacts with the environment (physical and human) and changes as a result of that experience" (p. 132). Such methods can promote the development of students' competence in such areas as problem solving (Brush & Saye, 2000), and are characteristics of contemporary education (Walker & Soltis, 1992). A shift from traditional to more contemporary teaching methods represents a prominent feature of EFL curriculum reform in China.

Traditional methods such as grammar translation may not be appreciated or accepted in the current EFL teaching and learning practice, nor be suitable for all students because of individual differences within cohorts of students (Brady, 1995; Marsh, 1992). Research indicates that EFL teachers prefer to assume their familiar or conventional teaching methods rather than adopt new ones (Brady, 1995;

Richards, 2001). As van Driel (2001) argues, it is difficult for teachers to change rooted teaching ideas as they are reluctant to risk changing teaching practice which has long proved workable and satisfying. Traditional methods, then, are still employed in classrooms; they are adopted by teachers around the world, and not just in China. This is one of the issues which I will discuss in further detail below as part of a framework for language pedagogy as this relates to my research.

3.3.5　Evaluation and Assessment

Evaluation and assessment are influential factors involved in curriculum development, as discussed above. I have addressed these in my consideration of the development of EFL curriculum reform in Chinese secondary schools. This is consistent with the view that a study of the terms of evaluation and assessment is to explore the underlying issues related to curriculum development (Auger & Rich, 2007; Brady, 1995; Hewitt, 2006; Marsh & Willis, 2007; Tanner & Tanner, 2007). As far as educators' purposes and perspectives are concerned, these two terms have their distinctions (Auger & Rich, 2007). Evaluation is a means for making judgments about the effectiveness of a curriculum in relation to student success (Auger & Rich, 2007; Brady, 1995). Evaluation usually involves assessment of students as part of its processes, but going beyond this to focus on examining components of curriculum. As Hewitt (2006) says, evaluation is the process of making decisions based on generating or conveying valuable and important information related to learning that occurs within a curriculum. Evaluation is to be considered as a necessary process for curriculum development.

Assessment is the means used by teachers to make judgments about expectations for changes in students (Brady, 1995). It is the term used to describe the activities conducted by teachers to acquire information relating to students' knowledge, skills and perhaps also attitudes (Marsh, 2004). Auger and Rich (2007) propose that assessment is a process of collecting information about students' understanding of course content designed for them, with the aim of encouraging students to demonstrate their knowledge and abilities. Evaluation, then, is a much broader concept than assessment, with assessment being included in evaluation (Brady, 1995). Hewitt (2006) further suggests that assessment may be the actual tool that is used as part of the process of assessing, such as testing, used in evaluation. Such discussions draw on different features of evaluation and assessment, and I have drawn of these in my own research as both assessment and evaluation play their roles in influencing teaching and learning in EFL curriculum and curriculum development.

I have given some consideration to issues of curriculum evaluation when examining the development of EFL curriculum reform in Chinese secondary schools. Curriculum evaluation is a systematic investigation of all elements included in the new EFL curriculum and taking up this issue suggests that such evaluation can promote EFL curriculum reform (Lee, 2005a). Marsh and Willis (2007) state that curriculum evaluation is an investigation of teachers and students, and their interactions with curriculum and its components, such as goals in a particular setting. Curriculum evaluation is a process that helps educators to select, to adapt and to support educational materials and activities (Scriven, 1967, cited in Behar, 1994). According to Wiles (2005, cited in Marsh & Willis, 2007), curriculum evaluation is intended as small-scale studies rather than large-scale ones, for such a focus helps researchers to keep in touch with teachers' perspectives, which is the case with my research.

The schools in which I have conducted my research, like any others in China, have their own protocols and processes for assessment. They use both summative and formative types of assessment. Summative assessment is that which is used at the end of teaching and learning; formative assessment is that which occurs regularly in the classroom, generally used as tools for data collection related to teaching and learning as well as for judgments on student progress or otherwise (Hewitt, 2006). These two forms of assessments have their respective foci in relation to teaching and learning. Summative assessment focuses on the outcomes of assessment while formative assessment addresses the processes of assessment, which implies that an integration of these two assessments in a curriculum would provide a complete picture of student development in relation to teaching and learning. As Brookhart (2001) proposes, it is possible and effective to use both formative and summative assessment. These two types of assessments are to be considered by teachers in the schools that I have selected to examine the EFL curriculum reform and ways in which it is to be implemented.

The new EFL curriculum has established new principles for assessment with "a shift from a focus on a purely exam-based to a more performance and progress-based one" (Wang, 2007, p. 99), a shift in focus from summative to formative assessment. EFL teachers are encouraged to adopt formative assessment to assess students' learning progress at the secondary schools level (Wang, 2007). This is a significant change in Chinese EFL curriculum as China has a long history of employing summative assessment, starting from 200 BC, or perhaps even earlier (Niss, 1993). Changes to assessment systems in the current EFL curriculum reform in China indicate that EFL curriculum reform can take into account perspectives such as those of Niss (1993), that working with assessment is pivotal to curriculum reform, and I will discuss this further in Chapter 6.

3.4   Curriculum Implementation

Curriculum implementation is the application of a curriculum designed for classroom practice, part of the process of curriculum development (Lee, 2005a; Richards, 2001; Tanner & Tanner, 1995, 2007). Curriculum implementation is also an interpretation of ways in which teachers carry out their teaching to achieve the aims of the curriculum designed (Behar, 1994; Rogan & Grayson, 2003). Curriculum implementation is a process of transformation which applies a written curriculum to classroom practices (Marsh & Willis, 2007). I have drawn upon such ideas of curriculum implementation to inform my research.

Effective curriculum implementation rests on a variety of factors, including "leadership, culture and contexts, planning and resources, participants' training and development, assessments and continued support" (Hord, 1992, cited in Gwele, 2005b, p. 9). This suggests that curriculum implementation is a complex process influenced by various factors. It requires consideration of participants' perceptions of the new curriculum, including whether or not they would like to accept it, and whether or not they would be able to cope with it in their teaching practice (Marsh & Willis, 2007). It also takes time for these participants to become competent and confident in adopting a new curriculum (Marsh & Willis, 2007). This suggests that teachers' professional knowledge and their relevant classroom strategies also play an influential role in implementing curriculum effectively. It is this perspective that has guided me to conduct an examination of issues related to teachers, EFL teachers in particular, as key players in curriculum implementation.

I will address the role of teachers and their knowledge base as influencing effective curriculum implementation in Chapter 10. In the following section, I will focus on a framework of language pedagogy, pedagogy in EFL curriculum reform in particular, that supports curriculum reform. This framework has provided me with a conceptual tool for examining the ways in which the content of the curriculum has been delivered, as Scott (2008) proposes. To this end, I will first draw upon the work of a number of scholars in their discussions of pedagogy to inform my research.

3.5 Framework for Language Pedagogy in EFL Curriculum Reform

Pedagogy is the way in which the curriculum is delivered (Scott, 2003). Edwards and Usher (2008) also say that pedagogy is the ways in which knowledge can be delivered, a concept which ties pedagogy closely to curriculum in practice. I have included an examination of pedagogy in my research as a means by which to study the classroom applications of EFL curriculum reform in Chinese secondary schools. Pedagogy is not the same as teaching, teaching method or curriculum programing (van Manen, 2003), but "the art of teaching" (Mckernan, 2008, p. 157). Pedagogy is the ways in which teachers think and behave with a view to promoting learning in relation to expected outcomes (Bygate, Skehan, & Swain, 2001). As McKernan (2008) says, pedagogy is a strategy used to promote student learning by guiding them to develop towards new requirements. I have taken up this consideration of pedagogy as being useful in examining not only ways in which the current EFL curriculum reform has promoted EFL teaching and learning effectively but also ways in which it has facilitated new relationships between EFL teachers and students. As Ireson, Mortimore and Hallam (1999, cited in Zheng & Davison, 2008) say, the concept of pedagogy provides a useful conceptual structure to examine professional practices, providing the means by which to understand complex approaches. I will focus on discussions of theoretical bases for EFL pedagogy as well as teaching and learning methods used in the implementation of EFL curriculum reform.

Current teaching methods advocate language proficiency and enhanced cultural awareness as goals of the language curriculum, which have been spurred by an increasing interest in communicative skills (Herschensohn, 1990). As Donato and MacCormick (1994) argue, in current EFL teaching and learning, teachers expect students to develop English communicative competence. This is the case with the goals of EFL curriculum reform examined in my research, to develop students' competence in using English language. In this section, I will discuss a number of theoretical bases for EFL teaching and learning in relation to the Chinese context that I have examined. I will focus on issues related to Transformational Grammar (Chomsky, 1957; Lakoff, 1973) and Vygotskian (Goodman & Goodman, 1990) sociocultural perspectives. Omaggio (1993) argues the case for an exploration of underlying perspectives of teaching methods and curriculum in order to obtain an understanding of those methods and that curriculum. Lack of relevant theoretical bases for teaching may lead to weaknesses in comprehending and then teaching a second language (Herschensohn, 1990). Learning a language, a foreign language in particular, requires linguistic competence which focuses on lexis and syntax of the new language, and it also requires related abilities of using these components in cultural and intercultural communication (Byram, 1997; Lantolf, 1996; Lantolf & Pavlenko, 1995; Lantolf & Thorne, 2006; Lantolf, 1994; Larsen-Freeman, 2000; Modiano, 2001; Mondada & Doehler, 2004). These issues in the development of linguistic competence have led me to a discussion of Transformational Grammar and Vygotskian sociocultural perspectives.

3.5.1 Transformational Grammar

Transformational Grammar is a particular form of linguistic knowledge for examining language structures proposed by Chomsky (1957), as it aims to understand ways in which sentences are generated in a language without any apparent formal application of grammar rules. It is one of a number of linguistic concepts developed in language teaching in the 1960s and early 1970s (Hubbard, 1994). Transformational Grammar, as part of Chomskyan linguistics, has become as a major concept in Second Language Acquisition (SLA) (Atkinson, 2002; Lantolf, 1996). The concept of Transformational Grammar has challenged structural and behaviourist views of language and language teaching and learning (Zheng & Davison, 2008).

Transformational Grammar distinguishes competence and performance and focuses on the study of the syntactic structure that linguistic competence requires (Chomsky, 1957; Kato, 1998; Larsen-Freeman, 2000; Ortega, 2007). Chomsky (1957) contends that language is not a conventional structure, arguing that it is an innate capacity of the human mind engaging grammatical rules and ordinary sentences. As Zheng and Davison (2008) say, Transformational Grammar is the innate capacities of one's mind to generate infinite sentences and patterns through abstract engagement. Transformational Grammar highlights ways in which sentences are generated from a language as it provides an appealing explanation of ways in which language learners master grammatical regulations and structures as they generate limitless grammatical sentences in a language (Lívia, 2006). This feature of Transformational Grammar has a number of implications for EFL teaching and learning, and for engaging grammar as part of this (Hubbard, 1994).

Chomsky (1957) calls humans' innate capacities the Language Acquisition Device (LAD). The LAD represents a major feature of Chomsky's work, work initially received as a unique but logical explanation of issues related to language learning or language acquisition (Hawkins, 1999). Chomsky represents the LAD as part of the brain, something one is born with (Hawkins, 1999), arguing that language acquisition occurs because of a child's brain growing towards maturity and experiencing a process of interaction with their environment to facilitate and promote language skills (Clahsen & Muysken, 1986). The suggestion is that children have innate capacities of language acquisition influenced by the frequency and type of interaction with the speakers of the target language. The argument goes further to suggest that children's language acquisition needs neither linguistic knowledge nor communication. All that they require is to be exposed to interaction in language (Salo, 1998).

Critiques of Chomsky's work have pointed up further areas for consideration. According to Donaldson, a British psychologist (1978, cited in Salo, 1998) comments on Chomsky's argument as being based on:

> A failure to pay enough attention to the difference between language as it is spontaneously used and interpreted by the child and language as it has come to be conceived of by those who develop the theories (p. 75).

Donaldson's view takes issue with Chomsky's posited LAD, suggesting that language acquisition and development occur not because of an innate LAD that children might have, but because they have other cognitive capacities, one of which is a highly developed capacity for understanding human settings (James, 2004).

Bruner (1983) calls it the Language Acquisition Support System, or LASS, extrapolating from Chomsky's LAD but going further to incorporate social contexts for language acquisition. Bruner's (1983) posited LASS acknowledges the deficiencies of LAD alone to explain language acquisition. He proposes that language development also needs something or someone else more capable than the language learner for assistance to promote language acquisition:

> The infant's Language Acquisition Device could not function without the aid given by an adult who enters with him [sic] into a transactional format... In a word, it is the interaction between LAD and LASS that makes it possible for the infant to enter the linguistic community—and, at the same time, the culture to which the language gives access (Bruner, 1983, p. 19).

Bruner (1983) argues that language acquisition does not depend on LAD but on LASS. It is a point picked up by Salo (1998) , who says, "If a child has no chance to interact with others, it cannot acquire a language" (p. 85) , emphasizing the significant role that LASS has to play in language acquisition.

Transformational Grammar emphasizes the idea that a language has both deep structures and surface structures (Lívia, 2006). A deep structure is an abstract body which conveys the meaning of a sentence, while a surface structure constitutes the form of a sentence (Jacobs & Rosenbaum, 1968). As Chomsky (1969) says:

> The deep structure of a sentence is the abstract underlying form which determines the meaning of the sentence; it is present in the mind but not necessarily represented directly in the physical signal. The surface structure of a sentence is the actual organization of the physical signal into phrases of varying size, into words of various categories, with certain particles, inflections, arrangement, and so on (pp. 4-5).

The deep structure of the relations between the components of a sentence underpins a language; a similar deep structure may underlie all languages (Lívia, 2006). Switching between deep structures to surface ones can help humans to distinguish particular languages such as English as they obtain further understanding of a language (Lívia, 2006). Such consideration is based on the assumption that a basic structure, such as word rules, underpins any language (Lívia, 2006). As

Smith, Vellenga, Parker and Bulter (2006) argue, the concept of Transformational Grammar is a tool that may be used to explore language structure as it illustrates and delineates the features used in the creation of language. It is a conceptual tool that may be used to engage the syntactic structure of a language, a tool which influences EFL teaching and learning.

One such influence is teacher understanding that language is not necessarily learned by students observing them explicitly addressing grammar rules in their teaching (Lívia, 2006). This view shows up audio-lingual method and grammar-translation method as inappropriate approaches to be used in EFL teaching in China, especially in a context of globalization, where language competence is required. As Hu (2002a) argues:

> The traditional approach to ELT in the PRC has been a curious combination of the grammar-translation method and audiolingualism, which is characterised by systematic and detailed study of grammar, extensive use of cross-linguistic comparison and translation, memorization of structural patterns and vocabulary, painstaking effort to form good verbal habits, an emphasis on written language, and a preference for literary classics (p.93).

Chomsky (1957) argues that language is learned not through the repetition of structural patterns, but rather by experiencing it in contexts where language learners are active processors of language, not passive receivers of language teaching. Transformational Grammar, then, challenges prevailing Chinese EFL teaching approaches such as grammar-translation and audio-lingual methods (Adamson, 2004; Lívia, 2006).

The audio-lingual method is based on the idea that students learn a language by repeating certain specified language formations until automatic levels of skills are achieved (Lewis, 1972). It is an approach that may not promote student development of their learning of the target language (Herschensohn, 1990) as it is a mode of learning a language, rather than acquiring a language, by analysing its grammar rules in detail and then applying these to bilingual translation (Richards & Rodgers, 2001). Language learning is viewed as mechanically memorizing language rules to achieve an understanding and engagement of the morphology and syntax of a foreign language (Richards & Rodgers, 2001). A problem that teachers and scholars have identified with this approach (see for example Bruner, 1983) is that students may only have knowledge of grammar, but they may not know how to use it in practice, so that the development of their competence in using language is adversely affected. Audio-lingual method and grammar-translation method both present their respective problems in language teaching and learning, as discussed above. I have taken up such considerations as grammar-translation and audio-lingual method have dominated EFL teaching in China for a long time, perhaps even too long a time (Adamson, 2004). Students subjected to such language teaching methods have found themselves exposed to failure by lack of competence in using the English language and have often failed communications requirements (Adamson, 2001; Adamson, 2004; Hu, 2002b, 2005b).

My discussions of Transformational Grammar do not mean that grammatical knowledge is expected to be ignored in EFL teaching. Rather, I have taken the position that grammar is a part of language teaching but has limited application in relation to obtaining language competence. Grammar teaching incorporated in appropriate ways in language teaching, linked to direct and interactive contexts, has its role to play in teaching and learning in EFL contexts (Herschensohn, 1990). As Chomsky (1986) argues, grammar is not a set of statements about externalized objects constructed in some manner; it is to be linked to the language experiences of the learner. The issue of grammar in whatever form it presents in language learning and teaching, and language acquisition, continues to be a topic of some concern to scholars, teachers and students alike.

According to Seguin (1995, cited in Renou, 2001), knowledge about the grammar of a foreign language is essential in language teaching and learning, as it can enable students to have more explicit, comprehensive knowledge of language which may enhance their confidence in learning a foreign language. The concept of Transformational Grammar has made significant contributions to an understanding of language structures (Hubbard, 1994). Hubbard argues that if the concept of Transformational Grammar is approached pedagogically, teachers may be able to generate valuable insights that they can pass to their students. I have taken the position that this is the case in the context of EFL teaching in China, especially as research has indicated that EFL teachers mostly accept grammar-translation method as their conventional ones used in their teaching. It is a method that sits well with the cultural context within which they have been operating (Jin & Cortazzi, 2002; Yu,

2001; Zheng & Davison, 2008), but not with the EFL curriculum reform.

Chomsky's (1957) concept of Transformational Grammar in language acquisition in native language speakers has been taken up by a number of teachers of second or foreign languages (Lívia, 2006; Yong, 2006). Despite critiques of Chomsky's posited LAD, aspects of Transformational Grammar have their implications for the current EFL teaching and learning in Chinese secondary schools (Yong, 2006). I have taken the concept of Transformational Grammar in light of Hewitt's (2006) proposition regarding reform, which is to "take what exists—the curriculum, schools, and the kinds of work done—and reform them, not do away with them" (p. 354). Based on this, possibilities emerge for Chinese EFL teachers to consider as they engage relevant features of Transformational Grammar and incorporate them into their EFL teaching. Li (2005) for example, suggests that acknowledging Transformational Grammar provides opportunities for EFL teachers to explore general rules in language to obtain an understanding of human cognitive systems. Yong (2006) argues that EFL teachers need to consider insights to issues of LASS to provide students more exposure to and support for language practice so that they can gradually achieve required language outcomes.

Yong (2006) argues that Transformational Grammar may help EFL teachers in China to focus on successful individual student development by acknowledging students' innate capacities in learning a language with EFL teachers' assistance. Emphasizing individual student development is a focus of the current EFL curriculum reform in Chinese secondary schools (Ministry of Education, 2001a). EFL teachers in China are expected to consider relationships between linguistic competence and linguistic performance in their EFL teaching in order to implement effective teaching and learning activities, such as pair work or group work (Yong, 2006). Such classroom strategies may be adopted as part of developing individual students' linguistic competence to achieve the required levels of linguistic performance (Yong, 2006). This sort of consideration is in line with the focus of the reform under study, with its stated emphasis on enhancing students' competence in using the English language. I have drawn on the work of such scholars that I have discussed in the foregoing to explore the possibilities that an understanding of Transformational Grammar in EFL teaching and learning in Chinese secondary schools may have in helping educators in developing appropriate teaching methods as part of EFL curriculum reform. Transformational Grammar has the potential to provide insights for curriculum design, and even examination design, in relation to ways of presenting classroom activities or exercises to engage students as successful and productive learners of the English language in Chinese contexts.

I have considered Transformational Grammar as a part of necessary linguistic knowledge providing EFL teachers' insights to EFL teaching and learning as part of their pre-service teacher education program. I have taken up this issue, for as Lantolf (1996) argues, Chomsky's perspective on Transformational Grammar is the most developed and scientifically based among linguistic notions which are worth considering in the case of SLA. Chomsky's perspectives provide EFL teachers with a way in which to obtain an understanding of ways in which a language comes into being and develops, as well as ways in which language acquisition comes about (Lakoff, 1973). Working with the idea of Transformational Grammar may further enable EFL teachers to make clear ways in which to improve their teaching and enhance students' EFL learning competence. The concept of Transformational Grammar has also provided an underlying perspective for me to explore an understanding of language acquisition, language learning and language development, guiding me to Vygotskian sociocultural perspectives, as outlined in the next section of this chapter.

3.5.2   Approaches Based on Sociocultural Perspectives

One of the issues related to teaching and learning a foreign language is a consideration of ways of acquiring relevant linguistic competence. Linguistic competence in relation to language acquisition presents attractive contrasts to traditional grammar-translation approaches, considering grammar as not a single, logical, *a priori* system, but viewing it as a social achievement and tool (Atkinson, 2002). Such perspectives turn to Transformational Grammar, which aims to help language learners to achieve effective communication in language (Atkinson, 2002), and positions the acquisition of a language as being closely related to social practices and learners' participation in language (Mondada & Doehler, 2004). I have drawn on such sociocultural perspectives as theoretical bases for language pedagogy in the conduct of my research.

Sociocultural perspectives present possible pedagogical directions for EFL teachers as they implement the curriculum reform (Lantolf & Pavlenko, 1995;

Lantolf, 1994; Vygotskiy, 1978; Wertsch, Del Rio, & Alvarez, 1995). As Mondada and Doehler (2004) say, sociocultural perspectives are inspired by Vygotsky's work, but developed by neo-Vygotskian scholars (Larsen-Freeman, 2000; Lim & Renshaw, 2001; Ortega, 2007). Vygotsky views learning as embedded in social activities, a perspective that has been extended by researchers who use it as a theoretical position from which to investigate second language acquisition (Larsen-Freeman, 2000). Vygotskian perspectives emphasise learning as a process where individuals interact with each other, participating in tasks together, and attaining a certain level of competence with the help of adults or more knowledgable Others (McLoughlin & Oliver, 1999). The emphasis is on language cognition as social ability, an ability which emerges from the experience of language acquisition itself (Ortega, 2007). Ortega (2007) further argues:

> Learning (including language learning) is explained via processes by which the mind appropriates knowledge from affordances in the environment. These affordances, in turn, are fundamentally social: They arise out of our relations to others, via tools (including language) that mediate between us and our environment, and out of the specific events we experience (p. 229).

In such a scenario, learning occurs with the changing nature of defining or redefining these relationships and processes of participation (Lim & Renshaw, 2001), where individuals' cognitive growth and development are closely related to the central roles played by social interaction and cultural institutions, such as schools and classrooms (Donato & McCormick, 1994). Human development occurs because of meaningful interaction, which cannot be separated from its social context (Vygotsky, 1978). These sorts of conceptualizations of learning are evident in the goals articulated as part of China's EFL curriculum reform, with their focus on students being competent as citizens of the 21st century. Student development is seen to be part of keeping up with the social and economic development which the new curriculum has been designed to address.

Vygotsky first systematized his work on learning and learner development in the early 20th century (Goodman & Goodman, 1990; VanPatten & Williams, 2006, 2007). According to Antón (2002), Vygotsky considered that individual interaction stimulates higher psychological functions mediated by symbols and signs in language use, and that a shift of function from the social to the cognitive level then takes place within the Zone of Proximal Development (ZPD). The ZPD is:

> The distance between the actual developmental level as determined through independent problem solving and the level of potential development as determined through problem solving under adult guidance or in collaboration with more capable peers (Vygotsky, 1978, p.86).

According to Kinginger (2002), the ZDP is a pedagogical tool that may be used in an attempt to achieve those educational goals set for children. One of the contributions of the concept of the ZPD to education and other domains is rooted in its notion of assistance, which Bruner and Garton (1978) have developed into concepts of scaffolding, which has been further expanded by other scholars (Fernández, Wegerif, Mercer, & Rojas-Drummond, 2001; Lantolf & Thorne, 2007). Wood, Bruner and Ross (1976) say that scaffolding is the help provided by experts, or more knowledgeable Others, for novice learners to achieve goals which are beyond their current levels of ability. Bruner and Garton (1978) define scaffolding as a sort of cognitive assistance offered by pedagogues to learners, aimed at helping them to solve the problems they cannot yet work out without assistance. Fernández, et al. (2001) see scaffolding as the way in which learners can mutually support each other's development in learning by solving difficult problems together. The concept of scaffolding may be used by teachers to explore learners' potential and help them to achieve expected and ideal goals. Scaffolding, then, emphasizes the strength of interaction, cooperation, negotiation and collaboration in learning, all of which are closely related to the stated teaching and learning processes of the reform under study where task-based learning is encouraged. The aims are for more interactive activities with classmates and teachers in order to achieve the stated learning and teaching goals. I will discuss task-based learning later in this chapter.

The ZPD is a concept that does not sit easily alongside traditional Chinese use of tests and measures which only focus on examining learners' actual level of development, and which ignore explorations of learners' potential as influencing future learning (Lantolf & Thorne, 2007). The ZPD is a concept which may guide assessments towards levels which include both present and potential achievements of learners (Lantolf & Thorne, 2007). A number of studies has drawn on Vygotskian perspectives from which to investigate second language acquisition, EFL teaching and learning in particular (Antón, 2002; Lantolf & Pavlenko, 1995; Lantolf, 1994; Lantolf & Thorne, 2007), and my research is no exception as I have examined learner-centred and task-based methods that are to be employed as part of the EFL curriculum reform.

Vygotskian perspectives provide a guide for the teacher as they come to understand the emergence of learners' cognitive development in activities which are mediated by language (Kininger & Belz, 2005). Language is a symbolic tool, used as part of human consciousness that inform human activity (Appel & Lantolf, 1994). Vygotsky (1978) considers it to be better for language educators to help children to develop Reading and Writing skills through play rather than actually learning to read or to write; that people achieve language acquisition and development in the context of the application of that learning and development (Goodman & Goodman, 1990). Vygotskian perspectives provide part of a framework for language educators, specifically EFL educators, to understand and explore ways in which language teaching and learning can be achieved effectively and successfully (Donato & McCormick, 1994). I have drawn on such perspectives to underpin my research to investigate the sorts of EFL teaching and learning delivered by participant EFL teachers.

3.5.3　Link to Current EFL Teaching and Learning in China

Language, as a social phenomenon, is developed within cultural contexts (Berns, 1990), and language acquisition in social settings of native speakers occurs unconsciously (Neuman & Koskinen, 1991). Krashen (1985) argues that second or foreign language competence is acquired in similarly subconscious processes. Krashen's (1985) main contributions to theories of SLA is his *Input Hypothesis* in relation to comprehensible input as part of language acquisition (Zheng, 2008).

Neuman and Koskinen (1991) have taken up this idea of comprehensible input, arguing that language competence is "a function of the amount of 'comprehensible input' received, without formal instruction in reading or grammar" (p.3). Krashen (1985) represents comprehensible input as an understanding of messages or meaning, where humans move from the level of i (their current level) to the next or higher level of $i+1$ (where 1 represents the advanced level). The formula that he gives for successful language acquisition is *i+1* (Krashen, 1985). Krashen's concept of comprehensible input takes the position that second language acquisition only takes place when learners are exposed to certain input (Fotos & Ellis, 1991). In Krashen's view, language acquisition develops or advances on the basis of comprehensible input beyond learners' current level of competence based on *i + 1* (Grove, 1999).

The notion of comprehensible input is an influential factor in concepts of second language acquisition and linguistic competence (Zheng, 2008), an example of the application of the concepts of ZPD and scaffolding applied specifically to EFL teaching and learning. I have drawn upon such considerations to inform my research, drawing on concepts of learners' innate capacities, linguistic competence and performance, and deep and surface structures related to Transformational Grammar and ZPDs. As Abdalla (2005) argues, linguistic competence is an essential component in language teaching and learning, but it ought to be considered along with other issues, such as those associated with culture. On the basis of such discussions, I have examined appropriate teaching methods and approaches that have been promoted as part of the EFL curriculum reform.

A number of English language teaching and learning approaches have been employed in the reform under study. I have previously in this chapter alluded to the grammar-translation and the audio-lingual methods, based on teacher-centred approaches. Other approaches that have appeared in EFL teaching in Chinese secondary schools now also include Communicative Language Teaching (CLT) and Task-Based Learning (TBL). CLT started in the late 1960s in Britain and gained its status in EFL/ESL in the early 1980s (Hu, 2002a; Richards & Rodgers, 2001). This approach, as an effort to improve EFL teaching and learning, was imported to China in the late 1980s (Hu, 2002a), and it has come to the fore in ESL/EFL teaching (Hu, 2002a; Sun & Cheng, 2000). CLT is used partly in response to Chomsky's (1957) criticisms of structural theories of language, with Vygotskian perspectives playing an important role in theoretical bases for CLT (Hu, 2002a; Richards & Rodgers, 2001; Zheng & Davison, 2008). As Richards and Rodgers (2001) say, CLT positions communicative competence as the goal of language acquisition and is used to " develop procedures for the teaching of the four language skills that acknowledge the interdependence of language and communication " (p. 155). Zheng (2008) says that the primary role of CLT is to promote students' communicative language competence. This is the key feature that distinguishes CLT from other more traditional teaching methods which focus on linguistic knowledge and ignore the concept of linguistic competence. Littlewood (1981) says, "One of the most characteristic features of communicative language teaching is that it pays systematic attention to functional as well as structural aspects of language" (p. 1). It is a feature of CLT that distinguishes it from traditional approaches, especially as it is more concerned with the context of foreign language teaching than other possible approaches (Sun & Cheng, 2000). CLT focuses on "authentic language input, real life-like language practice and creative generation of language output", which at the same time "highly depends on its context" (Sun & Cheng, 2000, p. 4).

Hu (2002a) teases out the deficiencies of CLT used in the Chinese context as evident in the shortage of necessary resources, the large class sizes, the limited time allowed for classroom teaching, EFL teachers' limited English proficiency, and pressure exerted by examinations. Wang (2007) points out that although education departments have taken a very big step forward in promoting CLT adoption in China, acceptance of this approach is less than one third among Chinese EFL teachers.

3.5.4　Task-based Approaches

In the schools that I have studied, I have found EFL teachers encouraged to focus on task-based learning in favour of any other possible language pedagogies that may be used as part of the reform. Task-based learning is an approach where tasks are employed as the centre unit of planning and instruction in language teaching (Richards & Rodgers, 2001). Richards and Rogers view employing tasks which promote learner use of communication and authentic language in EFL language classrooms as having significant pedagogical value, where the tasks are pieces of planned work used in teaching and learning in classroom practice. According to Richards and Rodgers (2001) "task" is a core unit of planning and teaching. They further state that involving learners in tasks helps to develop better contexts for activating learning processes, providing better opportunities to engage in language acquisition. A task used in such ways as an activity to achieve a goal provides learners with experiences of processes of "negotiation, modification, rephrasing and experimentation", the core of EFL language acquisition (Richards & Rodgers, 2001). As they put it：

A task is a piece of classroom work that involves learners in comprehending, manipulating, producing or interacting in the target language while their attention is focused on mobilizing their grammatical knowledge in order to express meaning, and in which the intention is to convey meaning rather than to manipulate form. The task should also have a sense of completeness, being able to stand alone as a communicative act in its own right with a beginning, a middle and an end (p.228).

Donato (1994) represents tasks in language acquisition as cognitive activity, suggesting that they are internally defined "through the moment-to-moment verbal interactions of the learners during actual task performance" (p. 272). Myers (2000) interprets the notion of tasks from a Vygotskian perspective, focusing on internal verbal interaction. Lee (2000, cited in Myers, 2000) proposes adopting tasks in EFL teaching and learning to set the stage for implementing real communication. Communication, as Lee (2000, cited in Myers, 2000, p. 10) argues, is the expression, interpretation and negotiation of meanings, rather than answering teachers' questions. He further argues that using this approach means that language is used to accomplish tasks rather than practising particular language forms. I have drawn upon these discussions to obtain an understanding of task-based learning as it applies to the EFL curriculum reform.

According to Ellis (2000), tasks are interpreted differently in different contexts. Nunan (2004) argues that target tasks are based on the use of language that occurs beyond the classroom; pedagogical tasks are those based on the language which occurs within the classroom. I have emphasized pedagogical tasks as my research is concerned with studying teacher classroom activities. Bygate, et al. (2001) argue that pedagogical tasks highlight formal language teaching and learning and its assessment and, more specifically, emphasizing teachers' actions, learners' roles and learning processes as well as assessments and evaluations. Nunan (2004) defines pedagogical tasks as pieces of classroom work that involve learners' understanding, engagement, production and interaction with the target language, emphasizing organization of grammatical knowledge as they attempt to express or convey meaning. He further points out that pedagogical tasks involve communicative language, suggesting that language learners are required to focus on expressing their meaning rather than on grammatical form. With this concept in mind, I have investigated task-based learning which Chinese EFL teachers are encouraged to use in classroom teaching as part of the reform under study.

Task-based learning is an approach which offers learners tasks to engage, rather than items to learn, providing an environment which can best promote language acquisition in a natural process (Foster, 1999). This approach provides learners with opportunities for various interactions to promote language acquisition (Fotos & Ellis, 1991). Nunan (2004) suggests that task-based learning incorporates the following principles and practices:

A needs-based approach to content selection; an emphasis on learning to communicate through interaction in the target language; the introduction of authentic texts into learning situations; the provision of opportunities for learners to focus not only on language but also on the learning process itself; an enhancement of the learner's own personal experiences as an important contributing element to classroom learning; the linking of classroom language learning with language use outside the classroom (p.1).

Successful language acquisition on the basis of task-based learning, then, links learners with meaning, providing them with particular kinds of input to facilitate their learning (Richards, 2002), so that meaning and input are key issues in task-based language learning. Mackey (1999, cited in Bruton, 2005a; Bruton, 2005b) stresses that tasks be proposed as both input and interaction. Meaning, input and interaction are the key features of task-based learning, a concept which is consistent with the concept of Transformational Grammar and comprehensible input and Vygotskian perspectives. Transformational Grammar includes an understanding of deep structures of language, which underpins the meanings communication in language. Comprehensible input as part of language acquisition is based on the idea that human language is acquired through an understanding of meaning. Vygotskian perspectives focus on meaningful interaction in language acquisition. All three are fundamental concepts in relation to task-based learning.

I have considered task-based learning as a reaction to traditional teaching methods such as teacher-centred and grammar-translation in EFL teaching. As I have discussed previously, this derives from considerations of language acquisition as a developmental process that involves communication within social interaction. I have argued that task-based learning provides students with tasks to engage and appropriate environments designed to engage language acquisition successfully in natural ways. As Jong (2006) argues, task-based learning assists students in learning the target language more effectively through a natural exposure to meaningful task-based activities. Paired or group work is fundamental to activities that implementing task-based learning in EFL as part of language acquisition. In a task-based classroom, learners are guided "through cycles of task planning, performance, repetition, and, finally, comparisons with native speaker norms" (Willis, cited in Foster, 1999, p. 69). The curriculum documents which outline the EFL curriculum reform suggest that this is appropriate for EFL teaching and learning in China, especially as it fits into contexts of large class sizes and limited time described above, and has its focus on students' comprehensive competence in using English language.

According to Oxford (2006), teachers and students can play multiple roles in task-based learning, where the teacher may be:

> Selector/sequencer of tasks, preparer of learners for tasks, pre-task consciousness raiser about form, guide, nurturer, strategy-instructor and provider of assistance while the learner is "group participant, monitor, risk-taker/innovator, strategy-user, goal-setter, self-evaluator, and more" (p. 108).

Given this, task-based learning is a significant shift in pedagogy from "teacher-centred to student-centred; a shift from textbook-based to task-based learning and a shift from summative assessment to formative" (Ko, 2000, cited in Adamson & Davison, 2003). Such considerations of teachers' and students' roles in EFL teaching and learning, where both of these are designed for language acquisition, are also in line with the focus of the reform under study, where students are expected to change from passive listeners to active participants while teachers are required to change from main speakers to guides or directors in class.

EFL teachers in Chinese secondary schools are encouraged to adopt task-based approaches in implementing the reform. Teachers are to design appropriate tasks in order to provide opportunities for student language interaction. These tasks are also required to take account of the concept of ZPDs as this offers a theoretical basis for task-based learning, where various resources can be provided according to different individuals' requirements. Such considerations have provided me with insights to language pedagogy in relation to the reform under study.

3.6 Conclusion

In this chapter, I have given consideration to issues relating to curriculum as well as a framework for language pedagogy. I have approached the notion of curriculum to open up discussions of curriculum reform. I have explored the concept of curriculum reform in relation to issues of curriculum development, and I have further taken account of issues of curriculum implementation and curriculum evaluation which are tied to those of curriculum reform. These considerations have provided me with conceptual tools to generate further understanding of the implementation of the EFL curriculum reform. I have also given consideration to the issues of Transformational Grammar, Vygotskian perspectives and task-based learning methods as these relate to EFL teaching and learning in China. In the following chapter, I will discuss the methodological framework for my research.

Chapter 4
Methodological Framework

4.1 Introduction

In the previous chapter I have detailed issues related to conceptual tools used to examine the reform under study. In this chapter, I will examine issues of methodology to inform my research, based on the concept of methodology as "the study of, or a theory of, the way that methods are used" (Dunne, Pryor, & Yates, 2005, p. xxi). Babbie (2008) describes methodology as the way of finding solutions to problems. My engagement with issues of methodology has helped me to design my research program and to investigate appropriate research methods, as well as to evaluate the research design that I have developed, as Krippendorff (2004) proposes.

My research question is: In what ways is the current EFL curriculum reform in Chinese secondary schools linked to globalization? In considering this issue, I have developed a number of subsidiary questions, which are: for example, In what ways has the current EFL curriculum reform in Chinese secondary schools developed? My investigation has helped me to engage discussion on ways in which the current EFL curriculum reform has contributed to ways in which EFL teaching and learning in China have developed. I will detail considerations of methodology on which I have based my research below.

4.2 The Starting Point: Ontological Position

I have first given consideration to two principal concepts in relation to my research: ontology and epistemology. As Blaikie (2000) argues, ontology is a view of what the world is like and what it is made up of. According to Crotty (1998), the world exists independently of mind and consciousness; the world exists before human beings make sense of it. Winter (2001) argues that ontology is "what exists *a priori* to perception, knowledge, or language" (p. 587). Ontology, then, is a view of the world, its nature and structure (Crotty, 1998). As Packer and Goicoechea (2000) argue, ontology is "the consideration of being: what is, what exists, what it means for something—or somebody—to be" (p. 227). Ontology addresses the idea of the nature of reality, and I have drawn on this notion to give consideration to the reality of the researched world. It may be that this reality is conceived as being objectively experienced and objectively studied, but that does not preclude subjective perspectives of the world.

I have taken the research process as being dependent upon a particular way of viewing the nature of reality, as suggested by Dunne, et al. (2005) and Gwele (2005a). The world that I have researched, indeed anyone's research world, is a complex and socially constructed one, and nothing in that world can be seen as a single component or separated from other components, as Blaikie (1993) suggests. These components are part of one framework or process and they all have their particular relationships with each other, as is the case with my research, which focuses on the current EFL curriculum reform in Chinese secondary schools in a northeast region of China. I have approached my study of this reform as positioned in the context of economic development in China, which in turn has positioned the reform within considerations of globalization. My ontological position is based on a view of the world as socially constructed, and subjectively experienced. I have approached this reform as occurring in a context of the interaction of politics, the economy, culture and the wider education field in China, not as something to be considered in relation to its field alone. This ontological positioning has influenced my epistemological position, methodology and method, as Higgs (2003) suggests.

4.3　Epistemological Position

Babbie (2008) says that methodology is to be regarded as part of epistemology in research programs. I have drawn on the work of Crotty (1998), who describes epistemology as "the theory of knowledge embedded in the theoretical perspective and thereby in the methodology" (p. 3). I have drawn on this idea that a carefully considered epistemological position can provide researchers with solid theoretical foundations for methodology. Epistemology focuses on the nature of knowledge (Blaikie, 1993); it is a concept which provides a tool with which the researcher may explore ways in which knowledge is generated (Knight, 2002). The articulation of my epistemological position has provided me with an underpinning of my approach to managing and conducting my research. More specifically, my epistemological position has enabled me to focus on the meaning and understanding of the reform under study through an investigation of Chinese EFL teachers' lived experience, the relevant contexts and their mutual relationships. My exploration is based on an Interpretivist rather than a Positivist approach.

Positivism is generating knowledge from experiments, observations or direct experience in natural sciences (Blaikie, 2000). Interpretivism is generating knowledge of social and personal life in the human world, based on understanding and interpretation of that social, human world (Walter, 2006). I have taken an Interpretivist approach in conducting my research, which has meant a focus on the most salient elements of the reform under study as interpreted by those teachers who have been commissioned to implement it. It is a perspective which has helped me to open up discussions with EFL teachers in an analysis of the curriculum that has been implemented, but it has been an analysis that has focused on teacher perspectives and attitudes to the curriculum itself. I will detail the features of the analysis below.

4.4   An Interpretive Paradigm: Qualitative Research

Paradigm is a set of beliefs and relevant methods relating to the conduct of research (Lincoln & Guba, 1985, 2000), an overarching conceptual framework which provides researchers with a particular way of making sense of their research world, as Crotty (1998) suggests. I have turned to a paradigm informed by an Interpretivist perspective and based on qualitative research because of the suggestive possibilities it provides, for "its relevance and its richness" (Ansari & Weiss, 2006, p. 177). I have chosen Interpretivism with its focus on qualitative enquiry to base my examination of ways in which the current EFL curriculum reform in Chinese secondary schools is linked to globalization. This choice is based on my ontological and epistemological positions as feeding into the methodological dimensions of my research in the way suggested by Creswell (2007) and Crotty (1998). I have not generated data through laboratory experiments or laboratory observations, but through gathering data based on EFL teachers' perspectives of the phenomena in their schools, which are not visible or measurable in a Positivist sense. The data are descriptive in nature, and I have interpreted these data as part of a process of making visible meanings of EFL teachers' lived experience. I have further explored the world in which the reform is implemented to generate knowledge of this world through analysis of relevant documents.

Embracing Interpretivism

Positivism and Interpretivism are two general theoretical perspectives emerging from natural and social sciences (Crotty, 1998). Positivism accepts objective, empirically verifiable, accurate and visible, scientific cognition as scientific knowledge (Blaikie, 2000; Crotty, 1998; Scott & Morrison, 2005; Silverman, 2000). Phenomena such as meanings, understandings and experiences are beyond the scope of what Positivism entails (Clark, 1998). The nature of my research suggests that Positivism is not an appropriate perspective for me to adopt as I have conducted data gathering and analysis in ways which are different from ways in which Positivism works. I have been further informed in this by the work of Kuhn (1970).

Kuhn (1970) argues that scientific revolutions may be considered as a change of paradigms, where a new paradigm completely or partly replaces the older one that is to be overthrown. Kuhn (1970) also argues that science does not develop uniformly, but has certain alternating stages between normal and revolutionary, as he maintains:

> Normal science consists in the actualization of that promise, an actualization achieved by extending the knowledge of those facts that the paradigm displays as particularly revealing, by increasing the extent of the match between those facts and the paradigm's predictions, and by further articulation of the paradigm itself (p. 24).

According to Kuhn (1970), paradigms which have been designed to develop scientific truths, senses or practices shift when new knowledge is generated by the research world, and such shifts challenge traditionally accepted so-called scientific truths. He suggests that the unobservables denied by scientists are nonetheless present in all research, which challenges Positivist approaches. The argument is a critique of Positivism, and it provides a theoretical impetus to my research in providing a research perspective in interpreting the meaning of the participants' perceptions and attitudes to the reform under study, in full acknowledgment of my non-Positivist position. I have explored participant EFL teachers' perspectives in relation to the reform under study where their attitudes, feelings and beliefs are socially rather than scientifically constructed. According to Kuhn (1970), these perspectives may legitimately be included in scientific research paradigms.

Interpretivism is the idea that the generation of meaning in social and personal life in the human world is based on understanding and interpretation of the social, human world (Walter, 2006). Seale (1998, cited in O'Brien, 2003) argues, "An Interpretivist approach emphasizes the understanding of people's intersubjective worlds which produce corresponding action and interaction" (p. 10). Interpretivism provides the conceptual tools with which to explore underlying meanings within people's inner worlds, including their perceptions or attitudes (Blaikie, 1993), a different view of the world from that of Positivism.

My project has been designed to explore the research participants' perspectives and attitudes to the changes that the reform has brought. I have conducted a number of interviews and generated a number of interview transcripts for analysis. I have also examined a number of relevant documents, including *ECS* (Ministry of Education, 2001a), relevant policies and research literature. In my analysis of these I have identified what has emerged as meaningful or relevant to the teachers concerned in implementing this reform. As Neuman (1997) argues, an Interpretivist researcher aims to "develop an understanding of social life and discover how people construct meaning in natural settings" (p. 68), which is the case with my research. Acceptable knowledge for a Positivist researcher is "observable, precise, and independent of theory and values", while an Interpretivist researcher "sees the unique features of specific contexts and meanings as essential to understand social meaning" (Neuman, 1997, p. 72). It is for such reasons that I have selected Interpretivism as an appropriate approach for my research.

I have identified an appropriate theory to give coherence and rigour to my research. A theory is a system of ideas which condenses or organizes knowledge for the purpose of shifting people's view of the world (Neuman, 1997). Zeegers (2000) argues that a theory is used as a tool to guide researchers to conduct their research. I have taken up such considerations to investigate appropriate theories to guide my research, exploring two major theoretical perspectives: Phenomenology and Reconstructionism. Phenomenology applies to my research question in data collection and analysis. I have drawn on Reconstructionism as a tool in the analysis of the current EFL curriculum reform in secondary schools in Northeast China as part of a social dimension of the EFL curriculum reform. I will further explore links between Phenomenology and Reconstructionism below.

4.5　Phenomenology

Phenomenology is represented as a philosophy, a paradigm or a methodology tied to a qualitative methods in research, having been applied to education research as well as other academic fields (Creswell, 2007; Danaher & Briod, 2005; Ehrich, 2003; Goulding, 2005; Rehorick & Taylor, 1995). Whether one considers Phenomenology as a philosophy (Heidegger, 1988; Husserl, 1970; Merleau-Ponty, 1962) or a methodology (Schutz, 1963, 1973), it aims to extend and intensify understanding of direct experience (Spiegelberg, 1982). Danaher and Briod (2005) point out that, "Phenomenology remains research in the first person, one that describes from the explicit life-world experiences of individual Is, the shared structures of meaning implicit in the We" (p. 217). Phenomenology is used to examine first-person experience, predominantly in relation to intentionality as far as that experience is concerned (Grbich, 2007). It is the study of phenomena that occur in everyday life in the human world through the lived experience of people who encounter them (Creswell, 2007; Crotty, 1996; van Manen, 1990). In examining the current EFL curriculum reform in Chinese secondary schools and its relationship with globalization as a major phenomenon through EFL teachers' experiences of it, I have drawn on Metcale and Game's (2006) representation of Phenomenology as being concerned with "direct and specific descriptions of experiences, of the space and time of our relations with others" (p. 92).

I have, then, used Phenomenology as a conceptual tool to examine phenomena in the social world, as suggested by Lyotard (1991). A phenomenon is "anything that appears or presents itself, such as emotions, thoughts and physical objects" (Ehrich, 2003, p. 45), and Phenomenology is an attempt to understand and describe the phenomena of an individual's awareness (Phillipson, 1972, cited in Willis, 1999). It is a conceptual tool which has allowed me to see how the participants in my research live through and convey phenomena (Creswell, 1998, 2007).

Ehrich (2003) takes issue with Phenomenology as a research methodology, contending that it aims at describing phenomena, rather than explaining them, identifying Phenomenology as a tool for obtaining certain knowledge through description of experiences in the world, a departure from a Positivist perspective in this aspect of research, but no more than this. I have described the phenomena associated with the design and implementation of the reform under investigation, as Ehrich (2003) suggests, but I have also drawn upon Phenomenology as a conceptual tool for use in my analysis of the data that I have generated, having turned to the work of other scholars to inform my activity in this regard (see for example Lyotard, 1991; Moustakas, 1994; Neil, 1979; van Manen, 1990). Willis (1999) argues:

> Phenomenology is not so much a particular method as a particular approach by philosophers who wanted to reaffirm and describe their "being in the world" as an alternative way to human knowledge, rather than through the objectification of so-called Positivist science (p.94).

Phenomenology, then, is an interpretive approach which focuses on everyday subjective meaning and experience (Holstein & Gubrium, 1998), and I have taken up this perspective to study participant EFL teachers' experience of the reform under study.

4.5.1　The Selection of Phenomenology

Education research in the second half of the 20th century has seen a turning towards Interpretivist approaches based on qualitative research, and this development has included Phenomenology (Burns, 1994). Phenomenological research exhibits particular features which are different from any other type of research suggested by van Manen (1990), who argues:

> Phenomenology is the study of the lifeworld—the world as we immediately experience it pre-reflectively rather than as we conceptualize, categorize, or reflect on it. Phenomenology aims at gaining a deeper understanding of the nature or meaning of our everyday experiences (p.9).

It is a perspective that allows researchers not only to enter participants' lives, but also to gain insights to their lived experience. Phenomenology focuses on an understanding of the meaning of individual lived experience (Barnacle, 2004). Creswell (2007) argues that Phenomenology focuses on understanding the meaning of a concept or phenomena and that this can be extended to consider the meaning of individuals' lives. Phenomenology is a unique theory (van Manen, 1990) which I have used to obtain an in-depth understanding of lived experience of the participants in my research.

Grbich (2007) argues that Phenomenology is a tool with which to describe given phenomena as accurately as possible in order to achieve understanding of their essence, and I have applied this idea to my research. I have turned to Phenomenology as a theoretical perspective to underpin my research as it allows me to enter participant EFL teachers' inner worlds to gain an in-depth understanding of their lived experience, enabling me to understand its meaning for teachers as they implement the reform under study. This is of some importance as I have been able to approach my research questions by means of these EFL teachers' perspectives, attitudes, feelings, and reflections on their professional experience in relation to the reform. My research has focused on an investigation of EFL teachers' experiences as part of generating an understanding of the relationship between the reform and globalization. In drawing on Phenomenology in the design of my research, I have examined two pivotal terms that have emerged for address: intentionality and lived experience.

4.5.2 Intentionality

In Husserl's (1970) view, intentionality plays an influential role in gaining an understanding of the research world as it provides direction in guiding human mental processes and consciousness. This is a unique feature of human consciousness which other features cannot replace, as Moustakas (1994) argues, "Intentionality refers to consciousness, to the internal experience of being conscious of something; thus the act of consciousness and the object of consciousness are intentionally related" (p. 8) I have highlighted the concept of intentionality as it has helped to guide me to an understanding of the reform, as suggested by Moustakas (1994).

According to Budd (2005), intentionality is a cognitive demand, or an authoritative tendency that guides researchers to negotiate the research world. Intentionality itself suggests a relationship between the subject and the object of experience (Willis, 1999) a concept which can help researchers to understand that experience (Ehrich, 1999). Husserl (1970) comments on intentionality:

> We must say to ourselves again and again that without them (intentionality or intentional mental processes) objects and the world would not be there for us and that they are for us only with the meaning and mode of being that they constantly derive or have derived from these subjective achievements (p. 163).

My research draws on the concept of intentionality in its deliberate and conscious engagement with EFL teachers' descriptions of their experiences with the reform under study, where I have come to understand the meaning of the reform in this teacher world. Intentionality in my case are the processes that I have engaged to gain an understanding of EFL teachers' attitudes to and perceptions of EFL curriculum reform as a response to globalization. This has been based on considerations of their views as having influenced their behaviours or experiences as they have implemented this reform.

4.5.3   Lived Experience

Lived experience is another term used in relation to Phenomenology (Bresler, 1995). As van Manen (1990) argues, Phenomenology is the study of everyday life and lived experience, and obtains a reflection of that everyday life and everyday experience. According to Dilthey (1985, cited in van Manen, 1990), lived experience is "immediate, pre-reflective consciousness of life: reflexive or self-given awareness which is, as awareness, unaware of itself" (p. 36). This suggests that lived experience occurs out of direct contact with things in the world (Barnacle, 2004). The concept of lived experience has provided me with possibilities to explore participant EFL teachers' experience of the reform as well as my own relevant personal experience. As Barnacle (2004) says, the value of experience is extended to researchers' own particular experiences.

I have drawn on the idea of lived experience as referring to the professional experience of EFL teachers in secondary schools, experience which is related to their teaching and learning practice in classrooms. I have investigated participating EFL teachers' perceptions and attitudes to their experience of the current EFL curriculum reform and ways in which it is linked to globalization, and Phenomenology has provided me with an intellectual context in which to conduct my research. It also foregrounds "its logic and criteria" (Crotty, 1998, p. 3), in that it has enabled me to structure the research through its various phases. I have taken the study of the lived experience of the teachers concerned in the implementation of the reform under study as both the starting point and the end point for my research, which is in line with van Manen's (1990) views on lived experience.

I have already referred to Ehrich's (2003) taking issue with Phenomenology as a research methodology even as a number of researchers have turned to it in the conduct of their research (Barkway, 2001). Criticism has nonetheless emerged, particularly in relation to the idea of Phenomenology having lost its essence when it was adopted as a methodology in qualitative research (Les, 2005). Crotty (1996) argues that most Phenomenological-based research is not absolute, as it is descriptive, subjective and not critical. Bourdieu (1977) claims that Phenomenology is flawed as it attempts to comprehend "the world as self-evident", "taken-for-granted" through describing lived experience (p. 3). These arguments are based on the concept of Phenomenology somehow having missed or neglected an important research process: to study phenomena objectively (Willis, 1999).

Phenomenology as advocated by researchers such as Boss (1983) proposes a strict study of phenomenon and a generation of meaning via directly visible experience, and this has generated some discussion and debate among scholars in relation to their understanding of Phenomenology (Budd, 2005; Crotty, 1996; Danaher & Briod, 2005; Grant, 2008; Groenewald, 2004; Lyotard, 1991; Moustakas, 1994). Such scholars argue that Phenomenological studies exclude internal things such as feelings, perceptions, and attitudes, as Leech (1989) argues. Such discussions represent Phenomenology as not being an appropriate methodology in qualitative research (Willis, 1999).

In response to such discussions, I have drawn upon Giorgi's (2000) view, as he contends that choosing Phenomenology is an appropriate methodological approach as it enables the researcher to examine subjective experience objectively. I have also drawn upon Creswell (2007), Moustakas (1994) and van Manen's (1990) views of Phenomenology. These scholars argue that Phenomenology focuses not only on the processes of description of experience, but also on interpretation of experience. Their perspectives have provided me with a means of engaging the interrelationships of subjective and objective experience in developing my own understanding of the implementation of the reform under study as suggested by Ladki (2005). I have also drawn on the work of Grich (2007) to explore possibilities of research methods and strategies to investigate EFL teachers' experience. One of the strategies I have used in my research is to turn to the lifeworld existentials identified by van Manen (1990) for the purpose of data analysis. In relation to an interpretation of experience, van Manen (1990) provides a useful conceptual tool for researchers to explore the nature of lived experience with his concept of lifeworld existentials. These are lived space, lived time, lived body and lived other. Drawing on this concept of four existentials of lifeworld serves to engage data analysis as contributing to a deeper understanding of lived experience, as van Manen (1990) argues.

4.5.4　Lived Space

Lived space is a space in which people feel that they might be influenced by their accustomed or familiar working, leisure, social or studying environment (van Manen, 1990). Lived space is "the felt space", and it is, in a general sense, "the world or landscape in which human beings move and find themselves at home", rather than a mathematical space relating to height, length and depth (van Manen, 1990, p. 102). Given the sort of familiarity involved in occupying lived space, if that space is in some way changed, feelings may be affected, and ways of thinking may be influenced in any number of ways, as van Manen (1990) suggests. I have considered lived space as participant EFL teachers' felt space in which EFL teachers have been influenced by those environments, including the global and the Chinese contexts in combination with the regional and the school contexts, so that I have positioned the reform in both macro and micro contexts. I will discuss such issues further in Chapter 7 in relation to a general picture of the global and the Chinese contexts. I will detail my discussions on the global, the Chinese and school contexts in Chapter 8, and discuss the local contexts in Chapter 9.

4.5.5　Lived Time

Lived time is subjective time, not clock time or objective time, "the time that appears to speed up when people enjoy themselves, or slow down when they feel bored or when they are anxious, as in the dentist's chair" (van Manen, 1990, p. 104). Lived time is also "a temporal way of being in the world" (van Manen, 1990, p. 104). What is more, lived time can serve as a record of people's emotions in their lives, part of their lived experience. As far as my research is concerned, lived time is EFL teachers' temporal lived experience, the time during which they have experienced the reform under study. It includes the past, the present and the future. Examining EFL teachers' perspectives of lived time allows a dynamic picture of the reform under study to be developed, an exploration of which has provided a general picture of development of the reform under study through EFL teachers' perspectives. I will develop my discussions further in Chapter 7 and Chapter 10.

4.5.6　Lived Other

Van Manen (1990) suggests, "Lived other is the lived relation we maintain with others in the interpersonal space that we share with them" (p. 104). Lived other is a concept that highlights the relationships maintained between participants and those who may influence these participants' lives and experiences. They include social, organizational, familial membership and surroundings (Eggenberger, 2007). As far as my research is concerned, lived other is the other stakeholders in the EFL reform, who influence EFL teachers' experience of the reform under study. They include students, parents, principals, and governments, who have provided EFL teachers' support or pressure, or not, playing an influential role in their lived experience which will be discussed further in Chapters 7 and 9.

4.5.7   Lived Body

Lived body is ways in which people physically experience the reality of the world. As van Manen (1990) states, "Lived body refers to the Phenomenological fact that we are always bodily in the world" (p. 103). I have not drawn upon considerations of lived body, as I have focused on the reform through EFL teachers' perceptions and their attitudes, rather than through ways in which they physically experience this reform. This is because the reform under study is an intellectual, pedagogical, social, political, cultural and economic reform, not one that takes up issues of the physical bodies of teachers.

Lived space is the contexts within which the reform under study has been implemented; lived time is participant EFL teachers' temporal way of experiencing their implementing the reform under study, and both of these are part of their lived experience. That lived experience is their past and present experience as well as their future expectations. Lived other is the relationship between EFL teachers and other stakeholders in the programs they deliver, and these are students, parents, principals, their own colleagues, and governments. Drawing on the concept of lifeworld existentials in my research has assisted me in developing my own understanding and analysis of the implementation of this reform. To this end, I have adopted a certain research method, case study with data collected from interviews, a questionnaire and curriculum and policy documents. I will detail such considerations in Chapter 5. My focus has been on subjective experience of participants in my research, as suggested by Giorgi (2000), in this instance of the teachers concerned in implementing curriculum reform, as discussed in Chapter 3. A major consideration of my research design has been that of validity, and I will discuss issues related to this below.

4.6   Trustworthiness

The literature on qualitative research represents an increasing concern about assessing its quality (Creswell & Miller, 2000; Lather, 1986, 1993; Mays & Catherine, 2000). Issues of validity in relation to any research relate to ways in which it is possible to evaluate and identify effective research (Cohen, Manion, & Morrison, 2000; Mays & Catherine, 2000). I have discussed issues of validity as they emerge in relation to researchers' perceptions of validity and their choices of research paradigms as influencing their decisions. Cohen, Manion and Morrison (2000) identify issues of validity as important factors in considering effective research, that is, the quality of qualitative research. I have turned to the concept of "trustworthiness" in relation to issues of validity as far as my research is concerned because it is consistent with my ontological and epistemological positions in relation to subjective views of reality and knowledge generation, and allows me to ensure the quality of this research. This is consistent with Creswell and Miller's (2000) suggestion that choosing validity procedures is based on researchers' lens and their paradigm assumptions. As Lather (1986, 1993) suggests, researchers adopt different means or procedures to achieve validity, and this is related to the methodology employed. Winter (2000) takes up the issue of validity as being inherent in "the processes and intentions of particular research methodologies and projects" (p. 1).

I have addressed issues of validity drawing on the work of such scholars as Lather (1986) and Scheurich (1997). Lather (1986; 1993) reconceptualizes validity in what she represents as an emancipatory context of research. She argues that validity is a "limit question" of research: one that repeatedly surfaces; one that can neither be avoided nor resolved; a "fertile obsession" given its intractability (p. 674). Lather (1993) has identified validity "as a regime of truth" (p. 674) that has normalized researcher activities along lines established in Positivist traditions, and one which may be challenged in Interpretivist paradigms. This does not mean that issues of validity are not to be engaged, but that Positivist views of validity may be challenged. Reviewing this position, Lather (1993, cited in Scheurich, 1997) attempts to unsettle that regime of truth that she has identified and to implode those "controlling codes", and "work against constraints of authority" (Lather, 1993, cited in Scheurich, 1997, p. 89) as far as issues of validity for Interpretivist research is concerned.

Lather's (1993) perspectives on issues of validity also suggest that researchers situate their work within a methodological framework that provides for an examination of "the conditions of legitimation of knowledge in contemporary post-Positivism" (p. 673). She posits the idea of a kind of validity to be considered, established, and maintained, one which focuses on causality and faithfulness in research, moving towards a new epistemological perspective that is consistent with Interpretivist approaches (McTaggart, 1998). Scheurich (1997) contends that issues of validity are a mask which covers " a profound and disturbing sameness " in spite of its " ostensible differences " (p. 81). He suggests an epistemological mask which may preclude or distinguish the knowledge of the untrustworthy or the invalid from the rest (Aguinaldo, 2004; Scheurich, 1997). Scheurich (1997) accepts the socially constructed nature of knowledge and associated issues of validity that then emerge with Interpretivist approaches.

According to Golafshani (2003) , researchers' perceptions of validity are diverse and the research paradigms they choose may influence their concepts of validity in relation to their own research. According to Lietz, Langer and Furman (2006) concepts such as reliability and validity are generally used in Positivist approaches with quantitative research for pursuing objectivity, and, given this, do not pertain to my research. I have taken up the idea of issues of validity being based on the quality or trustworthiness of qualitative research (Davies & Dodd, 2002; Golafshani, 2003; Lather, 1993; Lincoln & Guba, 1985). Qualitative research emphasizes the study of phenomena as needing to be conducted in their natural settings, and interpreted in relation to meanings generated by people (Phillimore & Goodson, 2004).

Qualitative research, then, does not necessarily embrace quantitative research via measurement to engage with quantifiable and quantified data in an attempt to achieve objectivity (Davies & Dodd, 2002). Qualitative research entails knowledge being obtained through people's subjective and interpretive social interaction (Phillimore & Goodson, 2004). Davies and Dodd (2002) further argue that the quality or trustworthiness of such research is achieved by generating meaning subjectively and reflectively from the social interaction in focus. What this means is that issues of validity in qualitative research are related to data and analyses that are descriptive and interpretive, not to be considered as accurate and measurable features of a research problem, as may be the case in quantitative research projects. This is the way in which my research has been carried out.

Such consideration is consistent with Kuhn's (1970) perspectives on qualitative research. Kuhn (1970) calls so-called scientifically-based research approaches myths, a step that goes some way towards discrediting the claims of Positivist approaches. As Kuhn (1970) states:

Then myths can be produced by the same sorts of methods and held for the same sorts of reasons that now lead to scientific knowledge. If on the other hand they are called science, then science has included bodies of belief quite incompatible with the ones we hold today (p. 2).

I have drawn upon the term, "trustworthiness", used by Lather (1986, 1993) as a parallel concept to validity in Positivist research. My research methodology is Interpretivist, and I have worked with the concept of trustworthiness, as a measure of the success of my research outcomes, relying on the readers' confidence in them. Erlandson, Harris and Skipper (1993) propose that trustworthiness can "demonstrate truth value, provide the basis for applying it, and allow for external judgements to be made about the consistency of its procedures and the neutrality of its findings or decisions" (p. 29). Trustworthiness is the result of rigorous research, rather than a naturally occurring thing (Lietz, et al., 2006). Qualitative researchers take into account relevant influential factors which play key roles in research when establishing trustworthiness (Creswell, 1998, 2007; Lietz, et al., 2006; Lincoln & Guba, 1985). As Lincoln and Guba (1985) argue, establishing trustworthiness in qualitative research is a matter of establishing credibility, transferability, dependability and conformability.

Credibility is obtained through examining internal consistency in qualitative research (Lincoln & Guba, 2000), dealing with issues of ways in which outcomes are compatible with reality (Merriam, 1998; Shenton, 2004). Gasson (2004) argues that credibility attempts to explore ways in which researchers can ensure quality in the research processes they engage. This suggests that credibility can be questioned on the basis of the subjective nature of data collected as the relationship between researchers and their subjects are interactive, participative and cooperative (Decrop, 2004). This further implies that credibility is the issue most related to personal and interpersonal skills in qualitative research (Henderson, 1991). I have attempted to achieve credibility through those strategies such as researcher reflexivity, based on Cutcliff's (2003) proposition that researcher reflexivity is used as an approach to increase the credibility of the research which I will detail below.

Transferability is the extent to which research outcomes are applicable to other research contexts (Decrop, 2004; Koch, 2006; Merriam, 1998; Shenton, 2004).

As Gasson (2004) argues, transferability addresses issues of "how far a researcher may make claims for a general application of their theory" (p. 98). This requires that researchers provide details of their research context and to integrate outcomes generated with relevant literature or similar settings (Decrop, 2004). I have achieved transferability through providing sufficient information related to myself, contexts, process, and participants, as well as the relationships between me and participants in ways suggested by Morrow (2005), which has enabled readers to determine ways in which research outcomes may transfer (Morrow, 2005).

Dependability is the match between the data collected by researchers and what actually took place in settings (Decrop, 2004). As Gasson (2004) maintains, "The way in which a study is conducted should be consistent across time, researchers, and analysis techniques" (p. 95). The concept of reality in interpretive research is multiple and contextual, rather than isolated and permanent (Decrop, 2004). This further suggests that issues of dependability stress issues of the processes of research, which need to be clear and repeatable or reproducible (Decrop, 2004; Morrow, 2005). I have achieved dependability in that I have provided details of research activities and processes as well as identified emerging themes and categories. As Morrow (2005) argues, dependability is achieved by examining research design, "research activities and processes" as well as its "influences on the data collecting and analysis; emerging themes, categories" (p. 252). I have employed case study method, using two sites, to study details of the implementation of the EFL curriculum reform under study, and I have used the outcomes of this research to inform professional considerations of that reform for the rest of China, suggesting that this case study is reproducible. I will present the details of the research processes engaged in Chapter 5.

Conformability is one of the foundations of social research, capturing the features of objectivity (Decrop, 2004; Morrow, 2005). Patton (2002) links objectivity to instruments, rather than perspectives or beliefs of human beings, suggesting that objectivity is linked to quantitative research used by quantitative researchers, where qualitative researchers use conformability to show their "comparable concern to objectivity" (Shenton, 2004, p. 72). Morrow (2005) takes up this view, arguing that "conformability (vs. objectivity) is based on the acknowledgement that research is never objective" (p. 252). It is achieved on the basis of qualitative researchers taking steps to assure as much as possible that the research outcomes are generated from the participants' experiences and views, rather than from researchers' descriptions (Shenton, 2004). Shenton (2004) also suggests that researchers use triangulation to promote such conformability in qualitative research.

4.6.1 Triangulation

Triangulation is an attempt to gain multiple perspectives on a single issues, event, or phenomenon to demonstrate the quality of research (Patton, 2002). As Decrop (2004) argues, triangulation is a term used in social science research to address the information derived from different perspectives to illustrate the research problem. Triangulation allows for improvement in researchers' confidence when it comes to overcoming their bias in research (Murray, 1999). As Decrop (2004) argues, triangulation serves to confine biases in relation to persons and methodology and to increase the trustworthiness of research. Morrow (2005) identifies it as one important component to assure the quality of research.

According to Creswell and Miller (2000), "Triangulation is a validity procedure where researchers search for convergence among multiple and different sources of information to form themes or categories in a study" (p. 126). Using triangulation, data is sorted systematically to find common themes or categories by removing overlapping parts (Creswell & Miller, 2000). In doing so, triangulation starts "the way for richer and potentially more credible interpretations" (Decrop, 2004, p. 162). Triangulation has four basic types: data, methods, investigators and theories (Decrop, 2004; Denzin, 2009). Data triangulation is the use of various data sources in research; method triangulation is the adoption of several methods to study a single research phenomenon; investigator triangulation focuses on employing different investigators to examine the same body of data; and theoretical triangulation draws upon diverse perspectives to interpret a single set of data (Decrop, 2004). According to Dootson (1995, cited in Farmer, Robinson, Elliott, & Eyles, 2006):

The type of triangulation and the decision to employ single or multiple triangulation techniques depend on the nature of the research question and should complement the methodological paradigms (e. g. phenomenology) that informs the question (p.379).

I have drawn upon data triangulation as a major trustworthiness procedure as part of my research as this has allowed me to access various data sources: primary, secondary and tertiary, providing multiple perspectives on research issues, as suggested by Decrop (2004). I have adopted multiple strategies in the form of interviews, a questionnaire and analysis of documents for the purposes of triangulation. I have undertaken this to provide diverse forms of evidence rather than one sort of data as part of enhancing the trustworthiness of my research. As Creswell and Miller (2000) argue, multiple data sources allow the provision of various evidences in order to increase the trustworthiness of research. Creswell (2002) also argues:

> Triangulation is the process of corroborating evidence from different individuals, types of data, or methods of data collection... This ensures that the study will be accurate because the information is not drawn from a single source, individual, or process of data collection. In this way, it encourages the researcher to develop a report that is both accurate and credible (p. 280).

Triangulation allows researchers to obtain a holistic understanding of the research through various evidences (Anfara, Brown, & Mangione, 2002) which is the case with my research.

Creswell and Miller (2000) argue that trustworthiness is part of the process where researchers, in the early stages of their research, recognize their "entering beliefs and biases" and "then to bracket or suspend those researcher biases as the study proceeds" (Creswell & Miller, 2000, p. 126). I have used bracketing, discussed below, to demonstrate the issues of trustworthiness. My approach is also based on Winter's (2000) argument that an exploration of the involvement and role of researchers in qualitative research may enhance the trustworthiness of research.

4.6.2 Bracketing

I have employed Husserl's (1931) notion of bracketing in dealing with what scholars have represented as deficiencies in Phenomenology as an approach to Interpretivist research (see for example Bourdieu, 1977). Bracketing is a subjective and intentional intellectual device used in relation to reflection and description of researchers' own lived experience. As far as Phenomenology is concerned, bracketing is researcher reflexivity, used as one of the tools a Phenomenologist may employ to investigate the social world, and knowledge of that world (Gearing, 2004). This is achieved by consciously and deliberately placing themselves beyond their own constructions, preconceptions and assumptions that may be closely related to the experience being investigated (Gearing, 2004). It is also a means used by researchers to clarify the trustworthiness of a work, a means by which the degree of freedom from researcher influence can be assessed (Ahern, 1999, cited in Rolls & Relf, 2006).

Bracketing is carried out by researchers in the processes of research design, data collection and data analysis (Ahern, 1999; Gearing, 2004; Klein & Westcott, 1994). This process of bracketing suggests that researchers are able to achieve interpretative conclusions even as they acknowledge their personal experiences, ideas or feelings in conducting the research (Bednall, 2006). Bracketing, in this sense, allows "the voices of subjectivity to emerge authentically in coming to an understanding of what essentially the research respondents mean in their personal accounts expressed through the data collection devices" (Bednall, 2006, p. 126). As Husserl (1931) argues, bracketing is done not only by means of researchers' general sensory observation of the experience they are studying, but also by their primary and direct consciousness of the phenomena that is under attention.

Researchers have taken up bracketing for consideration in their Phenomenological study as their past experiences or perceptions might cause problems in interpreting the meaning of participants' lived experience (LeVasseur, 2003). They adopt bracketing as a tool to shed light on their preconception and related influences in their research (Ahern, 1999). Bracketing used in qualitative research emphasizes the nature or essences of lived experience (LeVasseur, 2003; Reitz, 1999). I have drawn upon the concept of bracketing throughout each of the distinct phases of my project, which include initiating my research project, collecting data and engaging in data analysis, drawing on suggestions in regard to each of these made by Gearing (2004). I have outlined my personal encounters with the new EFL curriculum at the beginning of Chapter 1 to show my experience of it in Chinese secondary schools. This is normal in a project such as mine, to "begin a Phenomenological investigation with an examination of the investigator's preconceptions of the phenomenon in question" (Reitz, 1999, p. 148). An acknowledgement of this kind serves to make researchers aware of their own biases (Reitz, 1999). I have at the same time clarified my ontological and epistemological perspective and explored the possibilities of a methodological framework for my research, identifying a specific orientation. This has also been part of the initial phase of bracketing which has helped me to set up the parameters of my research, influencing my entire research program. I have drawn on the concept of bracketing in establishing my research project, choice of methods and processes of data gathering and analysis. I have turned to interviews for data collection as they may be used to inform me of my own preconceptions of the phenomenon in question. I have done this in order to "take steps to minimize the limiting effect such biases might have on descriptions rendered by study participants in their interviews" (Polkingorne, 1989, cited in Reitz, 1999, p. 148). I have employed an additional step in relation to interviews, drawing on Colaizzi's (1978) suggestion that the final transcripts of interviews and preliminary outcomes of my research be discussed with the participants before further analysis or exploration be engaged. This has been done so that I might see whether or not the outcomes of my research are in line with participants' experience, and not just my experience, as suggested by Reitz (1999). The employment of bracketing in my research is consistent with the view that bracketing may enable the researcher to obtain trustworthiness in the conduct of research (Bednall, 2006; Creswell, 2007; Husserl, 1970; Rolls & Relf, 2006).

4.6.3　Reflexivity

Reflexivity is "the capacity of any system of signification to turn back upon itself, to make itself its own object by referring to itself" (Myerhoff and Ruby, 1992, cited in Ahern, 1999, p. 408). It is concerned with being able to expose and to examine the self. In research, reflexivity is researchers' capacities to identify the perceived influential elements involved in their engagement with research. As Horsburgh (2003) says, reflexivity is used by qualitative researchers to engage a process of identifying their own engagement in given issues which might influence their understandings of the meanings and contexts what it is that they are researching. Smyth and Shacklock (1998) argue that reflexivity is "an acknowledgement of the ideological and historical power dominant forms of inquiry exert over the researcher and the researched" (p. 6). Reflexivity, then, is researchers' capacity to put aside their personal biases and their feeling, beliefs and their preconceptions in research (Ahern, 1999).

Reflexivity allows researchers to acknowledge their own roles in influencing the meaning of the research in which they are engaged (Lietz, et al., 2006). It demonstrates the quality of research as it forms part of the focus of trustworthiness. As Cutcliff (2003) says:

> There appears to be a clear perception among methodological researchers that the purpose of reflexivity, at least in part, is to enhance the credibility of the findings by accounting for researcher values, beliefs, knowledge, and biases. Given that the relevant methodological literature indicates that reflexivity appears to involve accounting for oneself in the research, it is reasonable, therefore, to review briefly the techniques that have been posited as facilitating this process (p. 137).

I have drawn upon reflexivity as a further means by which to ensure trustworthiness in relation to my research. To this end, I have focused on presenting my personal experience at the beginning of my research project, as set out in Chapter 1, to indicate my awareness of potential biases that may emerge in the processes of conducting my research. This is also consistent with my use of bracketing, as discussed above. In similar vein, I have addressed my ontological and epistemological stances at the beginning of this chapter. I have also identified Phenomenology and Reconstructionism as theoretical perspectives that underpin my research. According to Ahern (1999), reflexivity addresses the capacity of researchers to address issues of their biases in research, part of which derives from their ontological and epistemological positions. Bracketing focuses on the processes of putting aside these biases in relation to data collection and analysis (Ahern, 1999), which I have discussed above. These are the steps that I have taken to address issues of bias, and in doing so, to establish trustworthiness in my research. In the following section, I will highlight Reconstructionism as a theoretical perspective within my research.

4.7   Reconstructionism

Reconstructionism is a theoretical perspective that applies in education in general and curriculum in particular (Adamson & Morris, 2007; Gwele, 2005a; Ornstein, 2007; Ozmon & Craver, 2008; Stanley, 1992). It is a challenge to the status quo of a given society to realize an improvement of life in that society. Reconstructionism assumes that a given society has its problems, and identifies those problems as "social injustice, problems and inequities" (Adamson & Morris, 2007, p. 268). A Reconstructionist perspective positions stakeholders in education programs as advocates of social equality, who aim to inspire people to rebuild a harmonious and sympathetic society, as Brameld (1956) states. Reconstructionists recognize education as a means to address perceived social problems and to seek educational methods of initiating change in social and economic systems (Brameld, 1977). A Reconstructionist sees education as being used to serve society and to promote social development. Society and education are the two main components for Reconstructionism to focus on, both of which require constant change and reconstruction (Ozmon & Craver, 2008). As Ozmon and Craver (2008) state, Reconstructionism looks to changes for a better life by embracing ways of knowing, democracy and a humane disposition towards members of a society. As Simmons and Robert-Weah (2000) argue, Reconstructionism challenges social organizations to accept diversity and achieve equality in society. My own research focus on the current EFL curriculum reform implemented in Chinese secondary schools investigates its aims to engage challenges of globalization at the same time as it challenges traditional education concepts, teaching methods, content, and assessment, as it assists Chinese students in taking up new roles as 21st century citizens.

Reconstructionism, as a struggle between conservation and innovation (Anthony & Kritsonis, 2006), implies a shift from a certain lower level of social, economic and political life towards a higher one (Oyelade, 2002), playing a significant role in promoting the reconstruction of society, especially as this relates to education systems and curriculum (Udvari-Solner & Thousand, 1996). I have drawn upon Reconstructionism as a conceptual tool that underpins the reform under study. By this I mean that Reconstructionism is in itself a phenomenon in the context of Chinese secondary schools that makes up part of the lived experience of teachers implementing the reform. I have drawn on the conception of Reconstructionism in relation to the discussion of education, curriculum, teachers and students, detailed in the following sections.

4.7.1 Reconstructionism and Education

I have taken the position that education as the centre of culture is a key factor in influencing transformations of a culture (Brameld, 1971; Thomas, 1994). As Robertson and Scholte (2007) argue, education may be regarded as not only a way to pass on knowledge and skills, but also the site in which a number of social problems in a globalizing world may be solved, underscoring the argument the potential of education to promote social change (Adamson & Morris, 2007). I have drawn on this perspective of education as significant in rebuilding society, particularly in the context of globalization in relation to my research.

Reconstructionists use education to challenge current social systems directly, and to achieve changes in economics, politics, culture and social institutions (Stanley, 1992). According to Counts (1934), Reconstructionism stresses the use of schools to challenge existing social orders and to achieve change. Reconstructionists encourage educators to engage with concepts of international peace and cooperation and social reconstruction in a globalizing world (Brameld, 1950, 1956), attempting to provide learners with a site of effective Reconstructionist learning and access to attainable Reconstructionist goals (Anthony & Kritsonis, 2006). A Reconstructionist perspective allows learners to be made aware of existing social issues and to empower them to rebuild their own societies to make new ones (Adamson & Morris, 2007). I have interpreted this as being one of the goals of the reform under study, as is also suggested by Zhong (2006).

Reconstructionism emphasizes citizenship, where teachers and students work within their own socially and culturally established roles to seek solutions for existing social problems (Howard, 1994). As Ozman and Craver (2008) argue, Reconstructionists consider that education is integral to social systems, with educators encouraged to be part of improving their own education system and through this, ultimately their society. Reconstructionists help learners to realize that the point of learning is to reconstruct a better society around them. It is a view which is consistent with Chinese cultural history and its overall education goals, which have been identified in Li's (2007) work. Since the Chinese cultural context has been influenced strongly by collectivism and socialism, results in relation to relevant motivation and goals of education may be seen as being embodied in teaching and learning and the curricula that are related to these (Biggs, 1996; Brislin, 1993; Rao, 2006). My research has further indicated that these influences have their effect on the attitudes and behaviours of educators and learners as well, as Brislin (1993) also states.

4.7.2 Reconstructionism and Curriculum

The term, " curriculum ", has a number of connotations or interpretations, depending on a variety of social and ideological perspectives (Gwele, 2005a). Marsh and Willis (2007) provide no less than eight definitions for consideration of curriculum. Adamson and Morris (2007) also generate seven sorts of categories related to curriculum, " classical heritage, established knowledge, social utility, planned learning, experienced learning, personal transformation and life experience" (pp. 264-266). I have considered all Chinese education departments, from central to local, as being responsible for the design and provision of relevant curricula for the learners for whom they are responsible. This is on the basis of Gwele's (2005a) argument that curriculum is planned learning experiences provided by education organizations for their learners. I have extended such considerations to my own research in the Chinese context.

From a Reconstructionist perspective, curriculum may be regarded as one of the tools to be employed for social reconstruction (Stanley, 1992). As Adamson and Morris (2007) argue, Reconstructionists regard curricula as agents for promoting social change, through which a world of economic development based on social prosperity, fairness, equality, and democracy, each of which is conceived as indispensable factors for humankind to survive in a globalizing world, may be built (Armstrong, 2005; Gwele, 2005a). I have considered such issues in examining the EFL curriculum reform. Drawing on Reconstructionist perspectives in my research has enabled me to examine ways in which this reform may be seen in relation to modification of relationships within society, in particular relationships between culture and curriculum. Such consideration is extended from the work of Udvari-Solner and

Thousand (1996).

Again, from a Reconstructionist perspective, change and adaptation is the means by which a country may achieve constant growth and development, as curriculum is changed so that education takes up new responsibilities for a society, rather than adhering to traditional ways (Armstrong, 2005; Glicksberg, 1944). Given such a perspective, Reconstructionsists further propose that curriculum be constantly modernized so as to involve all participating learners, for this is seen as an aspect which will lead them to build up their own knowledge actively, rather than passively accepting it. It is a typical Reconstructionist goal of curriculum reform (Armstrong, 2005; Udvari-Solner & Thousand, 1996).

4.7.3 Reconstructionism and Participants

The research literature explores the role of teachers in implementing education changes, and curriculum reform in particular, from a perspective of Reconstructionism (Adamson & Morris, 2007; Armstrong, 2005; Gwele, 2005a; Ornstein, 2007). As Liston and Zeicher (1991, cited in Parks, 2006) suggest, teachers have taken up the role of challenging the status quo of the society, being concerned with problems inherent in culture and education. They argue that teachers have the potential to promote the development of social and education philosophy through their roles in influencing education policy making (Liston & Zeichner (1991, cited in Parks, 2006). Drawing on such Reconstructionist perspectives (see also for example Gwele, 2005), I have considered EFL teachers in Chinese secondary schools as being positioned as maintaining a transformative position in implementing curriculum reform. Reconstructionism views teachers as playing a significant role in education reforms such as the reform under study.

I have not only focused on exploring EFL teachers' professional development, but addressed the roles of teachers in implementing that reform. I have drawn on the work of Brameld (1956) and Gwele (2005) as well as that of Ozmon and Craver (2008), who represent Reconstructionism as a theory which explains demands on teachers implementing curriculum reforms designed to produce specific social, political, cultural and economic outcomes, especially in countries that perceive such needs as priority areas in their developing nationhood. I have been concerned with

EFL teachers' perceptions of and attitudes to their direct experiences of this reform which have emerged from data collected and analysed. As van Driel, Verloop and Beigaard (2001) state, "A teacher's practice and his or her personal knowledge of this practice constitute the starting point for change" (p. 151). My interviews with EFL teacher participants have proceeded on such lines, providing me with data on their experiences of implementing the reform in their schools.

Reconstructionists position students as another important group of participants in any curriculum reform, as they attempt to use the knowledge learned in class to help seek solutions to social problems (Reed & Davis, 1999). From a Reconstructionist perspective, an ideal student responds to the call to adjust their own learning to fulfill the identified needs of the society in which they live; the needs may be social, economic, political, spiritual, or a combination of any or all of these (Tanner & Tanner, 2007). It may be the case that they are to act as revolutionaries in an identified cause as part of their contribution to social reconstruction (Tanner & Tanner, 1995, 2007). Positioning students in such ways suggests that they are subjects of reform rather than participants in it. Reconstructionist thinking, then, recognizes the student as the person who may be led to identify social, economic and political problems and then engage them in order to promote the desired social, economic and political development, as Simmons and Robert-Weah (2000) argue.

I have not focused on the students in secondary schools in China in my research as they have no experience of the previous reforms and they cannot provide significant information for my research in that regard. A focus on student responses to the new EFL curriculum is beyond the scope of my research, but that does not mean that it might not constitute the subject of further research in the field. My research has not focused on students, as the thrust of my research has been on the phenomenon of the reform and its implementation by teachers, and not on how this reform and its implementation has been received by students. A longitudinal study tracking such students would be required, and this is beyond the scope of my research. The result is that I have not focused on ways in which students may attempt to improve their society with the knowledge learned, which might be my future follow-up research; I am concerned only with the proposition that they are positioned in such a way by the reform under study that they may be expected to do so. My research focuses on ways in which the current EFL curriculum reform in Chinese secondary schools has been linked to globalization, partly through EFL teachers' professional experience as represented in their interview transcripts, including their attitudes to teaching and learning as part of this reform. I have explored the tensions that emerge as rhetoric of reform and practical considerations in the implementation of that reform are considered.

I have employed Reconstructionism as a part of the theoretical framework that supports my research because its approach is consistent with current Chinese political and sociocultural mores. Issues of culture play an underlying role underpinning a theoretical perspective chosen in conducting curriculum studies (Tobin & Dowson, 1992). Chinese culture has been strongly influenced by collectivism and socialism that addresses the significance of social requirements or concerns (Biggs, 1996; Brislin, 1993; Guan, Ron., & Xiang, 2005; Rao, 2006). Education in China "must serve socialist modernization drive, must integrate itself with production and labour, so as to cultivate socialist builders and successors featuring an all-around development in morality, intelligence, physique, etc", stated in the *Educational Law* of 1995 (*The Educational Law of the People's Republic of China*, 1995, cited in Yang, 2005, p. 28). The reform under investigation has been initiated to help China meet the challenges of rapid economic development in the 21st century (Li, 2007; Ministry of Education, 1998; Wang, 2007; Zhong, et al., 2001). This action is also consistent with a Reconstructionist perspective of social outcomes. Basic tenets within Chinese cultural history have created a fertile ground for Reconstructionism to be considered as part of my research.

A Reconstructionist perspective recognizes education as a transformation agent in society (Brameld, 1971; Ozmon & Craver, 2008; Thomas, 1994). In Cuffaro's (1995) words, educational theoretical foundations symbolize "choices, values, knowledge and beliefs" as well as "aspirations, intentions and aims" as they contribute to social and community decision making (p. 1). On the basis of this, I have turned to Reconstructionism as I have engaged the lived experience of EFL teachers in China. It is they who have been charged with implementing the reform that I am investigating. Reconstructionism, then, is part of the Phenomenological perspective that I have drawn upon to inform my research into the realities of current English language education in China in the context of globalization. Further, Reconstructionism has drawn my attention to developing an understanding of social issues related to the popular injunction: "think globally and act locally" (Thomas, 1994, p. 77).

My research has focused on the current EFL curriculum reform in Chinese secondary schools which involves processes of reform of the EFL curriculum, which has emerged from a view of Chinese society being in a constant state of change, with its citizens' proficiency in English becoming an education priority as part of that change (Zhu, 2003). It is a requirement that is consistent with a Reconstructionist perspective, which encourages students to apply their learning to social practice (Ozmon& Craver, 2008). It is a perspective that suggests that students are to be exposed to Reconstructionist ideals for their own and their country's future development. It is a perspective which also requires curricula to be responsive in corresponding fashion. Reconstructionism has provided me with a further conceptual tool with which to examine processes of the reform under study that is inclusive of policies and the curriculum itself. I have adopted both Phenomenology and Reconstructionism in my research as they serve their different purposes. These two perspectives are not necessarily to be used in tandem; I have not attempted to use the concepts interchangeably or as equating with each other. Both are powerful conceptual tools that I have used at various points in the research.

Phenomenology is concerned with the meaning of individuals' experience of a phenomenon or phenomena (Creswell, 2007), and I have linked this with Reconstructionism as one of the phenomena that individuals concerned with this reform experience, and make meaning from. Counts (1978) first published his work in 1932, and he represents Reconstructionism as focusing on social phenomena as part of an attempt to rebuild a new vision of human expectations and experience. I have linked these two perspectives with the term "phenomenon" and have conducted my research on the basis of that link.

I have used Phenomenology as a tool to enable me to focus on examining an education phenomenon, the current EFL curriculum reform in Chinese secondary schools through EFL teachers' professional experiences. Phenomenology has provided me with conceptual tools that I have used to set up research procedures for my data collection and data analysis. Reconstructionism has allowed another set of conceptual tools in analyzing data generated in transcripts of interviews and examination of curriculum statements and policy documents in the context of China's growing presence on a globalizing world stage as it has hosted the Olympic Games in 2008 and achieved entry into the World Trade Organization in 2001.

4.8 Conclusion

In this chapter, I have outlined the methodological framework for my research. This framework includes my ontological and epistemological positions, an interpretive paradigm that I have chosen, an investigation of the rational for qualitative research that I have chosen, and a consideration of the theories of Phenomenology and Reconstructionism. I have discussed ontological and epistemological positions as having accommodated my starting point in the conduct of my research, and I have discussed an Interpretivist paradigm as having provided me with a particular way of making sense of my research. My choice of paradigm signifies ways in which I have situated myself—the particular stance I have adopted—in the conduct of my research. Phenomenology has provided me with a focus on research through an examination of EFL teachers' lived experience. This theoretical perspective has enabled me to obtain a deeper understanding of the reform under study and its implications for EFL teachers' professional lives. Phenomenology has also provided me with a conceptual tool that has helped me with designing this research in relation to my data collection and data analysis. Reconstructionism has allowed a significant perspective underlying curriculum studies in examining the current EFL curriculum designed for Chinese secondary schools.

Research methods can be classified as two main types: quantitative and qualitative (Blaikie, 2000; Creswell, 1998; Crotty, 1998; Ezzy, 2006). I have selected a qualitative approach to pursue my research questions. Research conducted with a Positivist's perception might engage in a quantitative approach; for Interpretivists, qualitative research might be employed (Creswell, 1998; Crotty, 1998; Denzin & Lincoln, 2000; Newton Suter, 2006; Walter, 2006). Qualitative research may be said to be subjective, inductive, multiple and small-scale, with data represented through words, pictures and thematic analyzes; quantitative research may be said to be objective, deductive, singular, large scale, with data represented through numbers and statistical analysis (Creswell, 1994; Crotty, 1998). Based on such distinctions, I have adopted qualitative research method in my research, using case study as the method to be employed. Given this, I have further explored relevant theories to underpin my research. In the following chapter I will detail case study as the research method that I have employed.

Chapter 5
Conducting Case Study

5.1 Introduction

In Chapter 4, I have outlined the methodological framework that I have employed in my research, discussing the theoretical perspectives which underpin it. In this chapter, I will discuss the research method that I have employed, and describe the data collection and analysis strategies that I have used in the design and conduct of my research, as well as ethics issues. In designing my research, I have turned to case study method. I have used the strategy of a questionnaire and interviews to generate data from participant EFL teachers' perspectives on the EFL curriculum reform that they have been required to implement, and analysis of policy and curriculum statements as they relate to this implementation. I have transcribed the interviews and read and re-read them to examine themes that have emerged for further discussions. I have designed interview questions to engage directly with participant EFL teachers' professional lives, including their perceptions, thoughts, experiences, impressions, feelings and beliefs as these relate to my research questions, as Welman and Kruger (1999, cited in Groenewald, 2004) suggest.

The dimensions of my research question have determined the criteria for choosing participants to be approached for my research. These are the EFL teachers who have experienced the reform under investigation, and because of this having been positioned to make sense of it (Hycner, 1999, p. 36). A further focus of my research has been on the meanings of the reform under study reflected in the EFL teachers' responses in the questionnaire and the interviews conducted, drawing on the work of Bednall (2006). Bednall (2006) considers the meanings of this reform developed out of reflection as providing possibilities for research foci. I will discuss issues of choosing case study as my research method before turning to research strategies used.

5.2 Case Study Method

Case study is an investigation with a focus on a certain aspect of a particular phenomenon to gain an understanding of its meaning in its own and possibly wider situations. Yin (2006) argues that case study may be used to tease out the specificity of the phenomenon selected for the research, a specificity which makes it different from other phenomena, but which may produce research outcomes from which generalizations may be made to a wider context. Merriam (1998) argues that case study is used to generate a deep understanding of contexts and meanings in relation to what is being investigated. Case study method, then, allows researchers to conduct detailed investigation of particular phenomena of interest in particular contexts (Hartley, 2004; Stake, 1995).

Given Yin's (2006) view of case study as being based on real life experience rather than what may occur in laboratory or clinical trials, it is a method that is appropriate in interpretivist qualitative research. Case study as a method, as George (2006) argues, allows the researcher to conduct a detailed examination of an aspect of a phenomenon in order to develop an understanding of it as a whole. The strength of case study lies in its focus on interactive processes within specific phenomenon to identify in some detail all that may come into play (Bell, 1993). The very specificity of detail allows for fine-grained research foci that allow the researcher to avoid the broad brush stroke approaches of other methods. In my research, I have applied that detailed focus to a specific area of Northeast China, and then on two regions within it, and then on school sites within those regions in order to pick up on details of EFL curriculum as they play out in individual teachers' classrooms within the larger context of the vast country that is China. This has allowed me to pick out details for focused attention, and on the basis of these, generate a number of knowledgeable insights to the national EFL curriculum reform and national outcomes of its implementation. According to Merriam (1998), case study focuses on studying the key features of a case—processes, contexts and discoveries—a concept on which I have drawn in designing my research.

According to Yin (2006), researchers taking up case study method consider three factors: research topics, contexts and data sources. This is particularly so with regard to a focus on an investigation of a current phenomenon in a real context (Yin, 2003a, 2003b, 2006). Hartley (2004) points out that case study "is particularly suited to research questions which require detailed understanding of social or organizational processes because of the rich data collected in context" (p. 323). I have drawn on these perspectives to take up case study as it has allowed me to highlight major issues raised by my research question: In what ways is the current EFL curriculum reform in Chinese secondary schools linked to globalization? This question has guided me to an emphasis on the contexts in which the reform under study has been positioned, and ways in which it has been initiated and implemented on the basis of documents, interviews and a questionnaire. Such consideration feeds into what case study elaborates.

Case study has allowed me to approach the selection of one province, Liaoning Province in Northeast China, and two sites within that province as being typical of representative features of the case, a bounded study, as suggested by Stake (1995). I have approached EFL curriculum reform in China as not being an isolated education phenomenon, having situated it in the context of constantly changing and complex political, social and economic developments. Such an approach to my investigation has enabled me to generate a general view of the reform being implemented throughout China as a whole. As Yin (2003a) argues, case study is to "cover contextual or complex multivariate conditions and not just isolated variables" (p. xi).

Case study further allows the use of single or multiple strategies for in-depth analysis of a single phenomenon (Creswell, 1994, 1998, 2007; Jones, 2006; Kumar, 2005). As Yin (2006) argues, multiple data resources may be used in case study method as they may provide different "logics and evidences" (Hartley, 2004, p. 24), to approach issues of validity, or in my case, trustworthiness, in conducting research. On the basis of such considerations, I have used multiple research strategies: a questionnaire, interviews and document analysis. As Hartley (2004) argues, researchers use case study on the basis of rich data sources to explore the phenomenon under study in relation to detailed and complex interactions and processes that occur within a social context.

According to Stake (1995), case study enables the researcher to learn about a particular case on the basis of the researchers' interests, and this is consistent with my consideration of taking up this research. I have used case study as my research method to enable me to generate a deep understanding of what the reform under study means in the context of China. As Merriam (1988) points out, case study is used to "gain an in-depth understanding of the situation and its meaning for those involved" (p. xii).

As I have drawn upon Phenomenology to underpin my research on the basis of participant EFL teachers' lived experience of the reform under study, I have explored the EFL curriculum reform in relation to participant EFL teachers' lived experience of it in the context of globalization. I have done this to obtain relevant insights to the reform under study. My use of case study is an acknowledgment of the uniqueness of what these participant EFL teachers have experienced in implementing the reform under study because this has allowed me to, as Stake (1995) would have it, "come to know extensively and intensively" (p. 36) about the meanings and contexts of the reform implemented in Northeast China and ways in which these teachers have experienced implementing it. My study of two sites within one case has enabled me to emphasize the experience of participants by allowing them to reflect on it, contributing to an understanding of this reform, and sharing this with me. This has allowed me to generate what Stake (1995) refers to as "thick description" of their lived experience (p. 39). Those "thick" descriptions that Stake (1995) refers to are the in-depth and detailed reports of experience in research which, in the hands of a researcher, produce what may be considered virtual sentences that make the readers feel that they seem to experience the phenomenon being studied (Creswell & Miller, 2000). Thick description is to uncover what lived experience would convey in research (Stake, 1978, 1995, 2000).

Critics of case study as a research method focus on its very nature of being a single case. Criticism hinges on the suggestion that it is the single case that renders it ineffective when it comes to providing researchers with an acceptable research conclusion (Tellis, 1997). One of the earliest and most persistent criticisms of case study has been in regard to the extent to which it may be used to generalize to inform other cases or to apply to other settings (Sturman, 1999). As Flyvbjerg (2006) argues, a number of scholars consider that case study cannot allow generalizability on the basis of a single case, implying that such a process is subjective and illogical, and so do not accept it as appropriate method for research on that basis (Flyvbjerg,

2006). Such views of case study emerge from the literature, highlighting case study method's "lack of rigor" and "little basis for scientific generalization" (Yin, 1994, p. 10). Such perspectives raise issues of trustworthiness in relation to case study method.

In dealing with such concerns, I have drawn on the work of scholars such as Yin (2006), Stake (1995) and Hamel, Dufour, and Fortin (1993) in relation to these issues. They identify the uniqueness and specificity of case study not as weaknesses in the method, but strengths the researcher may draw on in those details are made visible in thick descriptions that demonstrate ways in which issues emerge from cases. These are, as Stake (1995) says, "...intricately wired to political, social, historical and especially personal contexts" (p. 17). It is the intricacies that give the case study its strength as a method, for as Hamel (1993) observes, "...case study has proven to be in complete harmony with the three key words that characterize any qualitative method: describing, understanding and explaining" (p. 39). My research has focused on "describing, understanding and explaining" the lived experience of EFL teachers in a region of China in the sort of detail that case study method enables, and from this I have been able to identify features and intent of the curriculum reform as played out successfully or otherwise in the individual teachers' professional lives.

5.3   Selection of Sites for Research

I have selected two representative sites, an urban one in a developed area and another in a less developed rural area in Liaoning Province in Northeast China for a focused investigation within the broader EFL curriculum reform. I have made my selection on the basis of "suitable" and "feasible" considerations, first of all, identifying features that suit the focus of my research and secondly those that make it feasible for data collection (McMillan & Schumacher, 2001, p. 432). I have selected two sites rather than one as considerations of at least two sites has enabled me to engage comparisons and contrasts in ways suggested by Yueh (2007) which I will detail below.

Liaoning Province, one of three provinces in Northeast China, is located in the south of Northeast China, and administered by the Chinese Central Government

(China Travel Guide, 2007). This province is a mid-level developed region with political, economic, cultural and educational development typical of other areas in China. The current EFL curriculum reform initiated by the Ministry of Education has been implemented throughout this province, as is the case in most other provinces, including the other two Northeast China provinces (Zhou, 2002). In Liaoning Province, as in all other provinces, primary and secondary schooling is compulsory, with English a compulsory course in secondary schools (Adamson & Morris, 1997). Since the implementation of the new EFL curriculum reform, English is a compulsorily taught in Grade 3 in all Chinese primary schools, as discussed in Chapter 2 and in more detail in Chapter 6.

I have chosen Site A and Site B from two different regions in Liaoning Province as they are under the same provincial administration, but rural Site A and urban Site B are different in relation to economic and social development within the same province. This has raised issues of glocalization and globalization to be explored in my research. These two regions have both adopted the *English Curriculum Standards* (*ECS*), but use two different versions of series of textbooks based on the requirements outlined in the *ECS*.

While there are contrasts between the two regions, both have faced with similar requirements in implementing the same EFL curriculum reform in their schools. I have chosen one school in Site B and five schools in Site A as the relatively small size of the EFL teaching staff in any one school in Site A cannot provide equal numbers of participants as those in Site B. The school in Site B and those in Site A are different in relation to background, size, and availability of resources, which I will illustrate in more detail in Chapter 8.

I have obtained my initial knowledge of Liaoning and selected sites from literature consulted, from my former classmates and current colleagues, as well as my own personal learning and teaching experience in this region. This includes my experience in the province as a student from primary school to teachers' college, followed by a normal university and then employment as an EFL teacher in secondary schools for more than 20 years. According to Patton (2002), researchers themselves act as an instrument in conducting their research, and their knowledge, experience, perceptions and perspectives can help to enhance the validity of the research. This suggests that researchers engage issues of validity in research as part of using their personal experience and their own perspectives. Such perspectives have guided me to examine issues of trustworthiness in relation to issues of validity in my research, as I have discussed in Chapter 4. In the following section I will give details of the participants in my research.

5.4 Selection of Participants for Research

I have drawn on Grant's (2008) perspectives to inform my reasons for selecting participants in my research: "to generate as full a range as possible of elements and relationships that can be used in determining the essential structure of the phenomenon" (p. 2). I have invited those participants who have experienced the reform under study in their schools and who may provide information on that reform. I have invited a total of 42 EFL secondary school teachers in Liaoning Province to complete a questionnaire. I have used the questionnaire to generate an overall picture from these participants' perspectives on the current EFL curriculum reform which they have been commissioned by education authorities to implement. Using a questionnaire as one of the research strategies in my research is also a way to strengthen research outcomes and the trustworthiness of my research in relation to triangulation that includes interviews and documents analysis. I have then selected 16 teachers from those 42 to participate in an interview, during which I have investigated their responses to the reform in greater depth than responses to the questionnaire have allowed. I established two criteria on which to base the selection of teachers to interview: they would be available for interview, and they would have at least 18 years of relevant professional experience in secondary schools. This would mean that they would have experienced the previous reform of 1993. On the basis of this I could anticipate that they might offer perspectives that could be used to compare the reforms of EFL curriculum between 1993 and the current one. I have chosen equal numbers of participants from each region to provide items for comparison on these two sites.

6 EFL teachers from each site who met the criteria were available to participate in the interviews, making a total of 12 participants. There are a number of younger EFL teachers who did not meet the criteria of having experienced the previous reforms, but they volunteered to be interviewed, and I accepted their offer because they met the other criteria which my research focuses on. I then included 2 such younger teachers from each site for interviews, and they have contributed perspectives

that represent between 5 and 10 years teaching experience. These younger teachers have provided perspectives that are limited to the implementation of the current EFL curriculum reform, but they have experienced the effects of the 1993 reform as they were students themselves at that time, so that their perspectives provide a further dimension to my considerations of the lived experience of the teachers who have been charged with implementing the current EFL curriculum reform.

While engaged in data collection, I used my personal networks—my former classmates or colleagues who work in these two regions—to help me to identify potential participants to invite, particularly for interviews, taking up the suggestions of McMillan and Schumacher (2001) and Patton (2002). I gave them the selection criteria so that they could suggest those who met the criteria in these schools, and with their assistance I found teachers who were interested and willing to participate in my research. All the participants were informed of the purpose and methodology of my research, in accordance with my university's Ethics Committee requirements, before they made their decisions to participate or not. Since my research focuses on exploring participant EFL teachers' lived experience, I have not approached other stakeholders such as students, parents, principals or education bureaucrats for the purpose of data collection. I have approached issues as they relate to these stakeholders by examining participant EFL teachers' perspectives on these, as discussed in Chapter 9.

5.5   Data Collection

I have used a questionnaire, interviews and their transcripts, and curriculum and policy documents to generate data for my research. I have used a questionnaire to allow me to explore the EFL teachers' characteristics, attitudes and beliefs in relation to my research question. As Marshall (2006) argues, a questionnaire aims to help researchers to explore participants' perspectives on the related research questions. I have used a questionnaire with two groups of teachers. One group comes from one school selected in Site B, where all the EFL teachers at that school were willing to participate. Since all the schools are under the same municipal and provincial administration, they have similar characteristics and deliver the same EFL curriculum. Given the situation in this part of the province, any school in Site B could have provided sufficient EFL teacher data sources for my research. This has not been the case in relation to any one school in Site A, where numbers of EFL teachers in any of those schools are low. I have had to invite teachers from a number of schools within Site A to match the numbers of those in Site B. I have done this on the basis of Neuman's (1997) suggestion that choosing equal numbers of participants means a basis for comparison that enhances the trustworthiness of the research.

The questionnaire has been designed in the form of Likert Scales, which are "a measurement scale whose response categories require the respondent to indicate a degree of argument or disagreement with each of a series of statements" (Malhotra, Hall, Shaw, & Oppenheim, 2006, p. 333). I have drawn on the idea of Likert Scales because the form used in such scales has allowed me to represent a visual representation of a continuum in relation to each question on the questionnaire. I have not allocated numbers to the range of possible responses, but I have asked participants to indicate on the scale where their response fits best. In this way I have been able to generate a visual representation of the strength of participant attitudes in relation to each of the items canvassed. Armstrong (1987, cited in Busch, 1993) argues that scale formats which are explicit, graphic, or bipolar may have little effects on outcomes, and I have adopted explicit labels such as *strongly agree*, *agree*, *slightly agree*, *slightly disagree*, *disagree and strongly disagree* rather than a range of scores, with the aim of signifying intervals along a continuum as well as to facilitate respondents interpreting these category labels meaningfully and consistently, as Busch (1993) suggests. This is consistent with requirements of qualitative research which I have discussed in Chapter 4. I have employed 6 response categories in my research.

Copies of the English version of the questionnaire were sent to the participating teachers' schools in the two regions selected for my research. With the help of the heads of schools, they were sent to the identified potential participants and I received a high rate of return: a response rate of 98 percent in Site A and 95 percent in Site B. Some returned questionnaires with a small number of questions not answered. I followed these up, asking for the blanks to be filled. The group of participants from Site B in Northeast China responded enthusiastically to the questionnaires, so that I only had to distribute and then collect them. As the group from Site A had not been similarly enthusiastic in returning their completed questionnaire, I followed this up as well. I found that this initial lack of enthusiasm had occurred because these teachers were not confident in their understandings of the questions in English, and were concerned that they would provide insufficient or even incorrect information. They suggested that they were also concerned that they had insufficient professional knowledge or ability to answer my questions, thinking that wrong answers would reflect badly on their schools, perhaps even their jobs. Given their concerns, I readministered the questionnaire, and I was always present during these readministrations. I explained the process of answering a questionnaire and sometimes also the meaning of individual items as these participants were not used either to completing questionnaires or having to draw on their comparatively low (with site B) levels of English comprehension.

Interviews comprised the second phase of data collection. Selection of participants for interviews was made on the basis of the initial processing of data collected from the questionnaire. I have used interviews with the aim of generating in-depth and specific information from these participants to describe how they perceive the researched phenomenon in the way suggested by Merriam (1998). He also says that using interviews can help researchers to obtain an understanding of in-depth and particular information from participants' descriptions of the phenomenon under study. I have audio-taped and transcribed the interviews for detailed study from which to generate in-depth understandings of teacher experiences of the reform under study, representing these as descriptions of their lived experience. This has been the most important phase and instrument of data collection in my research because it has enabled me to step into participants' inner world to research their understandings of the EFL curriculum reform.

I have designed the interview questions on the basis of questionnaire responses, to allow entry to participants' inner worlds to know more about their perceptions, thoughts, experiences, impressions, feelings and beliefs in relation to my research questions, in the way suggested by Welman and Kruger (1999, cited in Groenewald, 2004). Interviewees met the criteria described above. Each interview lasted 15-60 minutes, depending on the participants' knowledge and experience. The interviews were carried out in a conference room and they were recorded and translated and transcribed in full. I had already conducted a pilot investigation in order to modify or expand the proposed questions for both questionnaire and interviews, in ways suggested by Bryman (2001). The questions for these interviewees were given in simple English and required participants to answer in English. The majority of participants suggested that they preferred to use Chinese for interviews. They said that although they were able to converse in English, speaking Chinese meant that they could express themselves more easily and clearly as this was their native tongue, used in personal and professional conversations. I have, accordingly, in the main used Chinese for interviews. I have then translated the Chinese in the transcriptions into English and drawn upon them in my analysis of data.

I have also used my personal experience to enrich the study on the basis of having learned English and having participated in relevant programs in a foreign language normal school for two years, with three years in teachers' college and another two years of university as well as three years of a Master's Degree study. I have experienced more than 20 years of English teaching in secondary school in China and one year of being a Visiting Scholar in Australia, as well as the years of PhD study at an Australian university. This indicates that I am competent in both English and Chinese. I have also been invited to act as an interpreter or a translator in various contexts, such as in a museum, a school, a university and at an international conference, as well as a number of companies which requested my bilingual expertise. These experiences have provided me with the competence and expertise that have enabled me to take up the role of an interpreter and a translator in my research. I work on the principle that while the skills of translation and interpretation are similar, they have their distinguishing features as Hoffer (1989) suggests. Translating is a process of communication, where what translators take into account is "the effective transfer of the meaning because that is precisely what clients want and need. Their concern is not the formal features but the context of the text" (Nida, 2001, p. 2). Translation requires that a text of target language be reliable in relation to the original or native language text in regard to semantics and functions as well as cultures, a position which does not allow the translator to do much in the way of explanation and summarization (Han, 2008). Interpretation takes account of these aspects as far as the interpreter is concerned (Han, 2008). I have drawn on such concepts when translating the transcripts from Chinese into English.

Documents provide researchers with a means by which to gain entry into what may be expected to be diverse voices, meanings and interpretations of phenomena, which differs from the sort of access that may be gained by means of the data generated from such things as interviews and questionnaires in qualitative research (Love, 2003). This is a perspective that has guided me towards an analysis of documents as another source of data to be collected. I have collected and analyzed relevant documents in relation to my research questions, in this case relevant policy statements and curriculum documents. I have also sought access to published previous research done on public and personal records that relate to my research. As part of my initial investigations, I obtained a number of such documents and materials from publications and accessible government websites. These documents have enabled preparation for and grounding of my study.

Document analysis is a systematic examination of documents collected for research (Luo, 2007). I have turned to it to enhance and develop other qualitative research strategies that I have used, as a way of dealing with gaps in data as they provide supplementary information (Love, 2003). I have found it a useful tool to identify relevant changes and challenges as well as shedding light on possible future trends (Luo, 2007) in the EFL curriculum reform that is the subject of my research.

I have used document analysis to set against the analyses of the data from the questionnaire and interviews. I have systematically examined documents relevant to my research, such as *ECS*, following Love's (2003) suggestion that where documents "have been collected, catalogued, contextualized and assessed for their degree of authenticity, more in-depth analytic procedures can be undertaken" (p. 89). Analytical procedures include categorizing, coding, and content analysis (Love, 2003) and I have extended this to my research in relation to document analysis, which I will detail in Chapter 6.

5.6   Data Analysis

In the following section, I will address ways in which I have generated meaning from participants' perspectives on the reform under study. Willis (2006) argues that insights generated from data may work towards informing common education phenomena and events. I have drawn upon this perspective in my research to explore EFL teachers' perceptions in relation to this reform to make meaning of it in the context of secondary schools and their teachers in Northeast China. I have carried out my data analysis informed by Phenomenological considerations, particularly as this pertains to questionnaire data and interview data. As van Manen (1997) argues:

Phenomenological research, unlike any other kind of research, makes a distinction between appearance and essence, between the things of our experience and that which grounds the things of our experience (p. 32).

I have drawn on van Manen's (1997) work in relation to Phenomenological research to focus on the lived experience of the participants in my research, referring to those themes in relation to the four existentials posited by van Manen, detailed in Chapter 4. Such consideration has allowed me to examine the meaning of these participant EFL teachers' lived experience as suggested by van Manen (1990; 1997).

I have designed a number of closed- and open-ended questions in my questionnaire, but while participant EFL teachers across the sites have provided incomplete questionnaire forms I have not been able to include them for data analysis as the responses were not there for me to deal with. I have taken questionnaire responses and constructed a number of categories on the basis of three of van Manen's (1990) four existentials, those of lived space, lived time and lived other. I have not employed the theme of lived body for reasons discussed in Chapter 4. I have used the software program EXCEL to count responses and on the basis of these generated visual images in the form of pie charts and graphs for descriptive purposes. I have not used EXCEL for engaging a quantitative analysis of the data.

I have used the data from the questionnaire to generate an overall picture of the field under study in relation to participant EFL teachers in both sites. I have also highlighted a number of differences that have emerged in each site. I have represented the data in graphs or pie charts to illustrate the regularity of occurrence of respondents' comments on such issues, or otherwise. I stress that these questionnaire data are for illustrative purposes only, acting as guides to the more in-depth explorations of teachers' views of the current EFL curriculum reform in Chinese secondary schools in the interview data.

I have recorded all the responses to interviews and the questionnaire separately and then coded them in files stored in my computer. I have drawn upon a Phenomenological analysis informed by the work of van Manen (1990), which focuses on analysis of themes that I have teased out for detailed study. On the basis of van Manen's (1990) suggestions, I have firstly divided the transcripts into sentence clusters that may be related his suggested existentials of lived space, lived time and lived other that I have used to explore EFL teachers' lived experience. I have identified these significant themes as they have emerged from interview data. These themes have provided me with the framework for identifying the structures of participant EFL teachers' lived experience as meaningful in relation to the reform under study.

5.7　Ethics Issues

Habibis (2006) argues that ethics issues are central to the research process, as principles of ethics and values always dominate research involving humans. My research is no exception; it has been conducted in compliance with the requirements of the University of Ballarat Human Research Ethics Committee. My research has been conducted with the express intention of ensuring that no harm will be done to any participant. Harm, in this context, refers to not only physical harm, but also " psychological or emotional distress, discomfort and economic or social disadvantage" (Habibis, 2006). To this end, I first made contact with the heads of relevant schools and then the potential participants. After a detailed explanation of my research, I obtained the consent of these participants. I then sent them the relevant documents to obtain their written and signed consent. These documents include the *Plain Language Statement* and the *Informed Consent Form* approved by the Ethics Committee of the University of Ballarat. By means of these documents, the participants were also reminded that they had personal freedom and rights in relation to the research being conducted. These documents also provided them with the contact details of my university, my supervisors and me. This operation further confirmed that they were free to raise any issues or concerns related to my research with the relevant university personnel. They were told that their personal information would be kept confidential through these documents, and given details of how this would be achieved.

Copies of the questionnaire were distributed to the participants at their schools and collected from there as well. The participants were invited to complete the questionnaires at any place they felt was appropriate and comfortable. Interviews were conducted in meeting-rooms in the schools. Prior to each interview, participants were asked permission for their interview to be recorded and as this permission was given I audiotaped each interview. The interviewees were also informed that they were free to leave the interview at any time, and they had the right to ask to have their interviews withdrawn from the research at any time after the interview was conducted. None of the interviewees made such a request. The participants in my research comprise a total of 42 secondary school EFL teachers from one school in Site B and five schools in Site A within Liaoning Province in Northeast China, whose ages range from 20 to 59. None of these participants are in any relative, dependent or formal power relationship with me. The data collected for my research have been kept in a locked filing cabinet in my office.

5.8   Conclusion

In this chapter, I have given an overview of the case study method used in my research, as well as data collection strategies, data analysis, and consideration of ethics issues. I have described the selection of sites and participants for my research in some detail, and I have illustrated the procedures of data collection in the form of a questionnaire, interviews, and documents for detailed analysis. I have also presented details of data analysis, particularly of questionnaire data and interview data. In the following chapter, I will present the new EFL curriculum intent and its features on the basis of document analysis.

Chapter 6
New EFL Curriculum Intent and Its Features: The Curriculum Documents

6.1　Introduction

In Chapter 5 I have outlined the research method used in this research, which is case study. In the following chapters, I will take up my main research question which is: In what ways is the current EFL curriculum reform in Chinese secondary schools linked to globalization? I will also take up my subsidiary question which is: In what ways has the current EFL curriculum reform in secondary schools in China developed? In doing so, I will start my data analysis with a review of the new EFL curriculum intent and its features through an examination of relevant government policies and curriculum documents discussed in Chapter 6. The features of the new EFL curriculum include resetting the role of English, an emphasis on students' all-round development in EFL teaching and learning, continuity and flexibility of the new EFL curriculum, an emphasis on task-based learning and improving curriculum materials, establishing an effective assessment system, and an emphasis on teachers' professional development. I have not considered these issues in isolation, but as setting the stage for further understanding the participant EFL teachers' lived experience of implementing the current EFL curriculum reform. I will detail these issues below.

6.2　New EFL Curriculum Intent

Since government policies of reform and opening up of China have been accompanied by rapid economic development in the country, a shift from a centrally-planned economy to a market-oriented one represents economic development that has been given priority in China (Hu, 2005b, 2005c; Lam, 2002; Wang, 2007; Wang & Lam, 2009). In the last decade of the 20th century, China was faced with the unprecedented challenges of globalization as it presented alongside the country's increasing integration into the global economy (Hu, 2005b). In response to these challenges, the Chinese government has begun to emphasize reforming education as education itself has been positioned as having a significant role to play in promoting economic development (Hu, 2005b; Hunnum, 1999; Nunan, 2003). Relevant policies in relation to educational reforms have been released throughout the country, including those in relation to basic education in China (Hu, 2002b). Such policies include the legislation for nine-year compulsory education in 1986, amended in 2006 to incorporate policies of education equity as the centre of building a harmonious society (Chu & Li, 2007). They also cover relevant funding policies including those of further improving education conditions of rural or less developed regions (Wei, 2008). More specifically, the State Council promulgated *Strategic Plans for Reviving Education for the 21st Century* in early 1998 (Wang, 2007), one important part of which is to reform basic education in relation to curriculum, evaluation systems, content and methods of teaching (Hu, 2007). The *Decision on the Reform and Development of Basic Education* (Guan & Meng, 2007), which focuses on reforming basic education, was released at the Third National Conference of Education in June, 1999. Both of these policies stress reform of the present curriculum system for basic education and the establishment of a new one focused on promoting quality education (Ministry of Education, 2001d). These two policies suggest an emphasis on students' all-round development in the new curriculum system. I have considered these two policies as primary driving forces for initiating the reform under study. Investigating these relevant policies has helped me to generate an in-depth understanding of EFL teachers' lived experience as it has established the contexts for examining their implementing the current EFL curriculum reform in Chinese secondary schools.

In response to the release of these two policies, the Ministry of Education in June 1999 initiated a major project as it formulated the *Outline of Curriculum Reform of Basic Education* (Ministry of Education, 2001d). The *Outline* states that the overall goal of the curriculum reform is to promote a complete and comprehensive quality education on the basis of the former general designer of China's development,

Deng Xiaoping's announcement that education needed to be modernized, internationalized and developed (Ministry of Education, 2001d). The Outline clarifies the education goals in the current curriculum reform in relation to the perceived need to promote students:

> To have patriotism, collectivism and socialism; to carry on the fine Chinese cultural traditions; to have awareness of the socialist democratic legal system and to follow national law and social ethics; to gradually build a healthy outlook on the world, value and life; to develop a sense of taking up social responsibilities and serving the people; to develop creativity, practical abilities, scientific and human as well as environmental awareness; to have the basic knowledge, skills and techniques for life-long learning; to have a healthy physique, and positive attitudes; to become a citizen with ideals, ethics, cultural and disciplined awareness (Ministry of Education, 2001d, p. 1).

These goals for basic education articulated in the *Outline* indicate a focus on students' knowledge, skills, attitudes and values in relation to students' all-round development. This is a change from previous statements that emphasize knowledge and skills, rather than students' attitudes and values (see details in the following section with a focus on the new EFL curriculum features). It is a change born of those two policies on contemporary education in China. The *Outline* also includes detailed considerations of relevant requirements for the new curriculum system: curriculum reform; curriculum structure; curriculum standards; teaching procedures; compiling and management of curriculum materials; curriculum evaluation; curriculum management; teacher development; and teacher education as well as organization and implementation (Ministry of Education, 2001d).

All these have been designed to shape the new EFL curriculum system. I have taken the position that the *Outline* is a representation of major driving forces for implementing the curriculum reform throughout the country, including Northeast China. I have also considered the *Outline* as a major distinguishing feature between older and current EFL curriculum reform. It defines the new EFL curriculum system that has been implemented for Chinese secondary schools on the basis of its detailed descriptions of what a new curriculum system would look like. I have considered this in relation to the following examples.

In 1999, the Ministry of Education of China had already been commissioned by the State Council to produce a new curriculum that aligned with all subjects in Chinese primary and secondary schools, including the current EFL curriculum designed for secondary schools (Wang, 2007). The English curriculum project team was formed in June, 1999, with 13 members who acted on behalf of various groups of people, such as research scholars, teachers, educators and relevant advisors (Wang, 2007). The *ECS*, as one of the major components of the new EFL curriculum, was written, providing guidelines for EFL teaching and learning in basic education (primary, junior and senior schooling). It serves as an authoritative curriculum document in describing new goals, setting down contents to be explored, suggesting appropriate teaching methods and ways of assessment, and shaping the outcomes to be achieved by the new EFL curriculum (Wang & Lam, 2009).

In line with the *ECS*, new series of EFL textbooks have been written and published, and the piloting of the new curriculum started in September of 2001. The pilot version of EFL curriculum is the result of nation-wide consultation meetings organized at different levels, including the level of classroom teaching as it included teachers in its meetings (Wang, 2007). The piloting of the new curriculum with new sets of textbooks involved 38 districts, counties and cities as well as 700,000 students across the whole country (Wang, 2007). The *Outline* was shaped and issued out of processes of careful preparation, providing a basis for implementing the new curriculum. I have taken such careful preparation as constituting a major development in relation to EFL curriculum development in China at the secondary level, because the guidelines provided for educators in this instance are a departure from previous practice that ignored such details in relation to reforms to be implemented. Previous reforms provided syllabuses, certainly, but they were not accompanied by the sorts of detailed policy, teaching and learning strategies, textbooks, supplementary materials and professional development programs that have been associated with the current reform.

Exploring such issues has helped me to gain an understanding of how these education policy and EFL curriculum documents work in the Chinese context. As Finnegan (2006) argues in relation to this sort of documents, "...They are produced by human beings acting in particular circumstances and within the constraints of particular social, historical or administrative conditions" (p. 144). Exploring such issues is consistent with my ontological position, which stresses that the world is socially constructed, so that the relevant education policy documents are to be seen as being produced on the basis of social, economic and political factors in the Chinese context. As Swanson and Stevenson (2002) argue, policies are ordinarily considered as primary driving forces behind relevant education changes, and the policies discussed above provide such a case. Such consideration indicates that policies represent intentionality of the kind referred to in Phenomenological studies as considerations of that which is intentional, directed and purposeful (Budd, 2005). My analysis of data suggests that this intentionality has guided participant EFL teachers to implement new curriculum in their schools, contributing their own professional understandings of the reform as they have implemented it. Examining education policies has also served as a basis for exploring the features of the new EFL curriculum itself, leading me to an examination of the new EFL curriculum documents themselves, detailed below.

6.3   Features of New EFL Curriculum

The overall structure of the new EFL curriculum designed for secondary schools in China is the most comprehensive ever designed (Wang, 2007). Since the new curriculum has been implemented in an attempt to address the shortcomings of the 1993 English curriculum (Wang & Lam, 2009), I have presented its main features in comparison with that 1993 curriculum. I have outlined the following distinguishing features in comparison with the 1993 one. These main features (see Table 6. 1) include resetting the role of English, an emphasis on students' all-round development, a new curriculum with a focus on its features of continuity and flexibility and establishing a comprehensive assessment system. I will discuss the details below.

Table 6. 1   **Features of the New EFL Curriculum Adopted from Wang & Lam (2009)**

	English Curriculum Standards (2001 Pilot Version)	EFL Curriculum (1993)
The Role of English	English for Citizenship	English for International Communication
Goals	An Emphasis on All-around Development/Comprehensive Language Competence	An Emphasis on Two Basic Features: Basic Knowledge and Basic Skills

	English Curriculum Standards (2001 Pilot Version)	EFL Curriculum (1993)
Design	Compulsory (for Levels 1-8) Elective (for Level 9, Senior Secondary Schools) Additional Optional Units Offered for Students with Particular Interests for Greater English Language Study (Level 9) Nine-level System with Separate Goals (from Grade 3 in Primary School to Grade 12 in Senior Secondary School)	Compulsory One Set of Goals for Junior or Senior Secondary School
Methods	Task-based Learning	Communicative Language Teaching
Contents	Realistic, Modern and Healthy, Rich and Varied, Closely Related to Students' Life	Out-of-date, Like an Encyclopaedia, Restricted in Teaching Materials
Assessments	Formative Assessment and Summative Assessment	Summative Assessment
Teachers' Professional Development	General Requirements (Basic Knowledge for Teaching EFL); Continuing Education; Modernizing Teaching	General Requirements

6.3.1 Resetting the Role of English

In the following section, I will examine the 1993 EFL curriculum and the new EFL curriculum. The 1993 English curriculum designed for secondary schools stated that English was to be regarded as an important tool for international communication, requiring as many people as possible to learn it (National Education Committee, 1993). As Wang & Lam (2009) say, the 1993 syllabus emphasized "students' communicative competence, independent learning ability and use of English" (p. 69). A review of the 1993 EFL curriculum suggests that the authorities' perceptions of the role of English began to take on dimensions of its being a language of international standing (Wang & Lam, 2009), which was in itself a new feature of that curriculum of 1993. The *ECS* represents English as an important component of citizenship education, part of the design of quality education, and included within a basic education program (Ministry of Education, 2001a). In such ways has English been linked to contemporary social development, national policy and perceptions of citizenship in the 21st century in China, the Ministry of Education going so far as to suggest that every Chinese citizen requires knowledge of English. This resetting of the role of English in EFL teaching and learning represents a distinct development in EFL curriculum.

In China, the concept of citizenship and citizenship education has received little attention, being seldom mentioned for almost 60 years, between the 1950s and the 1970s in particular (Wang, 2004). The concept of citizenship varies in different political systems (Cogan, 1998). In Western democratic societies, according to Wang (2004), the concept of citizenship is essential for individuals' political socialization, and individuals are required to have "knowledge of social and political systems, attitudes and participation skills" (p. 356). This concept also emphasizes the relationship of individuals with the states in which they live, shouldering relevant obligations as well as duties for those states (Wang, 2004). I have identified the concept of citizenship education as a specific emerging aspect emphasized in the current EFL curriculum reform in Chinese secondary schools.

China is different from the West in its political system, with its concept of citizenship being an emphasis on individuals' participation in state affairs, but with "the public good over individual benefits, collectivity over self-interest, and responsibilities" (Figueroa, 2004, p. 218). Citizenship in China means that individuals need unconditionally to obey the demands of the state, the needs of which are to be regarded as their priority (Wang, 2004). This sort of stance minimizes the role of individuals in state systems (Wang, 2004). From the 1950s to the 1970s, teaching and learning in China had focused on the concept of collective rather than on individuals (Figueroa, 2004). China has been gradually changing over the last 20 years in the 20th century, implementing policies of openness and reform, but Chinese people's awareness of citizenship and citizenship education are still unclear because of influences of radical ideology that have dominated politics for so long (Figueroa, 2004; Wang, 2004). The curriculum reform implemented in Chinese secondary schools at the beginning of 21st century has incorporated goals of citizenship education, highlighting them in the new curriculum standards, contents and modes of instruction. As Wang (2004) argues, people's consciousness of citizenship in a country represents its degree of civilization, progress, and democratization. The emergence of awareness of citizenship for EFL teaching and learning suggests a prominent and new aspect in EFL curriculum development in China.

The current EFL curriculum emphasizes that EFL teaching and learning is an important component for citizenship education in China (Ministry of Education, 2001a). Learning English, as far as the Chinese people are concerned, has become part of what it means to be a Chinese citizen, rather than taking it as a subject required for study in school (Smith, 2007). Students are expected to take more responsibility for their own learning in English (Smith, 2007) at the same time as English is positioned as knowledge required for every Chinese citizen to possess. As Smith (2007) states:

> ...learning of English is quickly becoming a regular component of general education in the Chinese public education system. This is particularly evident in the stringent English requirements placed on all Chinese university students both for initial entrance and later eligibility to graduates (p. 179).

Education for citizenship described in the new EFL curriculum is consistent with a Reconstructionist perspective which emphasizes citizenship. Reconstructionism considers that teachers and students have the responsibility to assist social development by adopting roles of social development actors within their society (Howard, 1994). This is consistent with the requirements of a citizen in a socialist country such as China. Education for citizenship also engages challenges posed by globalization (Law & Ng, 2009), part of the intent of the new EFL curriculum reform. Resetting the role of English in the new curriculum is a prominent feature of the EFL curriculum reform, linked to globalization, and influencing the context in which teachers are to implement the reforms with which they are charged.

6.3.2　An Emphasis on Students' All-round Development in EFL Teaching and Learning

The 1993 EFL curriculum stressed only two basic aspects in comparison with the new one: language knowledge and language skills (Ministry of Education, 1993). By way of contrast, the overall goal stated in the new EFL curriculum is to develop students' comprehensive language competence on the basis of their language skills, language knowledge, cultural understanding, learning strategies, and emotions and attitudes (Ministry of Education, 2001a) (see the figure below). In comparison with the 1993 EFL curriculum, students are required to develop not only language skills and language knowledge but also specified attitudes to learning, learning strategies and cultural awareness (Ministry of Education, 2001a). As Guan and Meng (2007)

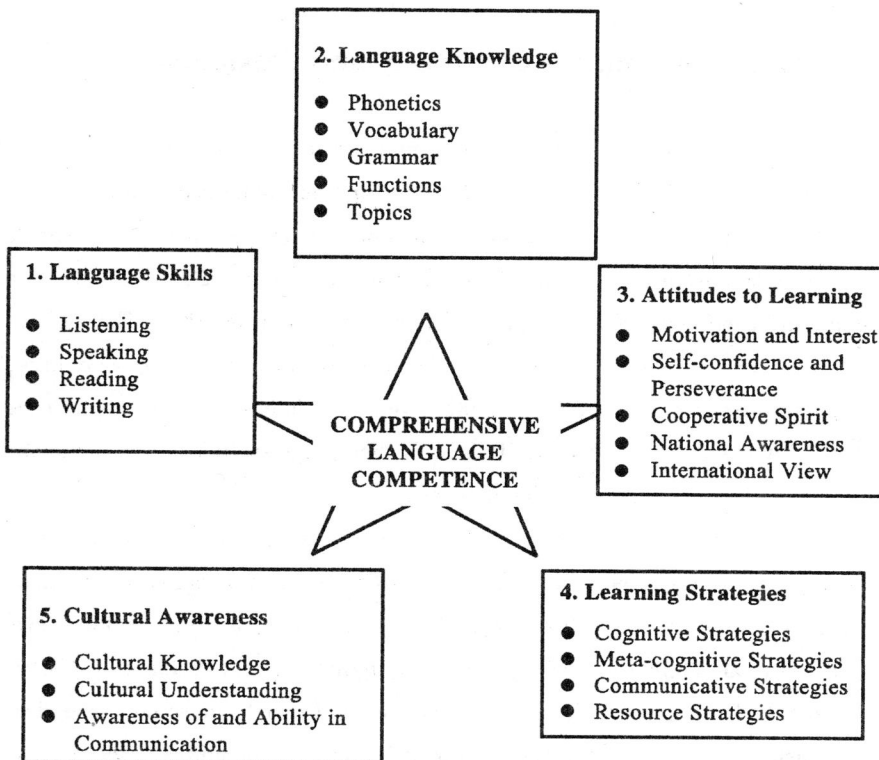

2. Language Knowledge

- Phonetics
- Vocabulary
- Grammar
- Functions
- Topics

1. Language Skills

- Listening
- Speaking
- Reading
- Writing

COMPREHENSIVE LANGUAGE COMPETENCE

3. Attitudes to Learning

- Motivation and Interest
- Self-confidence and Perseverance
- Cooperative Spirit
- National Awareness
- International View

5. Cultural Awareness

- Cultural Knowledge
- Cultural Understanding
- Awareness of and Ability in Communication

4. Learning Strategies

- Cognitive Strategies
- Meta-cognitive Strategies
- Communicative Strategies
- Resource Strategies

The General Goals Adopted from Martin (2005, p. 5)

say, the new wave of curriculum reform represents the three-part curriculum function: knowledge and skills; procedures and methods; and affect and attitudes (p. 587). Such emphasis on students' comprehensive language competence indicates that the new curriculum has moved towards a position of respect for the integrity of learners, taking individual development and their psychological and emotional factors into account. It suggests that the new EFL curriculum has moved significantly beyond learning English as a channel of knowledge acquisition (Johnson and Johnson, 1998, cited in Wang & Lam, 2009), shifting towards students' all-round development in EFL teaching and learning, another feature of the new curriculum. As I have discussed in my consideration of curriculum in Chapter 3, three factors need to be taken into account when establishing goals in a curriculum: knowledge, society and individuals. These three factors are to be given balanced consideration in relation to the goals of a curriculum (Brandt, 2007), which is the case with those set for the new EFL curriculum, as represented in the following:

6.3.3　A New Curriculum: Continuity and Flexibility

The 1993 EFL curriculum offered one compulsory unit designed for secondary schools, while the new EFL curriculum provides for one compulsory unit and one elective unit after the period of compulsory education, to be undertaken by students in senior secondary schools (Ministry of Education, 1993, 2001a). It is a progression within the new EFL curriculum compared with that of 1993. The elective unit delivered in senior schools offers students more flexibility and openness, providing possibilities for teaching in line with diverse levels of competence within the student body (Wang & Lam, 2009). It is a further progress in comparison to the 1993 EFL curriculum, which I will detail below.

There was one general set of goals and requirements for teaching and learning in secondary schools in the 1993 EFL curriculum (National Education Committee, 1993). The new EFL curriculum grades goals and requirements within a nine-level system. This is in an attempt to identify and codify requirements in relation to diverse levels of students from Level 1 in primary schools to Level 9 in senior secondary schools (Ministry of Education, 2001a; National Education Committee, 1993). The Ministry of Education (2001a) states that students in primary schools are required to start learning English from Level 1 to Level 2. Those in junior secondary schools are to learn from Level 3 to Level 5 and those in senior secondary schools from Level 6 to Level 8. Level 9 is offered for students involved in specific courses such as English for Special Purposes (ESP) courses or cultural and literary courses and so on (Ministry of Education, 2001a) (see Table 6. 2 for details). The new EFL curriculum is in such ways designed to bring both primary and secondary school English together, forming one developmental continuum in EFL teaching and learning as part of basic education. This is one of the most prominent features of the design of the new EFL curriculum.

Table 6. 2   **Levels and Grades of *English Curriculum Standards***

Adopted from Martin (2005, p. 4)

Primary Schools	Work towards:	Notes
Grade 3	Level 1	Students to Start Studying English in Grade 3
Grade 4	Level 1	
Grade 5	Level 2	
Grade 6	Level 2	The Required Standard for the End of Primary School

Junior Secondary Schools	Work towards:	Notes
Grade 7 (= Junior 1)	Level 3	Students to Build on English Language Knowledge from Primary Schools
Grade 8 (= Junior 2)	Level 4	
Grade 9 (= Junior 3)	Level 5	The Required Standard for the End of Junior Secondary Schools

Senior Middle School	Work towards:	Notes
Senior 1	Level 6	Students to Build on English Language Knowledge from Junior Secondary Schools
Senior 2	Level 7	
Senior 3	Level 8	The Required Standard for Senior Secondary School Graduation
	Level 9	An Extension Level for Specialist Schools and Able Students

This new design of EFL curriculum has English specified as a subject required in the primary school curriculum for students of Year 3, so that junior secondary school is not the starting point of English teaching and learning. A progression in primary schools and junior secondary schools in EFL teaching and learning is part of the design. EFL teaching and learning starting from primary schools is to be implemented first in cities, counties and provinces, and then gradually in towns and villages, suggested in the new EFL curriculum statements (Ministry of Education, 2001d). To ensure the success of the reform, there is a further requirement that the education department in each province work out its own strategic plan for implementing English teaching in primary schools in relation to starting age, timelines, and EFL teacher's professional development (Ministry of Education, 2001d). These are issues that have been taken up by the Ministry of Education, which has focused on a developmental approach in rolling out the new EFL curriculum (Ministry of Education, 2001d).

According to Wang (2007), the linking of both primary and secondary English language teaching and learning aims to make effective and better employment of EFL teaching and learning resources. It also shows flexibility and practicality in the curriculum as local educational institutions maintain control of decision-making regarding issues of when to learn English in primary schools and what level needs to be reached in relation to their own contexts (Wang, 2007). This change in attitude to curriculum implementation provides flexibility to both schools and students as they follow the nine levels as they progress, and it further provides flexibility for different regions in China as they consider their respective teaching conditions in relation to these nine levels (Ministry of Education, 2001d).

6.3.4 An Emphasis on Task-based Learning and Improving Curriculum Materials

The new EFL curriculum promotes task-based learning to achieve its overall goal in EFL teaching and learning. It emphasizes learning achievement and improvement to be achieved by tasks (Martin, 2005; Ministry of Education, 2001a). The curriculum document states that students, guided by EFL teachers, need to experience a process of senses, experiments, practices, participations and cooperation, as well as adjusting their learning strategies and emotions to these, and holding positive attitudes to learning when completing any one task (Martin, 2005; Ministry of Education, 2001a). It is an approach to EFL teaching and learning that indicates that the new EFL curriculum has moved towards a focus on procedures of teaching and learning, particularly on students' learning experiences, where students are positioned at the centre of EFL teaching and learning with the adoption of task-based learning (Wang, 2007). An emphasis of task-based learning as a teaching and learning approach is part of the design, to respond to policies of education for citizenship and students' all-round development.

Using task-based learning in the new EFL curriculum is consistent with considerations of curriculum in relation to issues associated with the development of an overarching framework for language pedagogy, as discussed in Chapter 3. I have discussed task-based learning as an approach that provides students with relevant and pedagogically sound tasks, creating an appropriate environment for students to learn a language as part of a natural language acquisition process (Foster, 1999). The new EFL curriculum suggests that a task-based approach to EFL teaching and learning offers students more opportunities for experiencing the processes of language acquisition. Task-based learning in the new EFL curriculum is based on pair work and group work (Myers, 2000), which is an appropriate strategy in the Chinese context of large class sizes and limited time available in a crowded curriculum for EFL teaching and learning. The CLT proposed in the 1993 curriculum produced difficulties in relation to its use in the Chinese context as it could not solve those problems described by Hu (2002a), presented in Chapter 3. Liao (2000) argues:

> These difficulties are related to the approach itself as well as the past teaching traditions and present situations of English language teaching and learning in China. They include the teachers' lack of language proficiency and cultural knowledge, no familiarity with the new method, and the negative influence educational traditions on teachers (p.5).

EFL teaching and learning in the Chinese context in 1993 did not provide adequate conditions for CLT to be embedded in an EFL teaching and learning program. I have viewed an emphasis on task-based learning in the new EFL curriculum as providing a more appropriate approach to be employed in EFL teaching and learning in the context of the schools that are to implement the new EFL curriculum, another feature that presents itself as a departure from the 1993 EFL curriculum.

The new EFL curriculum also stresses that the content of teaching and learning materials needs to be realistic, modern, and rich and varied as well as being closely related to students' life (Martin, 2005; Ministry of Education, 2001a). Students are encouraged to use various resources to experience language learning, such as the Internet, audio and visual materials, and taking up responsibility for developing learning materials themselves (Martin, 2005; Ministry of Education, 2001a). The Ministry also stresses that the new series of EFL textbooks to accompany the EFL reforms need to reflect students' life experiences as they emphasize appropriate teaching and learning strategies to affect this. In contrast, the content and curriculum of compulsory education that included the 1993 EFL textbooks restricted teaching and learning materials in relation to subject development, ignoring students' requirements for a life to be lived beyond the confines of the classroom (Guan & Meng, 2007). The curriculum content in 1993 could be considered in the same light as an outdated encyclopaedia, one which was not capable of matching the increasingly salient requirements of social development; these textbooks' contents did not relate to real life, lagging behind rapid Chinese political, social and economic development (Guan & Meng, 2007). Such contents also ignored issues of students' learning strategies and practical skills (Guan & Meng, 2007). The curriculum materials as they present in the new EFL curriculum are another feature that contrasts with the 1993 one.

Exploring the issue in relation to textbooks is part of generating an understanding of curriculum reform, for as Richard (2001) argues, a textbook is one of the most important components in considering curriculum reform. According to Marsh (2004), a textbook as part of curriculum materials plays a major role in everyday activities of teaching and learning. It is produced to engage the specific curriculum required in a particular context (Hewitt, 2006). Improving a textbook indicates the development of a curriculum (Bloom, 2007), and in this case forms part of the new features of the new EFL curriculum.

6.3.5 Establishing an Effective Assessment System

Another feature of the new EFL curriculum which is worth noting here is a corresponding assessment system that has been established. The new curriculum stresses introducing formative assessment in addition to summative assessment (Ministry of Education, 2001a). It also states that formative assessment needs to be positioned as the centre of this new assessment system in EFL teaching and learning, emphasizing students' active participation and confidence in EFL teaching and learning, while summative assessment will examine students' integrated language skills and their abilities in using language at the end of their programs of EFL study (Ministry of Education, 2001a). This inclusion of formative assessment as part of the new assessment system allows students to focus on the processes of learning through their active participation in it. It also helps them to develop their comprehensive language competence, as required in the new EFL curriculum, through that active participation, promoting a healthy personal development by emphasizing confidence in their own language learning. This new assessment system also promotes EFL teachers' concerns with student development as they adopt formative assessment that focuses on learning processes. Teaching processes are, as Harmer (2000, cited in Li, 2009) points out, "The basic building blocks for successful language teaching and learning" within which "learners need to be motivated, be exposed to language, and given chances to use it" (p. 26). Formative assessment addresses assessment as part of the processes of development (Li, 2009).

In comparison with the 1993 EFL curriculum, which mainly focused on summative assessment, this new assessment system is a change for the better. As I have discussed in Chapter 3, assessment is the means used by teachers to assess students on their expected changes in relation to students' knowledge, skills or attitudes, and it plays an influential role in curriculum reform (Brady, 1995; Marsh, 2004). Assessment includes summative assessment and formative assessment, which I have detailed in Chapter 3. In the case of the new EFL curriculum, assessment is considered more effective in relation to student achievement when both summative and formative assessment are used, in ways suggested by Brookhart (2001). As Guan and Meng (2007) say, the new curriculum proposes a much more effective assessment system as it focuses on students' learning processes, and involving formative assessment in summative assessment.

The new assessment system sits within the new curriculum as part of progressive phases of language learning embodied in those nine levels of basic education in China. As Wang and Lam (2009) say, "The formative element in assessment is in line with the new calibration of progressive states of foreign language learning into nine bands." (p. 71) Formative assessment, considered in this light, has a role to play in progressively developing language learning skills as part of the new curriculum, for as Wang (2007) states, the new assessment system shifts from a focus on "purely exam-based" to a focus on "a more performance and progress-based one" (p. 99) where EFL teachers are encouraged to adopt formative assessment to monitor students' learning progress. The new assessment system is a notable development in the new EFL curriculum, especially given China's traditional reliance on examination systems. As Priestley (2002) argues, assessment is an aspect to be included in such a major reform as it catches up with global trends.

6.3.6 An Emphasis on Teachers' Professional Development

An emphasis on teachers' professional development is another feature of the new EFL curriculum. As Huang (2004) states, teachers' professional development has attracted increasing attention in the current EFL curriculum reform. With various reform policies implemented, demands have been increasingly placed on teachers, including those that relate to "educational philosophies, standards of professional competences, curriculums, syllabuses, methodologies and teaching materials" (Gu, 1994, cited in Hu, 2005c, p. 686). These features constitute general requirements for teachers' professional development, including that of EFL teachers'. EFL teachers implementing the new EFL curriculum reform are also expected to update knowledge bases constantly to cope with the requirements based on areas of social development as far as English curriculum is concerned (Ministry of Education, 2001a). To this end, EFL teachers are:

To be familiar with language teaching and learning in relation to educational principles, goals, contents, and methods as well as psychological theories; to have the abilities for selecting and adjusting their teaching to engage diverse requirements of students; to develop their abilities in controlling their classroom teaching, adopting various teaching skills and teaching methods flexibly; to make good use of modern educational techniques, applying them to the process of their continuing study and their classroom teaching; to strengthen consciously their national and intercultural awareness; to explore an effective teaching method with an active and creative intention in response to the requirements of teaching and learning as well as local conditions; to reflect constantly on their own teaching practice in an attempt to become a teacher with the awareness of innovation and creation, and a research interest (Ministry of Education, 2001a, p.31).

Such statements provide guidelines for teachers' professional development under the new curriculum in relation to their knowledge, skills, methods, techniques, intercultural understanding and awareness and their awareness of innovation and creativity, as well as the development of the ability to put theory into practice. As Shao (2004) argues, an effective professional development system has to be in place for teachers to be able to translate research into classroom teaching practice.

This new EFL curriculum places a particular emphasis on teachers' abilities to adopt modern education resources such as information technology in EFL teaching (Wang, 2007), part of an attempt to modernize teaching. This consideration links EFL teachers' professional development to challenges for education posed by globalization. Teachers' continuing education in relation to professional development has been a major focus in the new EFL curriculum. As Hu (2005a) points out, the notion of teachers' career-long development has been developed and articulated, "to improve the professional quality of the teaching force through institutionalizing continuing education, enforcing a teacher licensure system, and upgrading the professional competence of core teachers" (p. 686). This too may be considered in relation to EFL teachers' professional development as progressive aspects in the new EFL curriculum in comparison with the previous one. According to Gu (1994, cited in Hu, 2005a), since the 1980s, teachers have needed to embrace new education ideas and professional competences. They also have needed to have developed an understanding of curriculum, syllabus, methodologies and relevant teaching materials (Gu, 1994 cited in Hu, 2005a). This concern signifies a progressive change in attitude to EFL teachers' professional development as part of the new EFL curriculum reform.

The foregoing discussion is consistent with considerations of curriculum discussed in Chapter 3 in relation to effective curriculum reform implementation, which take account of teachers' professional development as part of curriculum reform (Gwele, 2005). As Fullan and Hargreaves (1992) argue, reforms can only be implemented successfully when teachers have generated a deep understanding of the significance of changes. On the basis of such discussion, an emphasis on teachers' professional development in the new EFL curriculum may be seen as an attempt to move towards effective curriculum implementation.

The features of the new EFL curriculum discussed above present a picture of feasible and carefully considered strategies to be implemented in relation to each aspect of its reform. As far as teaching English from Grade 3 in primary school is concerned, the new EFL curriculum is to be rolled out first in cities, then in counties and provinces, and gradually in towns and villages. Education departments in each province need to have their own strategic plans to fit with diverse situations. The rolling out of the new EFL curriculum in such ways reflects a Chinese proverb: "Creep before you walk".

In my research I have considered the current EFL curriculum reform as constituting a significant feature of the participant EFL teachers' professional world. I have identified a number of features of this new EFL curriculum as providing possibilities for examining these participants' lived experience. As van Manen (1990) says:

> And every conscious experience is bi-polar: there is an object that presents itself to a subject or ego. This means that all thinking (imagination, perceiving, remembering, etc.) is always thinking about something (pp. 181-182).

Conscious experience is derived from an object which refers to *something*. The object in my research is the current EFL curriculum intent and its features presented in the reform under study. This object, as an inseparable part of intentionality, manifests as "the inseparable connectedness of the human being to the world" (van Manen, 1990, p. 181). I have considered the new curriculum intent and its features as the object of teachers' lived world, part of their lived experience articulated in their professional reflections. An exploration of these features of the new curriculum serve as a basis to generate an understanding of the participant EFL teachers' lived experience of implementing the reform.

6.4   Conclusion

In this chapter I have investigated the intent and features of the new EFL curriculum. I have first approached the new EFL curriculum intent as the basis for further examining its features. I have explored relevant education policies as primary and major driving forces for the EFL curriculum reform to be implemented in China. I have examined the features of the new EFL curriculum, including the resetting the role of English, with an emphasis on students' all-round development. I have discussed the new curriculum in relation to its focus on continuity and flexibility, its emphasis on task-based learning and its attention to improving curriculum materials with its focuses on new textbooks. Implementing the reform has included establishing a more effective assessment system than before, and emphasizing teachers' professional development. I have considered the intent of the new EFL curriculum and its features in relation to progressive aspects as compared with the previous 1993 one. My considerations have been further confirmed by participant EFL teachers' descriptions of their lived experience of the reform as indicated in my analysis of interview and questionnaire data. In the following chapter, I will focus on questionnaire data to explore some of the details of the lived experience of participant EFL teachers of the EFL curriculum reform.

Chapter 7
Lived Experience: The Questionnaire

7.1 Introduction

In Chapter 6 I have discussed the new EFL curriculum intent and its features as described in policy statements and curriculum documents. In this chapter I will explore participant EFL teachers' lived experience through an analysis of their responses to the questionnaire. I have given an overview of participant EFL teachers' lived experience of the reform under study as this emerges from the analysis of questionnaire data. My analysis is based on three themes—lived time, lived space and lived other—on the basis of van Manen's (1990) concept of lifeworld existentials. Van Manen (1990) argues that lifeworld is:

> The lived world is experienced in everyday situations and relations. Our lived experiences and the structures of meanings (themes) in terms of which these lived experiences can be described and interpreted constitute the immense complexity of the lifeworld (p. 101).

He identifies "these fundamental lifeworld themes" as "existentials" (p. 101), and I have adopted these perspectives, using the concept as a tool for data analysis.

I have taken the theme of lived time as relating to participants' experience of previous EFL curriculum reforms and the current reform as representing these teachers' temporal experience of the reform under study. As van Manen (1990) argues, "Lived time is also a temporal way of being in the world." (p. 104) I have taken the theme of lived space as participants' felt space within which they have found themselves affected. As van Manen (1990) argues, lived space is "felt space" (p. 102). I have highlighted stakeholder groups as they affect participant EFL teachers as playing influential roles in relation to the theme of lived other. Teachers' perceived influence of stakeholders initially emerged from questionnaire data, which I followed up in interview questions. I have considered stakeholders as part of the features of lived other in relation to lived experience. I have drawn upon participants' responses to the questionnaire to generate an overview of EFL teachers' lived experience as providing a basis for further exploration of that lived experience by means of in-depth interviews with selected questionnaire participants, discussed in later chapters.

7.2   EFL Teachers

As I have described in Chapter 5, 42 participants (EFL teachers) from Northeast China were invited to complete a questionnaire. In the following section I will give the participant EFL teachers' background in relation to their age, years of teaching, starting age of learning English, level of academic degrees, whether they learned English in China or overseas, gender, and any experience of traveling overseas. I have started my discussion on each site separately, and then discussed both sites together. I have viewed data as pertinent to my considerations of what underpins the EFL curriculum reform as far as participants' lived experience is concerned.

7.2.1   Site A

Questionnaire data from Site A with 21 participants (see Figures 7. 1 to 7. 4) show those participants' ages range between 20 and 59 years old, with the majority of them between 35 and 59 years of age. A number of participants started to learn English in junior secondary school, and less than half of them have at least 15 years of teaching experience. A number of participants are Teaching Certificate holders, which means that they graduated from 2 or 3 years of teachers' colleges, or have some other form of teaching certification as part of their own education backgrounds. The Teaching Certificate is an associate degree which is required by junior secondary school teachers in China (Hu, 2005c). 1 of them has a Bachelor's degree and none of them has a Master's Degree. None of them has overseas traveling or training experience; all learned English in China (see below). The majority of them are female; 2 of them are male.

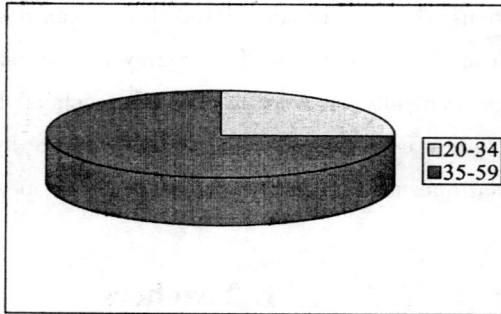

Figure 7. 1   Age Range (2008)

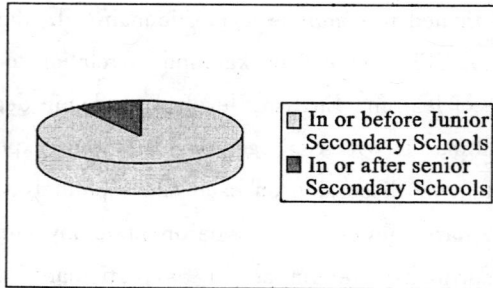

Figure 7. 2   Starting Years of Learning English

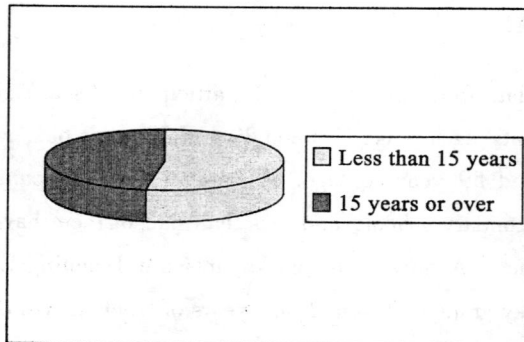

Figure 7. 3   Years of Teaching Experience

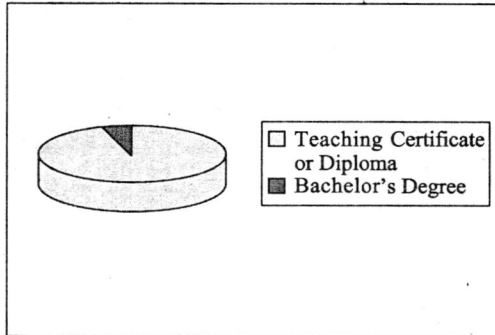

Figure 7. 4　Level of Degree

7.2.2　Site B

The questionnaire data from Site B with 21 participants (see Figures 7. 5 to 7. 8) show that ages range from 20 to 59 years old, and that most of them are between 35 and 59 years of age. More than four fifths of participants started to learn English in or before their junior secondary school years, and one third of them have at least 15 years' teaching experience. A number of these participants have a Bachelor's Degree and 2 of them have a Master's Degree. 8 of them have had overseas traveling or training experience (see Figure 7. 9), but they all started to learn English in China. 5 of them are female; 3 of them are male. As I collected my data in 2008, what is presented here only shows information up until 2008.

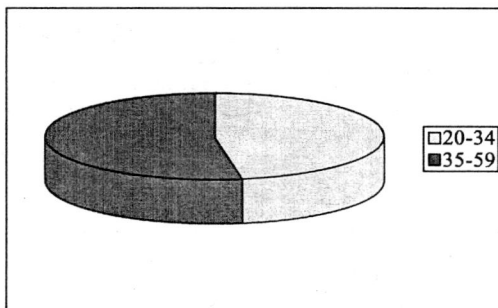

Figure 7. 5　Age Range (2008)

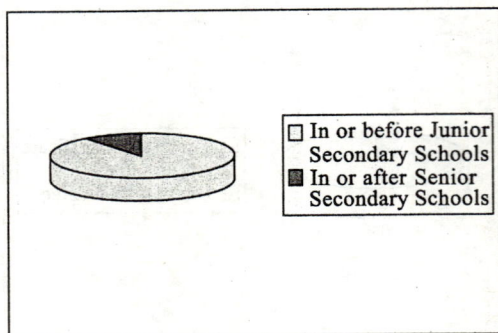

Figure 7.6 Starting Years of Learning English

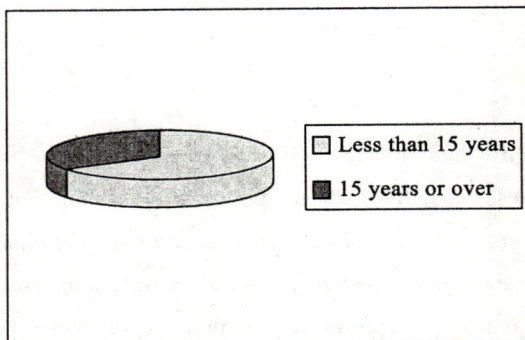

Figure 7.7 Years of Teaching Experience

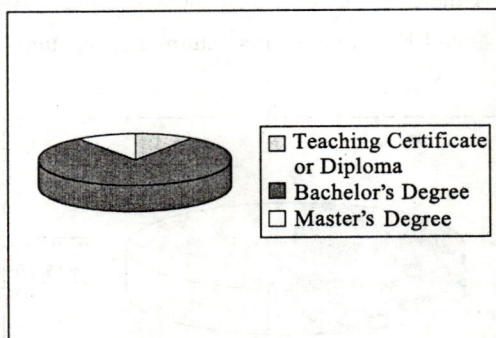

Figure 7.8 Level of Degree

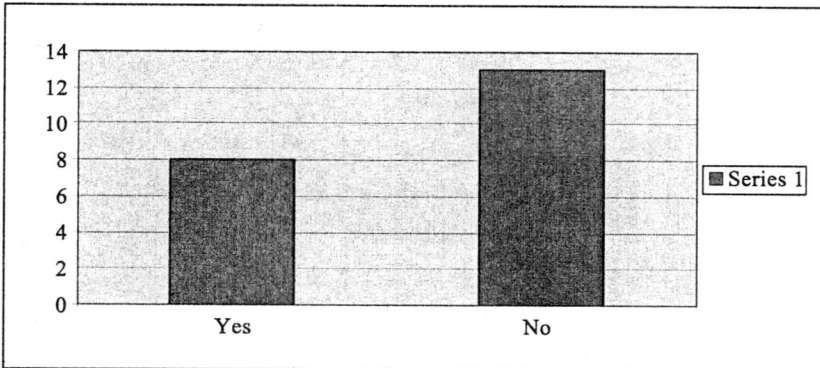

Figure 7.9   Experience of Overseas Traveling

7.2.3 Across Both Sites

Of the 42 participants, 37 are female; 5 are male. 17 participants of the 42 in my research project have at least 15 years of teaching experience and 16 of these accepted the invitation to be interviewed. The majority of participants learned English either before or while in junior secondary schools, and all of them learned English in China. 8 of the 42 participants have had experience of overseas traveling, and all of these are from Site B. The data show the differences between participants' backgrounds in the two sites. In relation to age range, there are more participants between the ages of 20 and 34 years old in Site B than in Site A, so that the ages of the participants in Site B are younger than those of participants in Site A (see Figure 7.1 and Figure 7.5). Participants in both sites are mostly aged between 35 and 59 years old (see Figure 12).

Questionnaire data also show more than half of participants have only a two or three years' Teaching Certificate. Less than half of the participants have a four-year Bachelor's Degree (see Figure 7.11). 2 of the participants in my research have a Master's Degree. Questionnaire data further show the differences in relation to teachers' levels of academic degrees (see Figure 7.4, compared with Figure 7.8). 1 of the participants in Site A holds a four-year Bachelor's Degree, while 19 in Site B have a Bachelor's Degree. The data indicate that participant EFL teachers' degree levels are lower than the average of those in China in general, where, according to

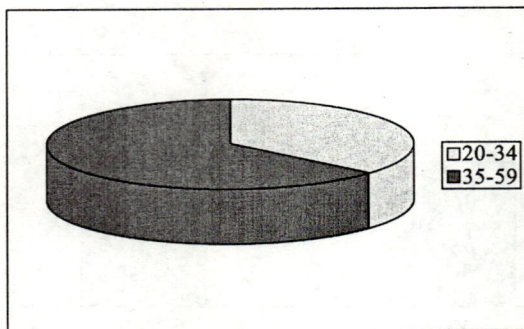

Figure 7. 10   Age Range

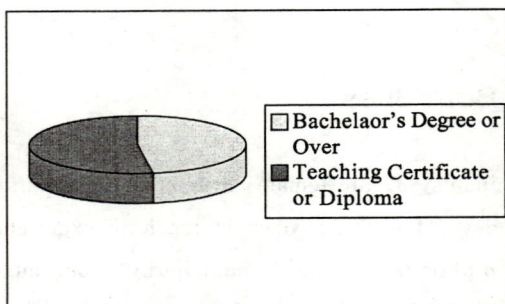

Figure 7. 11   Level of Degree

Wang (2004), 55 percent of teachers in secondary schools have a Bachelor's Degree. In Site A, that is, in the less developed regions where I conducted my research, this level is even lower, where only 5 percent of EFL teachers have a Bachelor's Degree (see Figure 7. 4 in Site A).

A 2 or 3 years EFL teacher education program is arguably insufficient to deal with the range of knowledge required because of the relatively short length of time of study. As Hu (2005c) states, 2 or 3 years teachers' colleges can only provide a small size of education courses and/ or school-based professional experience, and it is doubtful that such courses have the capacity to give the sort of attention to relevant knowledge and skills for a comprehensive pre-service teacher education. This has further implications for understanding and implementing the reform. As Shulman (2007) suggests:

Teacher preparation for reform efforts requires at least five years of higher education (because there is too much to learn) to be adequately equipped to organize elaborate programs of new-teacher induction and mentoring as the most important learning and socialization occurs predominately in the workplace (p. 127).

China has its own system of teacher preparation. normal schools, teachers' colleges and normal universities were the three major providers of programs for teacher preparation in China between the 1970s and the 1990s (Hu, 2005c). According to Hu (2005b), normal schools, as specialized secondary schools, provide 3 or 4 years of teacher education programs for preparation of primary school or kindergarten teachers. These schools cater for either junior or secondary school graduates. Teachers' colleges, as part of the tertiary sector in China, offer 2 or 3 years programs for preparation of junior secondary school teachers, taking in senior secondary graduates. Normal universities provide 4 years programs of pre-service teacher education programs delivered to senior secondary graduates. The pre-service teacher education programs in normal schools and teachers' colleges lead to Teaching Certificates while those in normal universities lead to a Bachelor's Degree. Of the participants in my research, more than half of the EFL teachers hold Teaching Certificates, representing more than half of the EFL teaching force in these schools, those in Site A in particular.

In both sites the majority of participants are female, but the issue of gender in my research has little influence on their perspectives in the course of my data analysis, and this is consistent with the research literature that also suggests little gender differences evident in teachers' perspectives (Li, 1999). I have also accepted 4 participants who have less than 15 years of teaching experience for interviews because of their availability, as discussed in Chapter 5. I have found similarities between this group of younger teachers and that group of older teachers who meet the criteria of selection for the interviewees, so that the differences that one might have expected between the two age groups has not been evident in interview data. Questionnaire data show that 8 of participants in Site B have experience of overseas traveling, compared with none in Site A, suggesting that Site B participants have had more opportunities to be exposed to the sorts of intercultural experience in foreign countries that may enhance their professional development. As Camenson (2007) argues, EFL teachers need to have experience of traveling or living in cultural settings other than their own as these sorts of experiences contribute to successful careers as language teachers. Participant EFL teacher backgrounds as identified from the questionnaire data have provided a basis for the selection of suitable participants to invite for in-depth interviews.

7.3 Lived Time

Phenomenological considerations of time do not look upon time as a measurable object, but identify temporality as one of the subjective aspects of the lifeworld (Rie Konno Rn, 2008). Van Manen's (1990) concept of temporality, which he calls lived time, is "subjective time as opposed to clock or objective time" (p. 104), which I have discussed in Chapter 4. This time cannot be measured, but can be experienced, developing a sense of continuity and identity, or otherwise (Brough, 2001). I have explored lived time as a feature of participant EFL teachers' lived experience. According to van Manen (1990), lived time may be considered as "our temporal way of being in the world" and "the temporal dimensions of past, present, and future constitute the horizons of a person's temporal landscape" (p. 104). I have taken up such considerations in this chapter to explore participant EFL teachers' past and present experience emerging as these emerge in their responses to the questionnaire. The past experience explored here is participant teachers' own experience of being a secondary school student during previous curriculum reforms, mainly between the 1970s and 1990s, given their age ranges. Some participant teachers were students themselves in the 1970s. I have dealt with this in Chapter 2 in my review of the literature. Participant teachers who were students in the 1980s experienced the ramifications of reforms of new policies that had opened China to the world, also detailed in Chapter 2. Other participant teachers experienced the specifically EFL focused curriculum reforms of 1993 as professional in the field.

In each of these cases, changes in EFL teaching and learning had identifiable common shortcomings, especially in comparison with the new EFL curriculum currently being implemented. On the basis of that commonality, I have considered previous reforms as a whole when analyzing participant EFL teachers' past experience, as there was more in common than was in contention. Considering the theme of lived time in relation to an overview of EFL teachers' experience, I have included an examination of participant EFL teachers' present experience of the reform under study with their views of *ECS* and the new EFL curriculum. This also includes their views of relevant teaching methods, content and assessment associated with the new EFL curriculum. This has enabled me to capture the views of participant EFL teachers as these relate to their lived experience, at the same time exploring ways in which these teachers' lived experience has played out in their implementing of the reform. As Benner (1994) says:

> The experience of lived time...is the way one projects oneself into the future and understands oneself from the past. Temporality is more than a linear succession of moments. It includes the qualitative, lived experience of time or timelessness (p. 105).

I have drawn on this concept to explore lived time as stemming from the past, and which provides the basis for exploring the present and the future. This has guided me to explore the participant EFL teachers' lived experience from their past experience, as detailed below.

7.3.1 Past Experience

In the following section I will investigate participant EFL teachers' lived experience of the current EFL curriculum reform as shown in their responses to the questionnaire on their experience of previous EFL curriculum reforms. Their reflections have opened up my exploration of lived time in relation to this. As van Manen (1997) states:

> Whatever I have encountered in my past now sticks to me as memories or as (near) forgotten experiences that somehow leave their traces on my being— the way I carry myself (hopeful or confident, defeated or worn-out), the gestures I have adopted and made my own (from mother, father, teacher, friend), the words I speak and the language that ties me to my past (family, school, ethnicity), and so forth...(p. 104).

He suggests that an exploration of the past provides possibilities for exploring present and future lifeworlds. I have drawn on his suggestion to inform my explorations of the past experience of participant EFL teachers, which has helped me to go a step further to explore their present experience of the reform under study as it relates to the theme of lived time. Crookes (1997) argues that past experience influences the ways of teaching, forming a major part of professional experience. In considering these perspectives, I have examined participants' past experience through their responses to the questionnaire to examine their lived time in relation to their lived experience.

When participant EFL teachers reflect on their time as secondary school students, the majority say that English teaching at the time was mainly teacher-centred and grammar-focused. They describe their EFL teachers as being the major speakers in class and as students, they had few opportunities to speak at all, let alone the new language of English that they were learning. They say that they found that EFL teachers mainly explained or practised grammar rules, seldom designing activities for students to communicate with each other in class. Participants also say that they seldom had Listening tests during their time as secondary school students. A recurrent note within the data is that they, as students, enjoyed taking notes in class as they were not often required to speak, and while they sometimes did have opportunities to answer questions, their EFL teachers often corrected their errors in front of the class. Such teaching practices tended to make students fear the prospect of communicating with others in English, even with the other students during or after class. Apart from these features of their education in EFL, the participants consider that their English teachers had limited English proficiency themselves. This was further indicated by their EFL teachers' instructional classroom language, being mostly in Chinese, rather than in English. This was more obvious in Site A than in Site B (see Figure 7.12 and Figure 7.13).

When participants recall their time of being secondary school students, almost half of them express an appreciation of teacher-centred and grammar-focused teaching, and nearly one third of them state that they still liked those traditional teaching methods. More than half of the participants across the two sites say that they were afraid of their teachers and seldom had any contact with them, particularly those in Site A (this is detailed in Figure 7.14 and Figure 7.15). Questionnaire data also

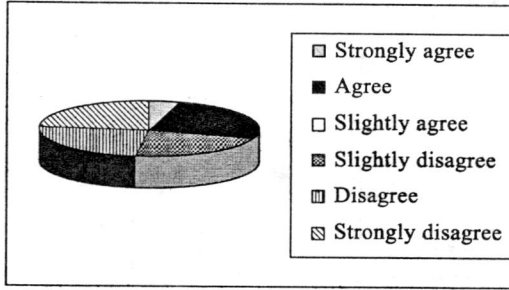

Figure 7.12   Instructional Language (Site A)

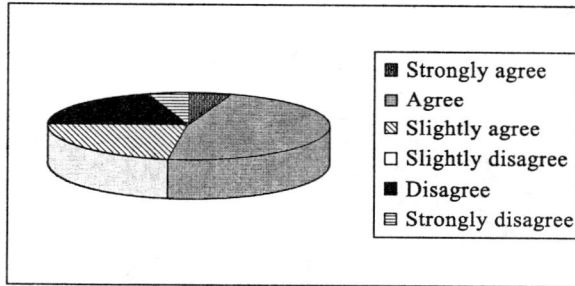

Figure 7.13   Instructional Language (Site B)

show that more than one quarter of EFL teachers across both sites complain that they had no extra learning materials outside the textbooks used, those in Site A in particular (see Figure 7.16 and Figure 7.17).

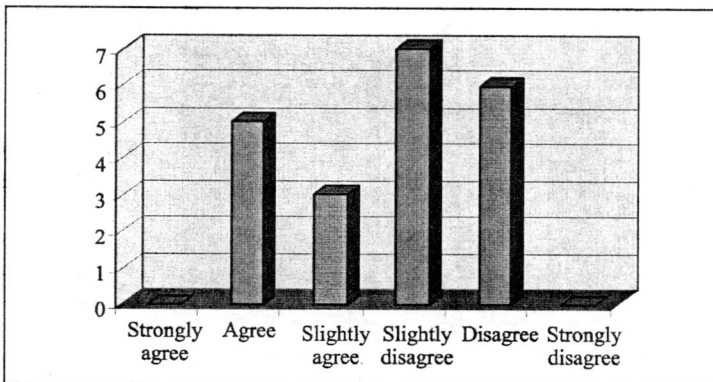

Figure 7.14   Feelings about Teachers (Site A)

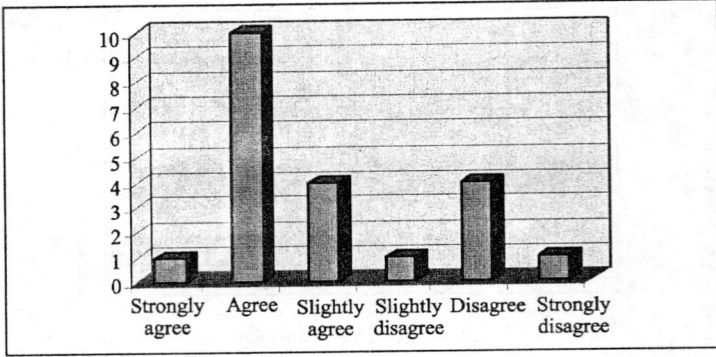

Figure 7.15　Feelings about Teachers (Site B)

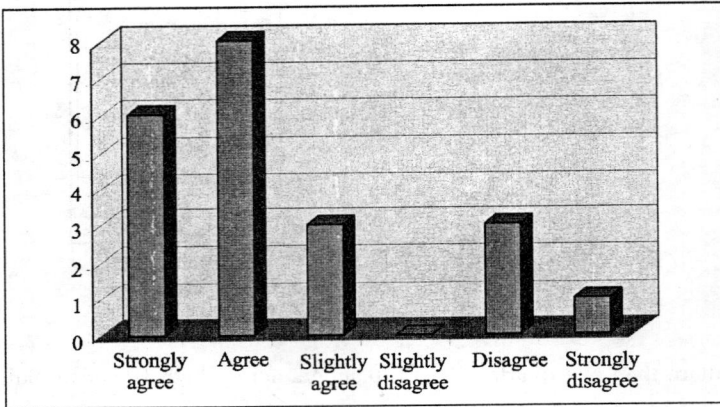

Figure 7.16　Extra Learning Materials (Site A)

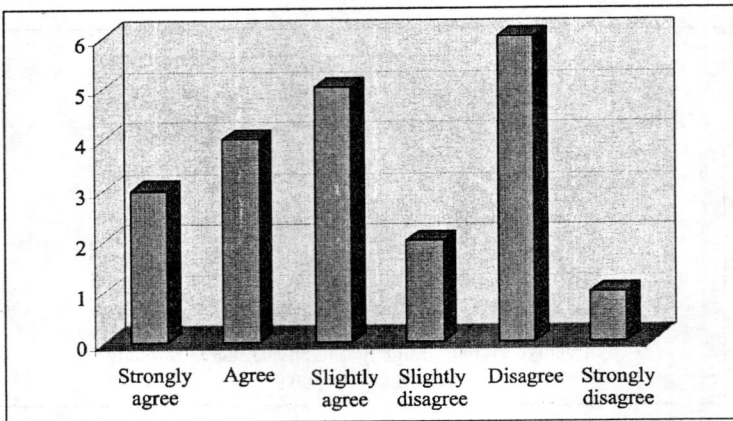

Figure 7.17　Extra Learning Materials (Site B)

Questionnaire data provide a general picture of participant EFL teachers' experience of previous EFL curriculum reforms through their reflections of being secondary school students themselves. The picture shows teacher-centred and grammar translation teaching methods dominating EFL teaching and learning in previous curriculum reforms. EFL teachers dominated the classroom while students were regarded as receptive vessels rather than participants in their own teaching and learning; they lacked opportunities for oral or listening practice in English in class, so that they found it difficult to communicate with others when learning English in secondary schools. Apart from this, they consider that their EFL teachers' limited English proficiency influenced their EFL learning and that dull and outdated teaching content resulted in them having a diminished interest in learning English. This is a particularly interesting point considering that they became English teachers themselves.

An exploration of participant EFL teachers' past experience as part of lived time indicates that they experienced shortcomings of previous reforms regarding EFL teaching and learning in relation to that lived experience. Teacher-centred methods focus on explaining grammar rules, conducting grammar practice and revision of these, giving prominence to the role in the classroom to the teachers, in the process constructing students as passive listeners. The emphasis is on language learning as learning grammar more than social interaction or learners' participation in the target language, marginalizing notions of comprehensive language competence as the final goal of language learning. Such teaching methods are not designed to have students achieve the specified competence that has been identified in the new EFL curriculum as enabling them to cope with the demands on Chinese society that is associated with rapid economic development. Generated out of the education contexts of the time before the current EFL curriculum reform, the teaching and learning approaches used are not consistent with considerations of Vygotskian sociocultural perspectives in relation to language learning, which I have discussed in Chapter 3. They are inappropriate when one considers the goals of the current EFL curriculum reform with its focus on students' comprehensive language competence, as this is the very thing that they ignore. They fail to position students as the centre of EFL teaching and learning, inhibiting student development in EFL competence. The data suggest that previous EFL curriculum reforms experienced by participating EFL teachers have been identified by these teachers as having been deficient. They have come to this conclusion through their present experience of alternative methods and approaches to language teaching and learning that are characteristic of the present reform, as "the past changes under the pressures and influences of the present" (van Manen, 1990, p. 104). These teachers' past experience has formed the basis for exploring their present experience, as discussed in the following section.

7.3.2 The Present Experience

Participant EFL teachers' present experience is also part of their lived experience, part of lived time in their lifeworld. My exploration of present experience includes examining participants' implementing of the reform in their schools, and changes in their own teaching practice. This exploration helps to identify ways in which these participants view the reform implementation in schools and its application in relation to teaching practice as part of their personal experience.

Participant EFL teachers' experience across both sites indicates that they have felt enthusiasm for the current EFL curriculum reform and have often conducted their classroom teaching with reference to *ECS*, considering that its goals are realistic, applicable, and achievable in relation to their classroom teaching. They say that they have emphasized students' comprehensive language competence in various ways, such as adopting task-based approaches, designing various activities to promote students interaction in English with peers, only infrequently correcting students' errors in class, and respecting students' personalities, attitudes and perceptions as part of improving their relationships with students and encouraging students to be more confident in communicating in English. To this end, they have made timely adjustments to their roles in teaching, considering that they have possessed adequate knowledge of language teaching to meet the challenges of implementation of the current EFL curriculum reform in their regions.

Nonetheless, there are some differences in relation to responses to questions in these two sites. For example, nearly half the participants in Site A say that they dislike the new textbooks designed for secondary school students (see Figure 7.18 and Figure 7.19). More than one third of them in the same region think that the updated content in students' textbooks are not appropriate in their schools, while none in Site B expressed such a view (see Figure 7.20 and Figure 7.21).

Almost half of the EFL teachers in Site A consider that they have inadequate

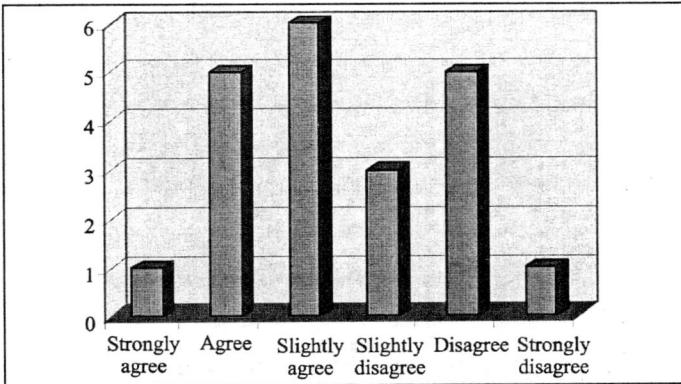

Figure 7.18   Enjoying New Textbooks (Site A)

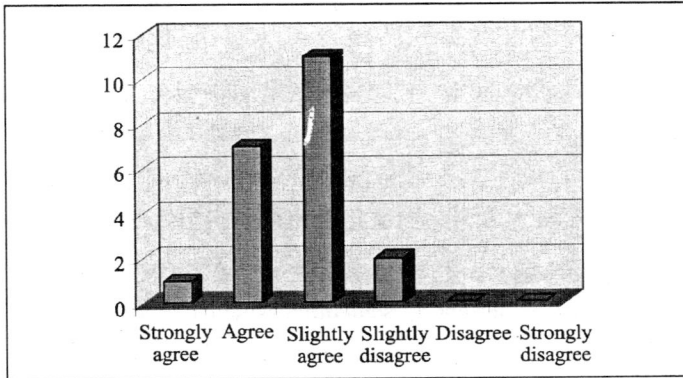

Figure 7.19   Enjoying New Textbooks (Site B)

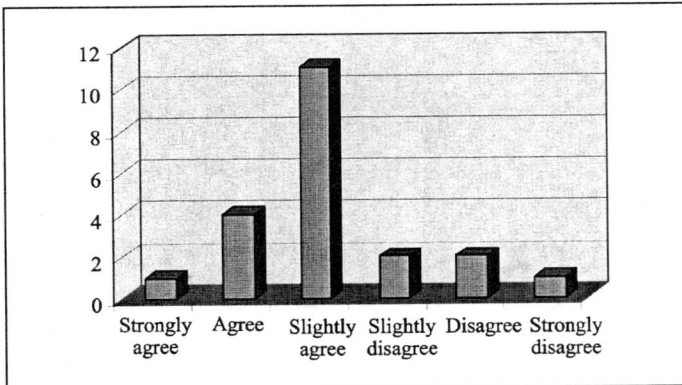

Figure 7.20   Appropriate Updated Content (Site A)

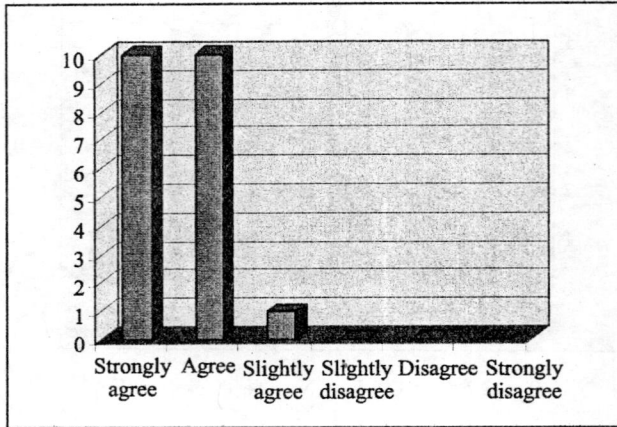

Figure 7. 21   Appropriate Updated Content (Site B)

knowledge of theoretical bases for English language teaching and learning, with 2 teachers in Site B voicing similar concerns about their knowledge base (see Figure 7. 22 and Figure 7. 23). I have considered such experience as linked with perceived inadequacies in the courses they have undertaken in their 2 or 3 years' teachers' college pre-service teacher education programs. Their present experience has been influenced by their past experience, something which has given rise to professional tensions as part of their implementation of the current EFL curriculum reform.

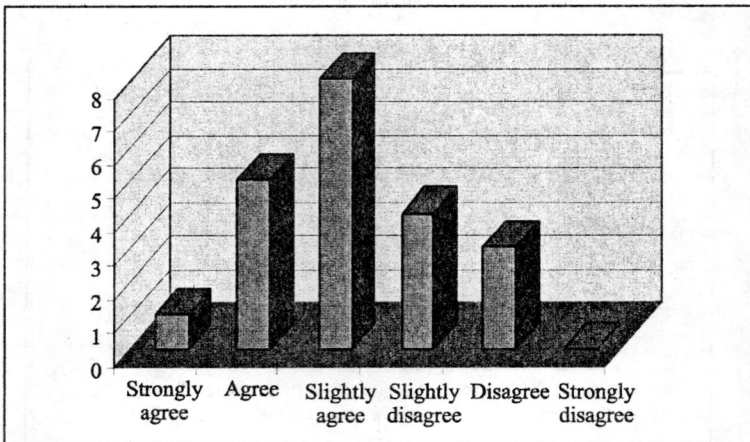

Figure 7. 22   Adequate Knowledge Base (Site A)

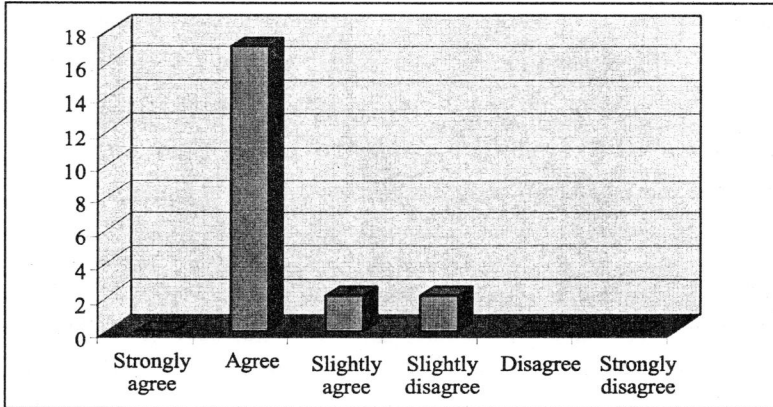

Figure 7. 23   Adequate Knowledge Base (Site B)

These teachers' past and present experience constitute significant features of the temporal ways in which they negotiate their lived experience. These teachers' present experience of inadequate knowledge influences their understanding of the reform under study and their practice of EFL teaching. As Shulman (2007) says, a teacher's knowledge base informs their understanding of reform as it relates to their teaching practice.

Exploring participants' present experience has also provided me with an image of ways in which participants have engaged an implementation of reform in schools and the personal professional pedagogical changes that have accompanied this. The picture that emerges is one where participant EFL teachers have already followed *ECS* in their teaching. For example, they have emphasized student-centred learning by employing task-based learning and new teaching and learning content. They have also created more opportunities for encouraging students to find confidence in using English, and to communicate with others in English in an attempt to achieve the goals of *ECS*. They have further adjusted their approaches to classroom teaching, suggesting that their approaches are different from the sort of EFL teaching they recall from their own past experience between the 1970s and the 1990s. Their responses to the questionnaire indicate that they consider their efforts to be part of an attempt to arouse students' interest in learning English and to develop their comprehensive language competence.

Explorations of participant EFL teachers' present experience indicate that they consider that the goals and relevant strategies of the current EFL curriculum reform are capable of engaging challenges of globalization. Emphasizing students' comprehensive language competence is the overall goal of *ECS*, a requirement that suggests itself as a response to globalization as they consider that it has turned the world into a global village in which people need to use the global language, English, to communicate and collaborate with people from different cultures (Zhu, 2003). Participants' present experience suggests their awareness that students need to have comprehensive language competence to serve both domestic and international purposes of education, vocation and society, and a means to access information sites in this global village as suggested by Zhu (2003). Approaches to EFL teaching and learning and teaching content of the current EFL curriculum reform have been concerned with positioning students as the centre of EFL teaching and learning, and with this an emphasis on individual student development, which also suggests itself as a response to challenges of globalization because it calls for education for a particular form of 21st century citizenship as a new focus for EFL teaching and learning. Participants' experience also indicates that they feel enthusiasm for implementing this reform in their schools as this manifests in shifts in teachers' role and teaching practice as suggested by Toombs (2001). Dilthey (1985, cited in van Manen, 1990) states:

A lived experience does not confront me as something perceived or represented; it is not given to me, but the reality of lived experience is there for me because I have a reflexive awareness of it, because I possess it immediately as belonging to me in some sense. Only in thought does it become objective (p. 35).

Goals, teaching methods and teaching content are key components of curriculum reform, which I have discussed in Chapter 3. Participant EFL teachers' descriptions of their present experience confirm that effective curriculum implementation rests on these factors. These teachers' descriptions of past and present experience has allowed me to examine dimensions which have constituted the horizons of their temporal way of experiencing their professional activities, as van Manen (1990) expresses it. In the following section I will emphasize participant EFL teachers' felt space in relation to the theme of lived space.

7.4   Lived and Felt Space

According to van Manen (1990), space in Phenomenological considerations is not objective or concrete, but subjective or abstract, a spatiality experienced psychologically rather than physically by individuals. It is something that is closely tied to human beings being influenced in regard to ways in which they feel (van Manen, 1997) because of their experience of a particular space or environment. I have taken lived space as the participant EFL teachers' felt space, suggesting their experience of implementation of the current EFL curriculum reform in the wider context of globalization. Graue and Walsh (1995) say that a context is "a culturally and historically situated place and time, a specific here and now" (p. 141), a concept which goes beyond the physical surrounding of settings such as classrooms and staffrooms. Such contexts are "constituted by what people are doing, as well as when and where they are doing it" suggested by McDermott and Roth (1980, cited in Graue & Walsh, 1995, p. 143), which is consistent with van Manen's descriptions of that felt space. To this end, I have initially explored participant EFL teachers' experience of lived space through their responses to the questionnaire. I have done this on the basis of their perceived understanding of globalization in relation to the current EFL curriculum reform as part of their relationship to ways in which this constitutes a new professional environment and their experience of new professional challenges that this poses for them which I will detail below.

Participant EFL teachers' descriptions of their experience indicates they see themselves as situated in a global context which requires their implementation of the current EFL curriculum reform in China. Their perspectives on their experience suggests that they have a general understanding of the concept of globalization and the current EFL curriculum reform; that for them globalization is a phenomenon that links national and local communities to a global one, thereby creating a need for relevant national and local changes in education. The EFL curriculum reform that has been implemented in China is one such change. They also recognize that globalization has had a number of influences on economy, politics, culture and education, and particularly on English with regard to all of these. On being questioned about the perceived influences of globalization on their lives, they say that they consider that nobody can avoid such influences, and that China is no exception, so that they think that it is impossible for the Chinese government to stop, or even reverse processes of globalization.

Their comments on their experience also suggest that they consider the current EFL curriculum reform as a priority because of the significant role of English in the global world and the pressures from China's entry into the WTO and the experience of Beijing 2008 Olympic Games. They indicate that the overall goal of the current EFL curriculum reform has shifted to enhance students' comprehensive language competence in response to challenges of globalization, and this indeed reflects the substance of the curriculum documents and policy statements. They say that the reform has highlighted student development, particularly individual student development, which again is a reflection of the curriculum document statements of outcomes. On the basis of their experience, they have come to the conclusion that the EFL curriculum reform that they are to implement emphasizes new teaching methods such as task-based approaches and updated teaching and learning content linked with contemporary social realities and students' life, especially as this involves material that deals with intercultural issues. These are issues that teachers have identified that constitute the lived space of teachers' lived experience, issues that are to be negotiated, managed, and dealt with as part of everyday professional life.

Participant EFL teachers' responses further indicate that they hold strong views regarding the idea of globalization posing challenges for human beings, and in particular for themselves, being EFL teachers. Across both sites, they share the view that they need to modernize their education ideas in order to keep abreast of social developments in China as part of their task of successful implementation of the current EFL curriculum reform. Apart from this common view, differences have emerged from the data in relation to details of implementation at school and classroom levels, shown in participant responses (see Figure 7.24 and Figure 7.25). The responses show that there is still a number of participants in Site A who think that they need to keep some traditional ideas or methods in their teaching, particularly given the Chinese context, while in Site B teachers have indicated a willingness to ditch them.

Participant EFL teachers' descriptions of their experience indicate their awareness of having been situated in a changing space marked by features of globalization. An analysis of participant perspectives suggest that, to them, globalization is a phenomenon whose influences are far-reaching, affecting every

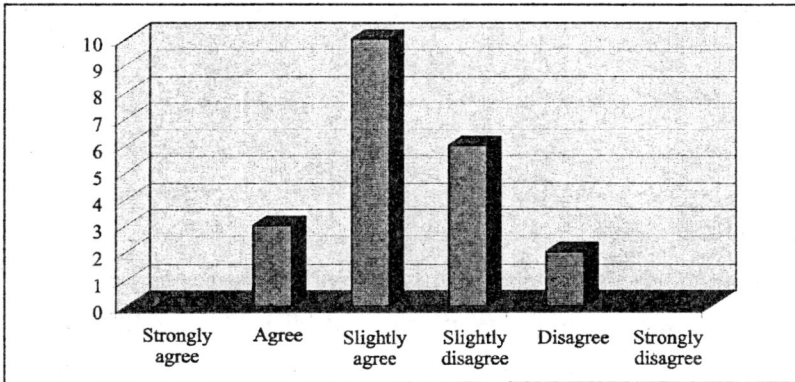

Figure 7.24　Keeping Traditional Ideas or Methods (Site A)

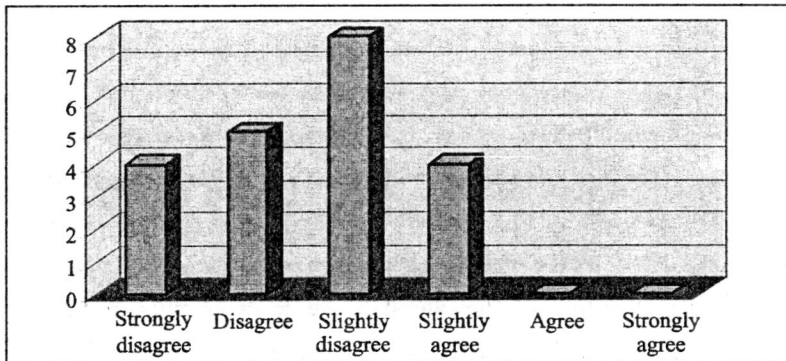

Figure 7.25　Keeping Traditional Ideas or Methods (Site B)

aspect of their life, particularly as this relates to EFL curriculum reform. Their responses to the questionnaire indicate an awareness that goes beyond information provided by the curriculum documents themselves; it is an awareness generated by an engagement with the lived space in which they are situated. Their responses go beyond considerations of EFL pedagogy to encompass the wider world of social, political, economic and cultural domains as they affect their professional classroom activities. An analysis of the questionnaire data regarding the lived space as part of participant EFL teachers' lived experience has suggested possibilities for further probing using individual interviews. As Warschauer (2000) argues, EFL teachers need to engage professional activities with an understanding of issues of globalization and their influences on their relevant fields and shape their teaching accordingly. The lived space within which participant EFL teachers have experienced the curriculum reform they are to implement has presented as a particular part of lived experience for me to explore.

7.5 Lived Other

According to van Manen's (1990) concept of lived other discussed in the forgoing, I have taken it as the relationships which participant EFL teachers have maintained with other stakeholders in the curriculum reform that is being implemented. I have not directly explored the relationship between participant EFL teachers and other stakeholders, having taken teachers' descriptions of those relationships as indicators of what these might be; stakeholders' roles have emerged from teachers' descriptions of these. What has emerged is the teachers' perceptions that stakeholders play an influential role in EFL teachers' experience of the reform. I will focus on the theme of lived other in the following section as ways in which these participant EFL teachers' experience of the reform has been influenced by stakeholders.

Participant EFL teachers' comments on their experience of implementing the current EFL curriculum reform indicate that the goals of students' progress and appreciation of their program of EFL study have been achieved. These results, participants feel, have provided an incentive for EFL teachers to pursue their implementation of the reform with some enthusiasm. They find that their students have already improved their comprehensive language competence, as seen in improved student skills in Speaking and Listening. They see this as being a result of their employment of new teaching methods, their use of interesting and challenging teaching content, as well as their increasing professional competence. Participant EFL teachers' questionnaire responses indicate that they perceive that their students have increasingly changed in their approaches to their own EFL learning as part of the reform. This suggests that the new EFL curriculum intent and its features have translated from statements of principles and goals in curriculum documents into EFL teaching and learning classroom practice. Teachers' responses to the questionnaire indicate that perceived constant improvement in students' EFL learning have led to teachers' confidence in implementing the EFL curriculum reform, leading to an enthusiastic pursuit of professional development as part of their lived experience.

Participant EFL teachers' enthusiasm for the reform has also derived from more cooperation, collaboration, and professional discussions with their colleges than before. They say that this has generated greater interest in undertaking relevant professional development activities to improve their teaching. Participant EFL teachers' responses to questions on their experience of professional development through cooperation and collaboration with their colleagues indicate another development in their implementing the reform. The *Outline* highlights teachers' reflections on their own teaching practice, encouraging them to improve their teaching constantly. Part of this feature of the reform is a new system of assessment that links principals, teachers, students and parents as they become more involved in this aspect of the reform (Ministry of Education, 2001d). Teachers, then, are required to develop a new awareness of new forms of cooperation and collaboration in the new curriculum. The new EFL curriculum documents, particularly the *ECS*, states that EFL teachers are to develop students' cooperative and collaborative awareness in EFL learning. It does not specifically suggest that EFL teachers themselves are required to have such an awareness of cooperation and collaboration in their implementing the reform. Such suggestions appear in the supplementary materials for in-service teacher education programs prepared as part of the reform. Zhong, Cui and Zhang (2001) state that teachers need to cooperate and collaborate with peers, parents and principals. Participant EFL teachers' experience of lived other has given them a sense of encouragement and enthusiasm for this feature of the reform, part of their lived experience of that reform. They have engaged a program of new forms of interaction with their colleagues and students, a program which, according to the questionnaire responses, has assisted them in professional development.

On the basis of analysis of questionnaire data, I have generated a general picture of the participant EFL teachers' lived experience of the current EFL curriculum reform in the context of globalization. It is a picture of participants in my research having a general knowledge and awareness of globalization and its influences in various aspects of their professional lives in relation to the reform under study. They consider that the reform was initiated to engage challenges of globalization, to cope with economic and political development in China. They perceive that the reform was initiated on the basis of economic and political stability in China, part of maintaining a balance between economic, political, and cultural and education factors. The current EFL curriculum reform has also been subjected to processes of investigation and careful preparation, indicating a depth of philosophical and practical concern that has gone beyond the superficiality that may be associated with propaganda campaigns. An examination of participant EFL teachers' lived experience of implementation of the reform indicates that, for these teachers at least, it is appropriate and practical. The responses the teachers have given to the questionnaire show positive attitudes and enthusiasm for the reform under study.

7.6　Conclusion

In this chapter, I have given an overview of participant EFL teachers' lived experience with an analysis of their responses to the questionnaire. I have first introduced EFL teachers' background in both sites. I have then explored these teachers' experience on the basis of three themes emerging from their responses to the questionnaire: lived time, lived other and lived space. In relation to the theme of lived time, I have focused on participant EFL teachers' past and present experience as constituting the temporal way of their lived experience. I have approached the theme of lived space as these teachers' felt space. In relation to the theme of lived other, I have highlighted the role of stakeholders as part of their lived experience. Such explorations have served to provide the basis for a general overview on which to base more detailed explorations with individual participants in individual interviews. In the following chapters, I will discuss the same themes as they have emerged from an analysis of interview data.

Chapter 8
Lived Space: Lived Experience and the Interviews

8.1 Introduction

In Chapter 7 I have explored participant EFL teachers' lived experience through an analysis of questionnaire data. In the following chapters I will focus on emerging themes from analysis of interview data which provide detailed insights into participant EFL teachers' lived experience of the reform under study. I have employed three of van Manen's (1990) posited four existentials of lived space, lived other and lived time within the concept of lived experience as a tool with which to explore EFL teachers' lived experience of this reform. I will discuss these three themes separately in Chapters 8, 9 and 10.

In this chapter, I will focus on issues as they emerge from the interview data in relation to lived space. As I have explained in Chapter 7, I have taken this concept of lived space as constituting participant EFL teachers' felt space. That felt space comprises the global context, the Chinese context and the school context. I have started this discussion by introducing the interviewees' before turning to emerging themes from interviews with them. I have introduced interviewees' backgrounds on each site separately, and then teased out main differences across both sites. This has provided a starting point for me to carry out an exploration of participant EFL teachers' lived experience of the reform under study.

8.2 Interviewees

I have selected 16 interviewees from the 42 participant EFL teachers who had completed the questionnaire and invited them to participate in interviews designed to generate more detailed data that would enable greater depth of discussions of the reform than the questionnaire allows. As I have discussed in Chapter 5, the criteria for this selection has been on the basis of their years of teaching experience and their availability at each school.

8.2.1 Site A

8 EFL teachers have been selected for the in-depth interviews on their work as EFL teachers in Site A (see Table 8.1). All of these teachers are Teaching Certificate holders. 6 of the 8 are female; 2 are male. None of them has experience of overseas training or traveling. Up until 2008, 6 of them have at least 15 years' teaching experience and 2 have at least 10 years' (details see Table 8.1).

Table 8.1   **Background of EFL Teachers Interviewed (Site A)**

Name	Age	Gender	Degree	When (Starting Teaching)	When (Starting Learning English)	Overseas Training or Traveling
Jiang	40-44	Female	Teaching Certificate	1991	Junior School	No
Xu	35-39	Female	Teaching Certificate	1992	Junior School	No
Jun	35-39	Female	Bachelor	1996	Junior School	No
Lian	45-49	Female	Teaching Certificate	1983	Junior School	No
Hua	35-39	Female	Teaching Certificate	1995	Junior School	No
Hong	40-44	Female	Teaching Certificate	1989	Primary School	No
Fen	45-49	Male	Teaching Certificate	1978	College	No
Wei	55-59	Male	Teaching Certificate	1970	College	No

8.2.2   Site B

8 EFL teachers have been selected for in-depth interviews from Site B. 7 of them (see Table 8.2) have a Bachelor's Degree; one of them has a Teaching Certificate. 5 of them are female; 3 are male. 4 of the 8 have had overseas training or traveling experience. Up until 2008, 6 of these EFL teachers have at least 15 years' teaching experience and 2 have more than 6 years' (Details see Table 8.2).

Table 8.2   **Background of EFL Teachers interviewed (Site B)**

Name	Age	Gender	Degree	When (Starting Teaching)	When (Starting Learning English)	Overseas Training or Traveling
Ju	35-39	Female	Bachelor	1991	Senior School	Yes
Qing	45-49	Male	Bachelor	1983	Junior School	Yes
Ying	35-39	Female	Bachelor	1996	Primary School	No
Fang	40-44	Female	Bachelor	1981	Junior School	No
Qin	50-54	Female	Bachelor	1976	Junior School	Yes
Xia	25-29	Female	Bachelor	2002	Junior School	Yes
Chu	45-49	Male	Bachelor	1980	University	No
Qiang	40-44	Male	Teaching Certificate	1984	Junior School	No

Half of the EFL teachers in Site B have experience of overseas traveling. None in Site A has. 1 of the teachers holds a Bachelor's Degree in Site A; 7 in Site B do. I have used these two main differences between teachers' backgrounds across two sites to serve as informing my analysis of the interview data in relation to ways in which participants have experienced implementation of the EFL curriculum reform, a significant feature of their lived experience of that reform. In the following section, I will examine participant EFL teachers' lived experience of the reform under study in relation to their felt space of professional experience emerging from interview data.

8.3   Felt Space

Investigating participant EFL teachers' lived space as felt space has enabled me to develop an understanding of this aspect of their lived experience in relation to EFL teaching and learning. This is also consistent with van Manen's view of lived space with a focus on felt space discussed in Chapter 7. Van Manen (1990) also argues that lived space is "a category for inquiring into the ways we experience the affairs of our day-to-day existence; in addition it helps us uncover more fundamental meaning dimensions of lived life" (p. 103). Van Manen's perspectives have provided me with a basis from which to generate an understanding of felt space as this applies in my research. Sub-themes that emerge from my discussion include those of the global context, the Chinese context, and the school context through exploration of the participants' felt space. Identification of these contexts has allowed me to focus on participant EFL teachers' felt space related to globalization and its influences on macro and micro levels which I will detail below.

8.3.1 The Global Context

In the following section, I will describe participant EFL teachers' lived experience of the current EFL curriculum reform through their felt space as being positioned in a global context. Such positioning includes influences of globalization on various aspects of English and EFL curriculum reform in relation to these participants' experience. As I have described in Chapter 2, globalization proceeds on the basis of extremely intricate processes that have considerably influenced the multidimensional aspects of societies at various levels (Krkgöz, 2008), Chinese society being no exception to this. I have drawn on the concept of globalization as a tool to be used to open up possibilities for analysis of current transformations or reforms that occur in various countries in general (Bradbury, 2007; Harris, et al. , 2002; Jay, 2001; Overholt, 2005) and China in particular.

Interview data show that participants have obtained an understanding of the concept of globalization and its influences on politics, economics, culture and education, with a particular focus on English teaching and learning. EFL teachers interviewed describe influences of globalization in such statements as "gradually involved in people's life" (Ju) and "the whole world is like a global village and it is becoming smaller and smaller" (Qiang). They say that because of globalization, there has been "more culture exchange" between countries (Qiang). Jiang also says:

> One change is to promote people to emancipate their minds and to improve the emancipation of productivity. The emancipations have also resulted in the economic boom and the economic development in China and they have really brought about great changes.

Qing says, "Globalization could promote people to have more convenient and more high-frequency communications, and people now are in an open world". These three examples of participant EFL teachers' are representative of similar comments on teachers' experience in these two sites, experience which has led them to generate an understanding of globalization as it affects their world. Participants' interview statements reflect not only their awareness of globalization, but an appreciation of it as being intentional, oriented and purposeful in their lived experience. Such awareness has given rise to changes in behaviour, suggesting an impetus to implementing the reform under study.

Globalization has also been increasingly associated with the prominent role of English in the world (Crystal, 2003; Crystal, 1997; Imam, 2005). According to Tsui and Tollefson (2007, cited in Krkgöz, 2008), English is one of two main mediation tools influencing the development of globalization. Chang (2006) states that the role of English as a global language has been further strengthened because of globalization. More specifically, the rapid popularization of information technology and Internet systems sets the stage for the growth of global English (Guan & Meng, 2007). Participant EFL teachers in my research are aware of the influences of globalization on the role of English in the global world. For example, EFL teachers in my research have accepted English as "a global language (Ju)," and "a bridge" to connect different countries (Qing). The increasingly important role of English as a global language has also posed new challenges for English language teaching and learning, including challenges for education philosophy, education concepts and the overall system of school management (Guan & Meng, 2007), each of which constitute part of felt space of the interviewees.

Participant EFL teachers' experience of being situated in a global context indicates that they have acknowledged globalization as an inevitable phenomenon in their world. Their comments indicate that they see this as influencing various aspects of their lived experience as it includes education, particularly in relation to the role of English as a global language. They see this phenomenon as posing challenges for the EFL curriculum reform they are to implement, including day-to-day experience of EFL teaching and learning. This is consistent with the literature discussed in Chapter 2 in relation to the issues of globalization and the role of English in a globalizing world. As Olssen, Codd and O'Neill (2004) say, globalization is a phenomenon serving as an invisible force assuring "sustainability and survival" in that world (p. 1). Globalization provides an impetus to the further spread of English as a global language, part of the challenges for EFL teaching and learning (Warschauer, 2000a). My examination of the interview data on these points provides a basis for further examination of participants' felt space in the Chinese context.

8.3.2 The Chinese Context

In this section, I will move from examining participant EFL teachers' felt space positioned within a global context to that of the Chinese context. In doing so, I have explored ways in which globalization has provided a stimulus for changes regarding the role of English and its influences on the current EFL curriculum reform implemented in Chinese secondary schools. I argue that this reform is part of China's response to globalization, a response which is both a proactive and reactive feature of the EFL reform under consideration in my research.

The current EFL curriculum reform prioritizes a study of English language in China in recognition of its role as a carrier of knowledge, information and skills underpinning social development, information technology and economic globalization (Ministry of Education, 2001a). The questionnaire data indicate that participants have recognized the significant role of English in the Chinese context. The interview data have confirmed this, suggesting that EFL teachers participating in my research have recognized English as a priority in the Chinese context. They have regarded English as not only "a useful tool" for students' future development (Qing), but also as integral to students' life, and not just for international communication. The interview data also indicate that their concerns in English teaching and learning emerge as a major feature of their implementing the EFL curriculum reform. Their stated concerns position EFL curriculum reform in secondary schools in China in the larger context that is dominated by issues of globalization, issues that go well beyond the concerns of their own classroom practices and protocols. As one EFL teacher, Ju, states:

> Globalization, after all, has become gradually involved in people's life, and children would feel that learning a language has already become a real and useful tool, rather than merely to get a diploma and certain marks.

Another EFL teacher, Ying, says:

> As an EFL teacher, I have to cope with international education. For example, we have been provided with so many platforms in my school. In the following semester, I might go to England as well. And thus, I would like to improve myself via collecting various teaching information from the world, English language teaching in particular.

These two examples of EFL teachers' perspectives are once again representative of similar comments in each of the two sites, which indicate that participants have recognized English as a tool for life, posing challenges for students and teachers alike in the Chinese context. Such comments couched in such terms by these teachers demonstrate the role of intentionality (Budd, 2005) as they indicate a particular teacher direction and purpose in implementing the EFL curriculum reform that is linked with the wider concerns of Chinese and international contexts in which their professional activities are situated. Teachers' comments demonstrate the awareness of the wider implications of their work for the country itself. In this sense this reform is not only one of curriculum development isolated from other events in the country but tied to promoting positive social, political and economic development across the country.

China has gradually changed its development direction and started to play a pivotal role in the world with its entering into the WTO in 2001 and hosting the Beijing 2008 Olympic Games (Zhan, 2008). I have explored these two events as a significant impetus for initiating the EFL current curriculum reform to be implemented in China. As I have illustrated in Chapter 1, English has been positioned as a priority in China's development as the two events have placed more pressure on English language teaching and learning. Interview data from participant EFL teachers' description of their experience have provided further details of teachers' understanding of the influences of these two events on English in the Chinese context, further confirming wider Chinese and international contexts as influencing the range and scope of their professional activities as EFL teachers in China. One EFL teacher, Fang, says:

> We have already seen that many old people in the streets and lanes in Beijing have their passions for the 2008 Olympic Games and attempt to take this further. Learning English is one of the most important things for them to take up as we all look forward to doing something for this significant event in China and expect this Olympic Games to be held successfully as well.

Another EFL teacher, Qing, states:

> People in China can see how important the role of English has become through its entry into the WTO. This event has also provided people in China with more opportunities to engage with foreigners in business and international trade.

These are two participant EFL teachers' statements which indicate that they have linked the two events of the WTO entry and the Beijing 2008 Olympic Games with the priority being given to the promotion of English in the Chinese context, and they are echoed in other participant statements across the two sites. Participant comments in this area have offered possibilities for further understanding the reform under study, as it has allowed me to examine in detail, in Phenomenological terms, felt space as part of the lived experience of the participants. For these teachers, it is not just a matter of events outside their work places forming abstract considerations for their professional activities; it is a matter of concrete manifestation of such events in what they do as teachers. This is also in line with the literature, such as the work of Hu (2005b), who states that these two developments provided an impetus for increasing demands for English in China.

The curriculum documents suggest that the current EFL curriculum reform has been initiated and implemented on the basis of globalization and its influences on the increasing role of English as a global language, particularly in the Chinese context (Ministry of Education, 2001a). In addition to this, the two events of the China's entry into the WTO and hosting the Beijing 2008 Olympic Games have provided an impetus to the current EFL curriculum reform being implemented throughout China. I have identified these two events as part of the contexts that provide direction for the participant EFL teachers in curriculum implementation, which has been confirmed by interview data. As van Manen (1990) argues, all human activity is always oriented activity, directed by that which orients it, part of "a person's world or landscape" (p. 182). Exploring the issues informed by such considerations has offered possibilities for examining participant EFL teachers' lived experience in relation to the reform under study.

8.3.3   The School Context

In the previous two sections, I have explored participant EFL teachers' felt space in relation to it as being situated within a global and a Chinese context. In the following section, I will investigate these participants' felt space within their school contexts in relation to the physical and academic environment in which they operate. I have done this on the basis of examining their descriptions of their experience and relevant government documents. This has enabled me to consider infrastructure as well as academic environment for the reform.

According to Priestley (2002), "Education reforms have been characterized by a tendency of central governments to divest themselves of responsibility for day-to-day management of schools" (p. 124). In line with this, I have examined the school context in which participant EFL teachers have been working, as the school context plays its own part in influencing lived experience of teachers implementing the EFL curriculum reform. As Goodson and Cole (1994) suggest, relevant micro-political and contextual realities of school life plays an important role in determining a successful curriculum reform. Remillard (1999) argues that different school contexts play a significant role in contributing to teachers' beliefs and understanding of teaching. On the basis of these discussions, I have considered that details of the school contexts provide the means by which an investigation of what EFL teachers may value and have concerns about the current EFL curriculum reform in Chinese secondary schools may be conducted. As Fullan (2000) argues:

> There was actually great pressure and incentives to become innovative, and this resulted in many schools adopting reforms for which they did not have the capacity (individually or organizationally) to put the reforms into practice. Innovations, thus, were adopted on the surface with some of the language and structures becoming altered, but not the practice of teaching (pp. 6-7).

8.3.3.1 Infrastructure

In the following section I will focus on new contexts in which participant EFL teachers have been situated, that of issues relating to schools' infrastructure. I have considered such issues on the basis of Fullan's (2000) suggestion, that no substantial reform can take place or be sustained if it lacks strong teaching work and corresponding infrastructure. As I have stated in Chapter 5, a total of 6 schools were chosen for my investigation, schools which exhibit 2 sets of contrasting features within Liaoning Province. There are 5 schools in Site A, as schools in this site tend to have between 3 and 5 teachers working in EFL. Such a small number in any one school is inadequate for my research needs in relation to data collection. 1 school constitutes Site B, as it employs more than 20 teachers in the EFL field, which provides me with a suitable range of teachers' experience to explore. Inviting between 3 and 5 teachers from a total of 5 schools in Site A has provided me with a similar range of experience as that of teachers in site B. Since the infrastructures of all 5 schools in Site A are similar, I have considered issues of infrastructure as they apply to the Site A schools as a whole, while using 1 school in Site B.

The schools in Site A are located in the mountainous area of a less developed region in Liaoning Province. The *Compulsory Education Law of the People's Republic of China* has experienced a number of amendments since its promulgation in 1986 (Wei, 2008). The current EFL curriculum reform began to be implemented throughout the whole country in 2001. The latest policies make it clear that the central and provincial governments are expected to take up the main responsibility for rural compulsory education (Wei, 2008). The policies have brought about a number of changes in these rural schools, including the reconstruction of school buildings and shifting from broken sheds or huts in which children had been schooled up until then. Some of the schools in rural or less developed regions have been equipped with teaching and learning facilities such as computers, tape-recorders, wall maps and supplementary teaching and learning materials. Such efforts have been aimed at narrowing the quality gap between rural and urban education provision and pursuing equity in education, which is also the focus of the current curriculum reform in Chinese secondary schools (Ministry of Education, 1998).

Despite such policies and their implementation, my research has indicated that there are still some problems regarding quality gaps and equity in education provision in some rural or less developed regions, particularly in Northeast China such as in Site A. I have come to this conclusion by examining participant EFL teachers' experience, which indicates that the infrastructures of their schools have been improved to some degree in consequence of government policies. Nonetheless, they still have inadequate facilities, with cassette recorders and tapes being the only provision of support for their language teaching on top of basic items such as classrooms, blackboards, chalk, and students' stationery and textbooks. These schools cannot afford to provide for themselves modern technological facilities such as desktops or laptops, computer software, video projectors or other such equipment. The majority of EFL teachers in the questionnaire state that they only have cassette recorders and tapes, and no other facilities, not even wall maps. Teachers in Site A indicate that their schools have no other financial sources beyond what they receive by way of government support. They accordingly have no sister school or exchange programs with overseas countries because of financial problems and their locations.

Interview data have further confirmed this point, as Jiang says:

> Our EFL teachers still do not have enough facilities, and they don't even have wall maps. At the moment, teachers only have one tape-recorder and sometimes cannot get the relevant tapes either.

This EFL teacher considers that although the governments in this region have endeavoured to improve the conditions of rural schools, and in the mountainous ones in particular, they still lack adequate facilities for teaching and learning. Her experience of inadequate facilities is at odds with documented teaching and learning strategies to be used to support EFL curriculum reform, which focus on encouraging teachers to integrate information technology with teaching and learning (Huang, 2004; Ministry of Education, 2001a). It is a comment that recurs in the interview data from Site A. It is also in accordance with a Chinese proverb: One can't make bricks without straw.

In the process of conducting data collection in Site A, I have been informed by teachers that their schools have not developed relationships with any other schools in any other countries. This, they say, is because of their remote location not making their schools attractive options to possible English-speaking exchange students. Their financial disadvantage has also meant that the schools themselves do not present as attractive propositions to such students. Aside from this, there is no money to send teachers or students to other countries for the sorts of exchanges envisaged in the *Outline*.

The school in Site B is located in a developed coastal city in Liaoning Province, and it is one of the key schools in this region. This school is a newly-established one which possesses what the teachers consider to be adequate facilities for teaching and learning, where each classroom is equipped with a whole set of modern teaching facilities such as a computer, a large-screen projector, and a television set. Most of the teachers in this school have computers, and relevant software, as well as the teaching materials they require to implement the current EFL curriculum reform. According to these EFL teachers, this school can provide almost everything required for teaching and learning in their field. The school has also developed sister school or exchange relationships with a number of secondary schools in other countries such as the United States of America, the United Kingdom, Korea, Singapore, and Japan. Because of this, teachers and students have opportunities to go abroad for exchange studies, suggesting that they have more opportunities to communicate and interact with foreign students and teachers than those in Site A. It is a school that has created an appropriate environment for EFL teaching and learning as outlined in the current EFL curriculum reform.

During the interviews, almost none of the EFL teachers in Site B talked about inadequate facilities as influencing their teaching. The funding for this school is not only obtained from central and provincial governments, but also from a number of sponsors in the form of parents and companies. Historically, the schools in this region receive strong support from parents' committees, especially for upgrading necessary education resources. Such infrastructure in this school provides a strong and stable basis for EFL teachers to implement the current EFL curriculum reform in their school. Interview data represents an impressive image of the school, which is different from those from Site A.

A comparison of the schools in both sites based on participant EFL teachers' stated experience of them has provided a general picture of infrastructure across both sites. Participants' descriptions of their experience in Site A indicate that they are provided with inadequate teaching facilities and no officially supported opportunities for travel experience abroad. Such problems relate to these 5 schools' location in less developed regions of Northeast China and being short of adequate financial support as they depend entirely on what support is provided by governments. These inadequacies act as barriers to their implementing the reform under study; they cannot comply with some of the requirements stipulated in the *ECS*, especially in relation to adopting modern information technologies as part of the teaching and learning engaged by teachers and students.

In contrast, participants' descriptions of their experience in Site B indicate that they are provided with adequate teaching facilities that match the requirements for EFL teaching and learning. Although the school also depends on government financial support, it has developed external supports such as those provided by the parents' committee and private corporations. In addition to this, they have taken advantage of their location in a developed region of China, building up relationships with other, both domestic and international, schools. Such relationships have set the stage for participants in Site B to go abroad for overseas English experience. These developments have created an environment conducive to EFL teaching and learning, supporting teacher and student motivation and passion for implementing the reform.

Features of infrastructure serve to construct the spaces in which participants have experienced implementing the EFL curriculum reform, and their various responses to their particular spaces, as I have discussed in the foregoing. Such issues provide a basis from which to explore in some detail the meanings of lived experience of the reform under study. I have considered differences in the sites in these two regions as a distinguishing feature that becomes salient in relation to concepts of glocalization, a related issue of globalization, which I have discussed in Chapter 2.

8.3.3.2   Academic Environment for Reform

In the following section, I will investigate issues as they relate to academic environments for reform, which have been confronted by the schools in both sites as they work towards supporting EFL teachers in relation to professional development needs that are associated with the reform under study. I have presented these separately in relation to these two sites. As Gordon and Yocke' (1999) argue, when teachers are acknowledged as a central link of reform process, the efforts of school improvement and educational reform will actually occur.

Fullan and Hargreaves (1992) say that reforms can only be implemented successfully when teachers have generated a deep understanding of the significance of change. I have drawn on the idea that even though teachers feel enthusiasm for reform or confidence in its conduct, they still require relevant and appropriate training or guidelines to help them (Pintó, 2004). On the subject of reform, Pintó (2004) argues that, "Given too much direction, and teachers lose any sense of ownership. Given too little, and they feel that they do not know what to do" (p. 2). The interview data from Site A show that EFL teachers have not been given too much direction, indeed they describe some inadequacies in training in relation to their implementing the current EFL curriculum reform. Jiang expresses it in this way: "Only one afternoon for this training, not for English as subject, but for general training in relation to the current curriculum reform." Wei also comments:

I do not think the training delivered in this region is good. We only had training at the beginning of the new textbook published, and it lasted for a short period and then it almost disappeared in mid process.

In contrast, interview data from Site B show that the training was conducted for reform in that place quite differently from that of Site A. Qin said:

5 EFL teachers were sent to England to study last year and they all got related certificates. Another example, an art teacher in my school was also sent to Australia to have 3 months' training.

Participant EFL teachers' statements from each site indicate that their schools have provided different professional development programs prepared for implementation of the reform in both sites. Participant EFL teachers' experience from Site B indicates that they have enthusiasm for new approaches to EFL teaching and learning as well as implementing the reform as they have been provided with various professional development programs, while those in Site A indicate that they feel helpless in the face of a lack of relevant professional development, influencing their understanding of the reform under study in negative ways. This can also be seen from the three statements above which are representative of similar perspectives in the two sites. Participants' experience in Site A has also given them a sense of expectation of equity of professional development programs such as that of Site B, but this has not been fulfilled. It highlights the significance of issues of equity of professional development. A balanced provision of professional development is the basis of realizing education equity and assuring successful curriculum reform (Zeng, Deng, Yang, Zou, & Chu, 2007).

These teachers' descriptions of their experience point to differences in relation to issues of infrastructure and academic environments. Their experience shows ways in which they have responded to their own school contexts. A tension has arisen as Site A participant EFL teachers experience a lack of adequate teaching facilities and professional development programs. Teachers are required to address issues of professional development and to modernize their teaching to engage challenges of the new curriculum. The inconsistency between the realities of a lack of professional development opportunities in Site A and the intent of the new curriculum reform has influenced their experience of implementing the reform. The requirements as specified in the *Outline* and *ECS* do not match the lived experience of Site A teachers. On the one hand this underscores issues of globalization and glocalization, where the demands of the two do not align, but it is also a matter of teachers' felt space marked by a lack of recognition of local issues in policy and curriculum statements, which raises issues of professional development that it was intended would be provided across the country. An examination of the details of the new curriculum implementation in this region shows that in relation to the felt space of a number of teachers in Northeast China, that is, in Site A, a general approach to EFL curriculum reform does not carry through to details of that implementation.

Representing teachers' felt space as discussed above in relation to participant EFL teachers' lived experience emphasises "the sense in which space is a constituent for the world that essentially belongs to our existence" (Baiasu, 2007, p. 329). These teachers' experience of their felt space has influenced their lived experience within a global context, the Chinese context and the school context. As Smith (2003) argues:

Human self-understanding is now increasingly lived out in a tension between the local and the global, between my understanding of myself as a person of this place and my emerging yet profound awareness that this places participants in a reality heavily influenced by, and implicated in, larger pictures. This calls forth from me not just a new sense of place, but also a new kind of response to the world. It is a response I may feel uneasy about making given that so much about what seems to be going on is experienced preconceptually precisely because no one, no authority, can tell me exactly what is happening (p.36).

My analysis of participant EFL teachers' experience in relation to the theme of felt space also serves as one example of education being used as a means by which China attempts to meet the requirements of social development and to promote students as 21st century citizens in response to challenges of globalization.

8.4   Conclusion

In this chapter I have examined the theme of felt space with a focus on participant EFL teachers' descriptions of their experience of it as one of the contexts in which participant EFL teachers have been situated while implementing the reform under study. In relation to a global context, these EFL teachers' descriptions of their experience indicate that globalization is a phenomenon that has influenced various aspects of their professional lives, specifically in relation to the role of English has to play as a global language. In the Chinese context, participant EFL teachers' descriptions of their experience indicate that the priority of English in China and two events—China's entry into the WTO and hosting the Beijing 2008 Olympic Games— have been identified by these teachers as the impetus for implementing the current EFL curriculum reform. In relation to individual school contexts, I have examined the infrastructure and academic environments for reform through these teachers' descriptions of their experience. The data indicate that schools in Site A have not been able to provide adequate teaching facilities and academic environments for teachers' professional development in comparison with those in site B, and that the problems which have emerged from this situation have influenced these teachers' understanding of how they are to implement EFL curriculum reform. In the following chapter I will investigate the theme of lived other via an analysis of interview data, with a focus on participant EFL teachers' descriptions of their lived experience.

Chapter 9
Lived Other : Lived Experience and the Interviews

9.1 Introduction

In Chapter 8 I have explored participant EFL teachers' felt professional environments in discussing the theme of lived space. In this chapter, I will focus on other stakeholders as lived other in relation to participant EFL teachers' lived experience of the reform under study. Stakeholders are groups of people who in the case of my research share with EFL teachers an interest in or responsibility for implementing the current EFL curriculum reform. They are people who make contributions to shape, support, or participate in some way in the implementation of the current EFL curriculum reform in Chinese secondary schools. I have not interviewed any of these people, but they have a presence in my interview data as they are referred to by participant teachers who have been interviewed. In my analysis of the interview data that refer to them, I have identified the stakeholders as being students, parents, principals and governments as part of the lived other of the EFL teachers' lived experience. Data suggest that these EFL teachers have experienced not only a sense of support and encouragement, but also pressure, which has affected them in implementing the current EFL curriculum reform; that a tension has developed between support and pressure, with teachers having to negotiate their way through this tension.

9.2 Students

Students' perspectives are present as part of EFL teachers' lived experience of other as they manifest in teachers' responses to interview questions. Participant teachers' accounts of their experience in both sites indicate that students are consistent in their expressions of enthusiasm for the reform; that they feel that their language competence has been developed as a result. Qin says, for example, "What has impressed me most is that children seem quite interested in the dialogues and texts in the new textbook". Wei says, "The main task for students is to do more practice. " Jiang also states, "When I changed my teaching methods, my students showed enthusiasm for learning English, and the class would become lively. " Qing adds, "You know when students themselves are capable of communicating with people or expressing themselves in English; they feel satisfaction in having such achievement. " These statements are indicative of general responses from participant teachers regarding student stakeholders as showing enthusiasm for what are for the teachers themselves new teaching methods and content that have suggested themselves as appropriate in the context of the new EFL curriculum implementation in their schools. What is more, it is indicative of students themselves having perceived their own progress in their acquisition of English in positive ways.

Students' enthusiastic responses to the reform and their progress in EFL learning suggest a certain measure of success on the part of the EFL teachers' implementing the current EFL curriculum reform in their schools, and that students perceive that they have had a measure of success in achieving what the current EFL curriculum reform expects of them. As I have discussed in the foregoing regarding the new curriculum intent and its features, the current EFL curriculum reform has as its overall goal the development of students' comprehensive language competence. To this end, the new curriculum emphasizes students' knowledge, skills, cultural understanding, learning strategies, emotions and attitudes (Ministry of Education, 2001a). Participant responses indicate that students have themselves been concerned with their own comprehensive language development regarding EFL learning. Teacher perceptions of student enthusiasm for EFL learning and perceived progress has confirmed the appropriateness of the design of the new curriculum in relation to its intent and its particular focus on individual skill development as far as the students in these Chinese secondary schools are concerned.

I have considered these students' enthusiastic responses to the new EFL reform and their progress in EFL learning as a feature that distinguishes this current EFL curriculum reform from previous reforms, and one which further highlights participants' perceived deficiencies in descriptions of their own past experience of being secondary school students, mainly between the 1970s and the 1990s, but particularly around the 1990s. The teachers are those same students who experienced the previous curriculum reforms during these periods, who were not positioned by their teachers as being at the centre of teaching and learning, and who were treated as passive listeners as their EFL teachers adopted teacher-centred and grammar-focused methods. Their descriptions of their experience as students under such regimes of EFL teaching and learning emphasize the intent and features of the new EFL curriculum as being focused differently, with a view to producing different outcomes than previous teaching and learning allowed for. The 1993 curriculum, for example, focused on the two aspects of students' knowledge and skills, tending to marginalize rather than foreground considerations of student emotions and attitudes, cultural awareness and learning strategies. Some participants were the very students of former years who say that they had no interest in learning English. They were the ones who found it difficult to communicate with others in English as they had no opportunities to practise the language in class. Interview accounts of their experiences provide a marked contrast with accounts of the present students' enthusiastic response to the reform and the progress that they have achieved, which indicates a development that features with some prominence in teachers' responses in interviews about their perspectives on the new curriculum reform.

This does not mean that teachers' perceptions of student enthusiasm are necessarily correct. Teachers' perspectives as they present in the interview data on the success of their own teaching are subjective impressions of their own success. It is possible that their perceptions are erroneous, and further research would have to be conducted on students' perspectives of the EFL curriculum reform to establish this. The point that I wish to make here is that the teachers have been able to make clear distinctions between what they have experienced as students by way of textbooks and teaching methods and what they experience now by way of new textbooks and new teaching methods associated with the EFL curriculum reform. They point out that they have not been able to turn to the models of previous regimes of teaching and learning in EFL as a basis for their own work as teachers; they have been required to make what they have represented in their interview responses as significant changes.

Given this, participants have indicated that their descriptions of their experience as EFL teachers of their own students' enthusiasm for changes associated with the reform have influenced teachers' lived experience of the reform, and not just in the sense of professional satisfaction with perceived classroom teaching and learning success. Jiang, for example, says, "It is the students who might promote teachers to learn more in order to improve their knowledge". Fang also says, "How can teachers teach in the future, if they fall behind their students in this?" These two EFL teachers at least consider that their students' involvement in teaching and learning activities have caused them as EFL teachers to focus on their own professional development, and it is a sentiment expressed by others from both sites as well. As Fisherman, Marx, Best, and Tal (2003) argue, EFL teachers have demands placed upon them for ensuring their own professional development when it comes to incorporating changes caused by students' behaviour in class, and this has been confirmed by participants in my research. This is also consistent with a Chinese proverb: "Teaching others teaches yourself", suggesting a Confucian education idea that is still relevant, in the context of EFL teaching at least, in China. Participant EFL teachers have themselves identified students' interest as acting as a stimulus to their engaging more effective teaching in implementing the EFL curriculum reform at the same time as concerns for comprehensive language development in their students' studying English has challenged them as far as professional development is concerned.

Teachers' perspectives on students' responses to the reform raise issues in relation to lived experience. According to van Manen (1990):

> Lived experiences gather hermeneutic significance as we (reflectively) gather them by giving memory to them. Through mediations, conversations, day dreams, inspirations and other interpretive acts we assign meanings to the phenomena of lived life (p.37).

The particular significance that teachers ascribe to students as influencing in positive ways their own professional development suggests an aspect of lived experience that has received little attention in the literature, and yet figures with some prominence in teachers' statements on this issue. This has been an unexpected outcome of my research, for while the literature acknowledges students as stakeholders in curriculum in general and curriculum reform in particular, such a specific detail as influencing professional development to maintain professional teacher standards has not been highlighted as a feature regarding the students in EFL curriculum reform.

Students as one of the stakeholders of EFL curriculum reform are considered by participant EFL teachers as playing a meaningful role in these teachers' lived experience as the current reform places students at the centre of their education system and its attendant curriculum, pedagogical, and teaching and learning activities (Gwele, 2005a; Stern & Riley, 2001). I have considered teachers' perspectives on students' progress and enthusiastic responses as inspirational as far as the teachers are concerned, giving an extra dimension of meaning to the current EFL curriculum reform as participant EFL teachers have experienced it. As van Manen (1990) argues, the distinguishing feature of lived experience is that it has a unity which makes it different from others and stimulates reflections. Exploring students as one of the stakeholders has been such a case as far as my research is concerned. Teachers' perspectives on students' progress in EFL learning and their enthusiastic response to the reform have made participant EFL teachers' lived experience meaningful in dimensions not anticipated in either curriculum documents or policy statements.

In relation to Reconstructionism, it is a research outcome that emphasizes the role of the student in relation to social, economic, political, cultural and educational development in the societies in which they live (Tanner & Tanner, 2007). My research suggests that students as well as teachers, principals, parents and governments are required to meet demands which globalization has placed on them in the Chinese context. Their enthusiastic responses to the EFL curriculum reform are more than what Reconstructionism looks towards in relation to education, but when this is coupled with China's stated needs for national perceptible and measurable progress in EFL skills and knowledge, it is consistent with a Reconstructionist view of education.

At the same time, my examination of teachers' perspectives on students' responses and progress in EFL learning suggests that teachers have positioned themselves as being required to maintain a transformative position in relation to the reform, which is also consistent with a Reconstructionist perspective. As I have discussed in Chapter 4, teachers viewed from a Reconstructionist perspective have the responsibility of promoting the development of social and educational philosophy through the significant roles they play in education reform (Armstrong, 2005).

Students as stakeholders add a dimension of meaning as far as investigating participant EFL teachers' lived experience of the current EFL curriculum reform in Chinese secondary schools in Northeast China.

9.3   Parents

In the similar vein as students as stakeholders, I have not approached parents directly for interviews, as discussed in Chapter 5. Rather I have generated a picture of parents' responses to this reform from EFL teachers' perspectives that have emerged from the data. In responses to the theme of lived other in the questionnaire, participant EFL teachers have not suggested issues arising in relation to parents in implementing the reform. These are issues that have emerged from interview data, suggesting that parents have also played an influential role in EFL teacher experience of implementing the reform under study. As Fullan (2001) argues, parents are where "the most powerful instrument for improvement resides" (p. 198).

Chinese education is highly competitive and Chinese parents have demanding standards as they are prepared to devote much time and effort to bringing up and cultivating their children in valued skills and knowledge (Ran, 2001). The interview data have confirmed this. Ying, for example, states, "Every parent would make an effort to help their children with greater opportunities to learn more. " Fang also states that parents are often asked by their children for "access to the Internet for more information" for helping with their learning, so that parents are urged by their children to provide the sort of learning assistance that this sort of 21st century technology represents. The statements of Ying and Fang are indicative of EFL teachers' experience of parents' efforts and strong expectations for their children in EFL teaching and learning. It is a situation consistent with the literature in its considerations of parents as education stakeholders in China. As Zhu (1999) states, since almost every family has but only one child in today's China, parents have increased and focused concern for their one child's education success. As stated at the beginning of this section, this sort of parent involvement has the potential to have significant influence on the teaching and learning engaged in schools, for as Fullan (2001) argues, "The closer the parent is to the education of the child, the greater the impact on child development and educational achievement. " (p. 198) This has been borne out by participant EFL teachers' perspectives of parents as represented in interview responses.

Participant EFL teachers' descriptions of their experience indicate that parents' expectations, as they put more emphasis on their children's academic achievement, also place pressure on teachers. Fang, for example, says, "Although the school attempts to reduce this pressure from maintaining a continually higher rate of success, parents and the society still watch or focus on the goal only." Xu says, "Students and their parents pay more attention to learning results." These two EFL teacher's comments on their experience of parents' expectation represent a general view held by participant EFL teachers across both sites. Teachers' perspectives on parents' emphasis on results are that these have indirectly influenced the purposes of teaching and learning. They see that a parent's focus on results are driven by traditional concepts of examination-oriented education, giving rise to a tension between what the current EFL curriculum expects of teachers and students as being contradictory to what the parents expect. Exploring such issues suggests that participant EFL teachers are confronted with tacit pressure from parents' expectations in implementing the current EFL curriculum reform that goes beyond the requirements of the EFL curriculum itself. As van Zanten (2002) argues, parents' expectations and attitudes play an influential role in education change which places pressure on individual teachers. It is a tension that has emerged in my exploration of participant EFL teachers' lived experience of the reform under study, and it is a tension that figures with some prominence in the lived other of the lived experience of the teachers who have participated in this research.

It is a tension that sits uneasily alongside Reconstructionist perspectives on education that focus on the common good of a community more than on educational achievement of individuals within that community. While Reconstructionism acknowledges that individual achievement is necessary, it does so in the context of a greater social, political and economic good. Chinese parents with one child, as they focus on the educational progress of that child, are positioned within the wider Chinese context of globalization, and they too find themselves conflicted within the tension. Committed, as good citizens, to political, social and economic policies, at the same time they have intensely personal commitments to the advancement of their only child. The situation is a part of the lived other that is to be negotiated by EFL teachers as they implement curriculum reform, and the interview data do not indicate that it is a tension that has been resolved as yet.

It is not likely to be resolved easily, given the change in policy regarding parents' roles in their children's education. As I have discussed previously, the *Outline* includes setting up a new system of assessment. It states that the assessment system will include considerations of parents, students, principals and peers as key influential factors in the new curriculum system that includes the EFL curriculum (Ministry of Education, 2001d). As Ran (2001) states, the influences of globalization in the 21st century means that parents' status and role in their children's formal education have been shifted from one of being kept away from schools to one of being invited to involve themselves in their Children's education. It is no small shift in emphasis; it is a shift of such dimensions that have made a complete break with traditional parental roles in Chinese schools, changing this feature of them at least beyond all recognition.

The role of English as a global language in a global world and in the Chinese context as having influenced parents' increased attention to their children's EFL learning has been confirmed by my interview data. Ju says, "People, including students' parents, in China, think that learning English is quite useful for their future development." Fen says, "English, as a global language has been recognized by parents and the society." Ying also says, "More and more parents and students pay greater attention to English language learning." Ying says, "The majority of parents in my school expect their sons or daughters to have the chance to go abroad to study in one of the world-famous universities." Chinese parents' increased concern about their children's EFL learning in the Chinese context has influenced participant EFL teachers' teaching as they have implemented the reform, which is also consistent with Fullan's (2001) argument in relation to such influence of parents. Chang (2008) argues that the influence of parents is central to their children's EFL learning, so that parents' perspectives about EFL teaching and learning, regardless of how educationally sound or not these might be, affect the success of the implementation of relevant curriculum reform. This stakeholder group, then, forms no small feature in a consideration of teachers' lived other in relation to lived experience.

In relation to the concept of lived other regarding participant EFL teachers' lived experience, parents' responses to EFL teaching and learning have exerted a tacit but discernible sense of pressure on participant EFL teachers, even as this pressure is seen as support for teachers' efforts in implementing the reform under study. The literature bears this out. Kenway (1994, cited in Ran, 2001) argues that different parents' expectations influence ways in which parents interact with teachers in schools, which affects teachers' classroom practice; Ryan (2001) argues that parents' expectations act as a spur to teachers to improve their teaching. This takes on a more specific form in China, where, as Phillipson (2007) points out, the values in the Confucian-Heritage Culture (CHC) in China and parents' expectations serve as influential factors in teaching and learning. I have drawn on such works in the preceding section to analyze the data. In the following section I will examine interview data in relation to principals, who are another group of stakeholders with whom these EFL teachers are to work, which I will detail below.

9.4　Principals

My consideration of the role of principals as one of the EFL curriculum reform stakeholders as seen through teachers' comments on their experience points to a central aspect of new policy statements and curriculum documents. The *Outline* highlights decentralization of curriculum and its implementation, suggesting that national, local and school forces need to be involved in the new curriculum system (Ministry of Education, 2001d). School-based curriculum development is accordingly part of this new curriculum system on the basis of principals being representatives of schools. The literature is consistent in its arguing that promoting school-based curriculum development is an important strategy that accompanies the current EFL curriculum reform in Chinese secondary schools (Huang, 2004). Giving prominence to principals' roles is part of an attempt to rearrange sources of educational power and resources to emphasize ways of harnessing EFL teachers' creative abilities in schools (Huang, 2004). Principals play a pivotal role in any education change, and curriculum reform in particular, as they, "Help create and sustain disciplined inquiry and action on part of teachers" (Fullan, 2003, p. 7), and are regarded as "the gatekeeper of change" (Fullan, 2001, p. 138). In similar vein to my discussion of students and parents as stakeholders, I have not collected data from school principals directly. Rather, I have generated a picture of their influential role in implementing this reform in different regions through EFL teachers' perspectives. In responses to the questionnaire, participant EFL teachers have not directly suggested specific issues in relation to principals but they have highlighted the role of principals in relation to their implementing the reform in their responses in interviews. Participant EFL teachers' experience in Site B indicates that they are satisfied with the leadership provided by their principal, including the role played in the provision of relevant effective and professional strategies used for assisting EFL teaching and learning in curriculum implementation. Ju says:

> My school has done its best. Since the reform has been implemented, the EFL teachers have been sent out to study and then they have been given opportunities to have seminars upon their return. Further, we attempt to expand or make comments on these activities. We might have open professional discussions on the same topics or problems. Thus, I think our school has made various efforts and the follow-up steps might be to take time to implement this reform. And so it is with any reform. In the process of promoting the reform, we may find out problems, and solve them, and then we would repeat the process over again until the reform becomes better and better implemented.

Another EFL teacher, Ying, states, "Actually, our school has done a lot to support EFL teaching," and, "I think that the principal has tried her best to help us." These two teachers' comments on their experience of their principal indicate that they consider that their principal has endeavoured to prioritize their professional development, creating an appropriate environment for EFL teaching and learning to help with implementing the reform under study; they have felt that they have been supported by their principal. As Fullan (2001) argues, "Change is only one of the forces competing for the principals' attention, and usually not the most compelling one" (p. 137). By way of contrast, the data present a different picture in Site A. Xu says:

> As far as English language teaching is concerned in this region, it seems that there are few principals who have the necessary knowledge of language teaching... Since there is a shortage of relevant experts, nobody is available to come out [to our school] to help these EFL teachers to develop further.

This EFL teacher considers that the principals in Site A lack knowledge of

English language teaching and so they cannot offer timely and appropriate guidelines for EFL teaching in their schools. She considers that such shortage of expertise in Site A has promoted ignorance rather than expertise in EFL teaching in this region, a negative influence on curriculum implementation. This participant's description of her experience of the influential factors for which her principal is responsible indicates that she has a sense of non-assistance, influencing in negative ways her understanding of the reform and her EFL teaching. Xu's is an experience that is repeated in the responses of other participants across the schools in Site A.

Interview data present teachers in Site A as experiencing a lack of support and assistance. This is at odds with the experience of participants in Site B, where the principal has created opportunities for EFL teachers' professional development, such as sending EFL teachers abroad for training and inviting relevant experts to her school, holding seminars and creating a suitable environment for EFL teaching and learning in accordance with the requirements of the EFL curriculum reform. Participants in Site B suggest that the principal has provided them with relevant support, including effective and professional strategies for teachers' professional development. By way of contrast, the experience of participants from Site A is that few effective professional development programs have been delivered, and that the teachers consider that this is because of their principals' lack of expertise, confirming points made in the literature in relation to principals being necessary for assisting teachers in a successful implementation of curriculum reform. This relates particularly to EFL teachers in China in this instance. As Fullan (2001) argues, the role of principals is central to school improvement, as they play a key role in influencing whether reform works or not, or making conditions in schools better or worse. Day (2000) states that "effective" and "professional" are two main terms used to describe the nature of a good principal in the school context, terms which may be linked to principals' commitment and capacity.

Interview data in relation to principals as one of the stakeholders in relation to EFL curriculum reform indicate that principals' professional competence has influenced teachers' teaching and professional development as well as implementation of the reform under study. As the teachers see it, principals need to develop their own professional competence and expertise in order to engage school-based curriculum development. I have generated this from teachers' perspectives on principals' responses to the reform. Ying, for example, says,

What our principal always says is that a teacher should not only be a teacher, but also be a researcher, and studying while teaching. That is what a teacher should be like today in China.

Ying's principal's concern about teachers' roles and their professional development in her school reflects that principal's own education conceptions, which have foregrounded the idea of professional competence in teacher development. As Fullan (2001) argues, "It is always the thinking leader who blends knowledge of local context and personalities with new ideas from the outside who is going to do best" (p. 149). Ying's principal in such ways displays a particular feature of principals' professional competence as a leader when it comes to school-based curriculum development. As Zhong (2001) argues, principals' roles in the new curriculum implementation are the key to promoting that implementation. Zhong represents principals as a tour guide, creating a cooperative and collaborative environment for assisting relevant teaching and learning in reform, a metaphor that is consistent with interview data in relation to teachers' attitudes towards their principals.

Participant EFL teachers' experience also points to areas where a perceived shortcoming in principals' expertise may have a negative influence on effective EFL curriculum implementation. Participant Ying's principal may be considered an example of the sort of leadership that the curriculum implementation requires, but that is not the case in all schools studied. This has been unexpected research outcome. Much of the literature acknowledges principals as playing a key role in any education change, discussing the issues in relation to their relevant professional standards, and the complexity of principals' work in schools (Fullan, 2001, 2003, 2007; Wildy & Louden, 2000). The issue of principals' incompetence and lack of expertise in curriculum reform that focuses on specific discipline areas, particularly in the current EFL curriculum reform in China, has not attracted attention in such literature. In Site A, teachers' perceptions of principals' lack of expertise in EFL teaching and learning have identified a negative influence on developing teachers' understandings of the reform and its relevance to its importance in globalization concerns for the country as a whole, and not just a region. Given the relatively innovative nature of the reform, and its early stages of implementation, this is hardly surprising. In developed parts of the province the principal does not figure in the data as having any sort of negative influence on the reform implementation. In the less developed regions of the province, the opposite is the case, where teachers specify and identify principals' lack of expertise in EFL curriculum reform implementation as a stumbling block to their efforts in relation to this important national reform of curriculum. The literature does not approach this as a problem; it is something which has emerged from my analysis of the data, and it is one that is still to be addressed as part of EFL teachers' lived experience in relation to a lived other in the form of one of the stakeholders with whom they are required to deal.

Perspectives on principals' professional competence and expertise have emerged from the data as an issue that has gone beyond details of implementation and orientation of the new EFL curriculum. The policy statements and curriculum documents are premised on an understanding that principals' professional competence and expertise may confidently be drawn upon to provide insights to the reform under study, and this would include principals' concerns for EFL teachers' development. Policy and curriculum may also take it as a given that principals' concerns would be translated into the creation of opportunities for professional training for teaching and learning as integral to curriculum implementation. Teachers in Site B exhibit a sense of support in implementing the reform that is generated by the principal in that site. By the same token, in Site A principals' perceived lack of professional competence and expertise emerge from interview data as providing teachers with little support and few effective strategies, so that teachers feel a lack of the required backing from principals in implementing the reform. This situation is consistent with the related literature, for as Hunnum and Park (2002) argue, the role of principals in rural schools draws less attention in human resource challenges in relation to their being schools with minimal resources, such as those in remote areas in China. Hunnum and Park (2002) further state that some principals in China are isolated from their peers or institutions because of their school locations in those less developed regions or remote areas. Here, as they describe it, the transport is inconvenient, and they lack opportunities for professional development in support of developing their own leadership skills, such as in the case of those principals in Site A. This indicates a shortcoming in policy making and implementation of the provincial government and its establishment of a consultancy team of experts that has overlooked that isolation and its potential to influence policy implementation in less than positive ways.

In exploring participant EFL teachers' perspectives on the issue of principals in their schools, I have found from the interviews that these teachers have experienced a sense of tension. It is a tension that sits alongside principals' professional competence and expertise or otherwise in relation to the reform under study, something which has provided a particular dimension of meaning to the reform as participant EFL teachers have experienced it. They have encountered it in the lived other of their lived experience, and they have had to deal with it as best as they could, given that nothing in the curriculum reform package has been designed even to anticipate this development, let alone deal with it. It is an aspect of the new reform that has emerged after the event, identified by the teachers, but absent from any other texts that have come out of the implementation of the reform. In the following section, I will focus on governments as stakeholders who form part of participant EFL teachers' lived other in their lived experience of the reform under study.

9.5   Governments

I have recognized central and local governments as one of the stakeholders in the EFL curriculum reform, part of the lived experience by participants of the reform under study. As Fullan (2001) states, governments, which are essential in implementing large-scale reform, are key forces for transformation. According to Huang (2004), governments play a significant role in promoting curriculum development in China, with the central government in the past having dominated curriculum decision-making through its centralized system. There has been a shift towards a decentralized and distributed system as part of the implementation of the current curriculum reform, where the central government has distributed some powers for curriculum decision-making to local governments and schools themselves (Huang, 2004). Central, provincial and local governments and schools themselves all share responsibilities for implementing the current EFL curriculum reform in China.

Decentralization in relation to national level has been witnessed since 1949 (Hawkins, 2000), and it represents one of the most important features of the reform under study (Huang, 2004). The decentralization of Chinese governments' authority as far as education programs are concerned provides a context in which to position the current EFL curriculum reform not only in regard to generating an understanding of the role of governments in relation to the reform, but also as part of lived other in relation to participant EFL teachers' lived experience. Decentralization may be further seen in the context of globalization and corresponding issues of glocalization in relation to that lived experience, discussed below.

At the beginning of this chapter I discussed the role of central government in relation to the reform under study and in relation to the new EFL curriculum intent and its features as part of teachers' lived time in a globalizing world. In this section I will continue the focus on the role of government in Northeast China in implementing the reform, but I have included a particular focus on the role of local government in influencing curriculum implementation in a provincial context. To this end, I have considered ways in which local governments have implemented the central government's policies of EFL curriculum reform in secondary schools in my research sites. I have focused on the Liaoning Provincial Government and in doing so, I have included an examination of relevant policies issued and released in the region. The local government that I have discussed here refers to Liaoning Provincial Government which manages the reform as it relates to Site A and Site B. I have not approached municipal or district governments in either Site A or Site B for similar reasons as I have not approached students, parents, or principals, but relying on teachers' perceptions of government activities as part of the lived other of their lived experience.

Liaoning is a developed province as far as education is concerned (see for example Liaoning Education Department, 2006), which has enabled it to focus on the development of its education system in line with central policies of curriculum reform, and EFL curriculum reform too. Its provincial government engages educational policy-making and curriculum implementation mainly in relation to organization and administration of support that derives from a number of sources (Liaoning Education Department, 2006). Until 2005, there had been 9,311 primary schools with 26,661,555 students and 163,589 qualified teachers, and 1,798 junior secondary schools with 1,570,269 students and 106,439 qualified teachers in this province (Liaoning Education Department, 2006). Since the opening up of the country in the late 1970s, education in Liaoning has also experienced constant innovation and reform, as has the whole education system in China, and its Education Department notes that it has achieved rapid development as it has established an education system designed for the challenges of 21st century and its associated phenomenon of globalization. These are the claims made in the official documents of the Liaoning Education Department. They do not come from any of the data that pertain to participant teachers.

A series of education policies related to education reform were developed in China in the 1990s, designed to engage challenges presented by globalization, and these have included policies of EFL curriculum reform in Chinese secondary schools. Such policies have implications for supporting the current EFL curriculum reform in Chinese secondary schools. A "strong and professional leadership team" who takes special responsibilities for current curriculum implementation, which includes EFL curriculum reform in secondary schools, has been established in the province, according to National Research Reports (Cui, 2005). "Strong" is not clearly defined in this context, but it is a word that suggests a certain commitment from the Liaoning Provincial Government, which has released a number of relevant policies to promote effective curriculum implementation in this region. In 2001, the Liaoning Education Department issued *Liaoning Education Department Guidelines for Continually Promoting the Teaching of English in Primary Schools* (Cui, 2005), which focuses on students in this province as they start to learn English as a compulsory subject in the third grade (Cui, 2005). This document deals with students who have experienced four years of English learning in their primary schools before entering junior secondary schools. The document also stresses that until 2002, the Department attempted to achieve a 50% rate of primary schools located in towns and townships developing the professional capacity to teach English. All primary schools in this region were assured of developing the capacity to be able to teach English up to 2003. It further states that English teaching and learning was expected to be carried out in Grade One if possible in some districts in the region, which means that students would have had an even longer experience of exposure to English learning than before this change in policy. It also indicates that the significant role of English among other compulsory subjects had been identified and supported by the provincial government, a particular effort of a provincial government to achieve the goals of the EFL curriculum reform.

On December 6, 2002, the Liaoning Education Department released another policy, *Printing and Distributing Liaoning Province Compulsory Education Local Curriculum Implementing Project (For Experiments)* (Liaoning Education Department, 2002). It addresses concerns regarding the establishment of a new local curriculum system with specific characteristics that include orientation of Liaoning Province and relevant education information. The new local curriculum has been designed to cope with three grade levels of curriculum administration (national, local and school) in the Chinese context. It is another response by the Liaoning Provincial Government in implementing the current EFL curriculum reform in Chinese secondary schools.

The Liaoning Education Department has also released a further series of documents which focus on teachers' professional development to implement the policies outlined in the document titled *Project Gardener*: *Crossing the New Century*, included in *Strategic Plans for Reviving Education for the 21st Century* (Wang, 2007) released by the State Council. Modern information technology, for example, has been included in the program of in-service teacher education (Ministry of Education, 2001b, 2001c). Relevant policies have been released separately in Site A and Site B. Having knowledge of modern information technology has been recognized by the provincial Ministry of Education as a necessary criterion for employing or evaluating a teacher in Liaoning Province (Ministry of Education, 2001b). These are some of the efforts on the part of local governments and departments across both sites that implement decentralization policies and procedures as far as curriculum implementation has been concerned. On the basis of these, the Liaoning Provincial Government has provided professional development training for all teachers, including EFL teachers, in the three full years of 2002-2004. These activities suggest that the Liaoning Education Department has endeavoured to support this reform, and has been active in an attempt to create a suitable environment for secondary school teachers' professional development, EFL teachers in particular, to implement the current curriculum reform in this region.

I have positioned my examination of the role of provincial government as part of lived other, linking this to participant EFL teachers' lived experience of the reform in my research. The Liaoning Provincial Government has provided these teachers with more detailed, authoritative documents and orchestrated as well as systematic advice programs on appropriate strategies for the implementation of the EFL curriculum reform in Northeast China than has the central government. The *Outline* provided by the central government has served, as the title itself suggests, an outline only (Ministry of Education, 2001e). The Liaoning Provincial Government has fleshed out the *Outline* and supported that fleshing out with a specially selected and appointed team of consulting experts (Cui, 2005). Liaoning Provincial Government activities in this area of the education program that it delivers in the province include detailed policy making in relation to local contexts, providing relevant training and necessary funding. Policy and curriculum documents have demonstrated their endeavours in supporting this reform implementation and the majority of these participant EFL teachers, particularly those in Site B, consider that they have support from governments. Some teachers in Site A point to lack of relevant support in relation to their professional development. The literature points to the role of governments as an important influential factor in teachers' lived experience of curriculum reform. As Fullan (2001) argues, governments are able to offer accountability, pressure and support, and promote developing capacity, or not. In similar vein as my approach to students, parents, and principals, I have taken teachers' perspectives on governments as providing insights to the ways in which policy and curriculum statements have been rolled out as part of the reform. As van Manen (1990) argues:

> Even if we learn about another person only indirectly (by letter, telephone, or book) we often already have formed a physical impression of the person which here may get confirmed, or negated when we find out, to our surprise, that the person looks very different from the way we expected. As we meet the other we are able to develop a conversational relation which allows us to transcend our selves (p. 105).

Central and provincial governments, and the Liaoning Provincial Government in particular, have provided support in the form of policies and delivery of relevant professional development for EFL teachers in relation to appropriate teaching and learning strategies. This is indicative of a focus by governments on the teasing out problems in the education system they administer, and seeking relevant solutions to achieve the changes they want to achieve. In the case of the current EFL curriculum reform, the documents indicate a carefully considered government approach to the reform, calculated to achieve optimum effect.

The central government in China has been aware of the problems in education domains, particularly in the old elementary curriculum system which has been found to be inadequate to engage challenges posed by globalization. Central government has looked to the establishment of a new curriculum system in an attempt to cope with those challenges, and a new series of national policies and strategies delivered. Provincial governments have also responded along similar lines, and released their own policies in relation to their own contexts.

I have explored the role of provincial governments as part of decentralization that has become visible as part of glocalization in the Chinese context. As Sharma (2008) argues, decentralization is a feature of globalization linked to glocalization, providing possibilities for maximizing positive effects of globalization through the establishment of "a stable, secure and just government" which would support glocalization (p. 3). The literature emphasises the twin features of decentralization and glocalization as integral to globalization, and in my research I have taken these twin features as forming a stimulus to the EFL curriculum reform being implemented in this region of China. The Liaoning Provincial Government, as a decentralized and in effect a glocalized body, has provided more detailed policy statements and relevant strategies than the central government regarding education reform. Having absorbed general policy outlines from central government, the Liaoning Provincial Government has focused on details of local issues in local contexts that the general policies from central government have not been able to approach.

9.6　Conclusion

In this theme of lived other, my discussion of other stakeholders in relation to participant EFL teachers' descriptions of their lived experience has identified students, parents, principals and governments in relation to the EFL curriculum reform. Their position as stakeholders in the current EFL curriculum reform provides a basis for comparison with previous attempts at such reform. I have taken into account influential factors in curriculum implementation in relation to other stakeholders as far as the EFL teachers' implementing the reform are concerned as governments have included relevant stakeholders' concerns in relevant policy-making. I have identified students' positive responses to the reform as a stimulus to EFL teachers' own enthusiastic participation in reformed EFL teaching and curriculum implementation. Teachers' responses in interviews regarding the expectations of parents with whom they are to interact suggests that parents have put teachers under pressure at the same time as they give support to their efforts. A further aspect of EFL teachers' lived other as part of their lived experience is that of principals' professional competence and expertise or otherwise, indicating that they have obtained support from that quarter in their implementation the reform under study, or otherwise. Government policies, curriculum documents, and teachers' professional development in relevant EFL teaching and learning strategies further suggest a feeling of support among participant EFL teachers. In discussions on lived other, I have examined participant EFL teachers' descriptions of their experience of other stakeholders which show that these teachers have a sense of support on the one hand and pressure on the other. In the following chapter I will discuss the theme of lived time.

Chapter 10

Lived Time: Lived Experience and the Interviews

10.1　Introduction

In Chapter 9, I have discussed the theme of lived other in relation to participant EFL teachers' lived experience. In this chapter I will examine interview data in relation to participant EFL teachers' lived time as part of their lived experience. I will firstly explore EFL teachers' reflections on their past experience of previous curriculum reforms, then on their present experience of the current EFL curriculum reform, and finally on their expectations for improving that latest reform. Participant EFL teachers' reflections include those on their past experience of previous EFL curriculum reforms, the 1993 one in particular, as well as their experience of pre-service teacher education programs. Teachers' present experience includes their experience of the current EFL curriculum reform as this is played out in relevant changes in EFL teaching. Teachers' expectations focus on their hope for further improving this reform. I will focus on the theme of lived time emerging from interview data as a means by which to examine ways in which the current EFL curriculum reform has developed. I have situated these issues within the theme of lived time, in accordance with van Manen (1990)'s suggestion, "The temporal dimensions of past, present, and future constitute the horizons of a person's temporal landscape" (p. 104). I will discuss participant EFL teachers' past experience in the following section.

10.2　Past Experience

The questionnaire data that I have examined provide an overview of participant EFL teachers' past experience of previous EFL curriculum reforms in Chinese secondary schools in relation to their lived experience as secondary school students, particularly during the 1990s. I have approached issues that have emerged from document analysis in relation the new 21st century EFL curriculum intent and features, which provides the basis for a comparison between the new curriculum and the previous one. My focus has been on the 1993 one because, by 2008, when I conducted my questionnaire and interview research, teachers who had taught in the 1970s had mostly retired, and numbers available for questionnaire or interview in both sites were too few to be used to good effect in my research. The number of teachers from both sites who had had experience of reforms in the 1970s numbered only three. For this reason, I have relied on documented accounts of teachers' experience in the 1970s, as explored in Chapter 2, to make comparisons with the 2000s. Teachers' descriptions of their experience of previous reforms, then, refer to those of the 1990s in the data that I have collected. In the interviews I have further emphasized comparisons between the current EFL curriculum reform and the 1993 one as this fits with one of the selection criteria of participants with at least 15 years' of teaching experience (see Chapter 5). In the following sections in relation to participant EFL teachers' past experience, I will use the term "previous" to refer to the reform of 1993. In doing so, I will generate a more detailed picture of their lived experience of previous EFL curriculum reforms, the 1993 one in particular, by analyzing interview data that has explored their lived experience of professional development, and pre-service EFL teacher education programs.

To this end, I will examine a number of sub-themes of EFL teachers' experience that I have categorized as "a word class and passive listeners", "spoon-fed mode", and "the divergence and the directing stick". I will discuss these in the context of participants' experience of teacher education programs as developing a knowledge base as part of their professional development. I have considered these issues as related to their lived experience as EFL teachers in China, as part of examining details of participant EFL teachers' experience of the current EFL curriculum reform, which I will detail below.

10.2.1 "A Word Class" and "Passive Listeners"

Teachers' responses to questionnaire items in relation to teaching methods indicate that the majority of participant EFL teachers' experience of EFL teaching and learning in China has been dominated by teacher-centred and grammar translation teaching methods that characterised previous curriculum implemented when they were secondary school students during the 1970s and the 1990s. I have detailed current EFL teachers' perceptions of shortcomings of EFL teaching methods couched in the 1993 EFL curriculums in Chapter 6, considering these in relation to the new curriculum intent and features. In the following section, I will further examine teaching methods in relation to previous curriculum reforms, the one in 1993 in particular, through analyzing participant EFL teachers' responses to interview data.

Interview data have confirmed both questionnaire data and that which has emerged from the document analysis discussed in Chapter 6 and Chapter 7. One of the participants, Fang, says that they continued to adopt "teacher-centred method" in their previous teaching in the previous reform, where students were regarded as "passive listeners" in class. Wei describes his previous EFL teaching as "a word class" where he as a teacher was the key speaker while his students were passive listeners. As EFL teachers themselves, Fang's and Wei's experience as students has made them aware of the shortcomings of traditional teaching based on teacher-centred and grammar translation methods. Teacher-centred and grammar translation methods emphasize teachers' authority and teachers' roles in EFL teaching and learning, ignoring students' roles as participants in their own learning, as well as the sort of individual student's development discussed in Chapter 3. Their experience is also consistent with the literature, such as that of Wang (2007), who argues that, despite the achievements of reforms since 1993, there still remain significant problems in need of address in the current EFL curriculum reform.

Wei's and Fang's past experience as teachers in relation to traditional teaching methods of the previous reform indicates that they have been aware of the problems as far as their own EFL teaching has been concerned. Their experience has prompted them to turn to new teaching methods proposed in the reform under study. I have considered these two teachers' reflections on their past experience as part of lived time in relation to their lived experience which I have discussed at the beginning of this chapter. Their experience is a common one described in the responses of participants across schools in both sites. Their experience serves as the basis for an understanding of their present experience and their expectations, which I will explore in the following sections.

10.2.2　"Spoon-fed Mode"

According to Zeegers and Zhang (2005), textbooks used in EFL teaching and learning in China play a significant role in processes of student learning in the Chinese context as textbooks constitute a major resource for EFL teaching and learning in China. Zeegers and Zhang (2005) have focused on textbook language and content, and the need for a textbook to match student's development requirements, something which applies to the new EFL textbooks developed as part of the reform under study. A new series of textbooks has been developed as part of the reform, consisting of Grade 3 to Grade 12 books that cater to the needs of students in primary, junior secondary and senior secondary schools. They have been based on the *ECS*, and designed to facilitate the changes in the EFL curriculum that the *ECS* supports. The textbooks used by teachers in primary schools are related to the particular level at which they are teaching, as are those in secondary schools. Each teacher would be given one copy of the new textbook for their classes, and each student would have theirs as well. Supplementary materials have also been developed as part of the EFL curriculum reform that all participant teachers may draw upon in the course of their professional activities.

In similar fashion, when the 1970s, 1980s and 1990s reforms were implemented, textbooks were produced as part of the exercises. Each series of textbooks was then replaced when each new reform was implemented. Older textbooks, and teaching materials, left over from the 1970s, 1980s and 1990s are no longer available in the schools. Participant teachers now rely on new textbooks that, while they incorporate elements of systematic grammar study, contain elements of contemporary foci on modern content more relevant to 21st century Chinese student life that were missing from the older textbooks. When I refer to a textbook, then, I refer to one of the new series that are used at each level of EFL study in Chinese schools. Old textbooks are those that were previously used, ones that focused on grammar and language items to be rote learned by students. Participant EFL teachers have indicated that they themselves generally do not consider the old series of textbooks to be as good as the new series.

Participants' descriptions of their past experience both as EFL students (as is the case for those participants who have 4-10 years of teaching experience) and as EFL teachers (as is the case for those participants who have at least 15 years of teaching experience) point to the textbook as the main source of teaching and learning content, and that previous ones contained material that was dull and outdated. Those textbooks did not, in their view, stimulate students' interest in learning English. This has been confirmed by both questionnaire data and the documents which I have examined and discussed in Chapter 6 and Chapter 7. Participant EFL teachers' experience of old textbooks refers to the one edited by the People's Education Press, adopted in both Site A and Site B as part of the 1993 reform. In the following section, I will address participant EFL teachers' past experience of the textbook used in the 1993 reform, with a focus on issues of what the teachers have themselves described as "spoon-fed mode" in their responses in the interviews.

I have borrowed the term "spoon-fed" from Guan and Meng's (2007) work on curriculum and associated teaching and learning strategies in China. This has been confirmed by my interview data. An EFL teacher, Chu, says, "There were some given patterns in the old textbook. For example, I told you how to make up a sentence and then the textbook would have relevant exercises." Chu considers that students and teachers who experienced the 1993 reform only needed to follow the instructions given in the textbook to conduct their teaching and learning activities, so that they were not required to think further about what methods were to be used in their practice. She says that such sorts of textbooks restricted students' and teachers' development, particularly in teaching and learning.

Another EFL teacher, Qing, says:

The layout of the old textbook emphasized that grammar points should be taught in a given order. As a result of this, the topics, the texts and the dialogues were all developed via grammar.

Qing discusses this in more detail, saying that since the old textbook emphasized grammar points, the textbook content design followed grammar orders that determined topics, dialogues and texts. Such textbook design would obviate the need for teachers and students to develop their thinking or imagination, which participant teachers have described as one of the shortcomings of the old EFL textbook that they used. These two EFL teachers' experience are two examples which are representative of similar teachers' perspectives from these two sites. They consider the old textbook's design and structure, which focused on ready-to-use traditional grammar points, was an example of the "spoon-fed mode". As Adamson (2001) states, the 1993 EFL textbook used:

> The technique of controlling the level of linguistic difficulty in a very structured way, either by restricting new items to a specific numerical quantity or by defining the language skills (listening, reading, speaking, writing) in which mastery is expected (p.31).

This feature of textbooks reflects certain traditional elements involved in the 1993 EFL curriculum design (Adamson, 2001). Guan and Meng (2007) also argue that textbook design and textbook content produced in the 1993 curriculum reform could be described as being based on a "spoon-fed mode" and that such materials tended to place little emphasis on students' learning abilities and the tenets of language learning. According to Poon, Tang and Reed (1997), teaching content in relation to "spoon-fed mode" would not play a stimulating role in promoting students or teachers to expand teaching and learning in language; that such content is to be seen as a restriction on both students' and teachers' language development. Particpants Xu and Qing's statements, which are representative of similar perspectives on teachers' experience in these two sites, indicate that they have been aware of the sorts of problems identified in relation to the old textbook. Their descriptions of their experience indicates that such features of the old textbook would inhibit the development of EFL teaching and learning in the previous reform as they restricted students' and teachers' language thinking and language imagination. Taking into account the demands of a rapidly globalizing Chinese context, this had the further implication that students would not effectively engage associated challenges that have been reconceptualized and incorporated in the new EFL curriculum reform and its approach to textbooks.

My research has confirmed the perceived shortcomings presented in the previous series of textbooks in 1993. Ju says, "The old series of textbooks only addressed grammar points." Lian, another EFL teacher, says, "The previous series of textbooks focused more on grammar"; "less on Listening and Speaking, and it might be useless in language applications that focus on such things as effective communication". She further says, "The textbook seemed to fall behind the times", and, "The articles and the vocabulary were all out of date". Qing, another EFL teacher, states, "The poor content or topics in the old series of textbooks bored the students; they could not arouse students' interest." These EFL teachers' experience, as three examples of common perspectives across schools in both sites, shows their dissatisfaction with the previous series of textbooks of 1993. It is not only dissatisfaction as far as teaching and learning is concerned; it is dissatisfaction on the basis of the textbook being inadequate to the task of students' and teachers' development that has emerged out of rapid Chinese economic and social changes in the context of globalization. This, after all, has been a major concern of the new EFL curriculum reform, and with it concerns for curriculum materials as they are focused on textbooks.

As I have discussed in Chapter 3, textbooks are one of the most influential factors in understanding the development of EFL curriculum reform in Chinese secondary schools. According to Richards (2001), a textbook needs to be constantly revised in line with the context in which it is to be used. The previous series of textbooks of the 1993 reform were produced to meet requirements of social development in the last years of the 20th century, rather than those of the 21st century. Teachers' experience suggests that it is not effective for EFL teaching and learning to adopt such textbooks in present EFL teaching and learning contexts.

Given such considerations, EFL teachers' descriptions of their past experience indicate a number of different perspectives, those from Site A in particular. Xu, for instance, says:

> We found that we could find some rules in the previous series of textbooks in 1993. At least it could be seen in its continuity in grammar. So I think the previous series of textbooks [in 1993] was concerned with grammar and also was linked to the current trend of the new curriculum reform.

Another EFL teacher, Wei, says:

> The old textbook was divided into a couple of parts and linked with tenses, eight tenses together. In Grade One the textbook involved in the present continuous tense and the present tense. In Grade Two, the past tense and the past continuous tense, as well as the present perfect tense. In Grade Three, the past perfect tense. I think the old textbook structure made it easy for us to learn these grammar points and also easy for teachers to cope with them.

Another EFL teacher, Hua, says:

> I think the current textbook is much briefer, but the previous one presented more details which could help students to [understand] what they learnt from it. However, the current textbook sometimes needs us to comprehend the content such as what is in Section A and what is in Section B, and sometimes we [become] confused about it. To tell you the truth, I still enjoy and appreciate the previous series of textbooks in 1993 more.

Some teachers, describing their past experience of working with textbooks, disagreed with their colleagues about the "spoon-fed mode" of the 1993 series of textbooks. As Xu, Hua and Wei describe it, their experience of the older textbooks was a positive one. These several EFL teachers' statements show that texts which emphasize systematic order of the grammar points distributed among a textbook's pages is professionally reassuring for them, at least. It is a view that is consistent with what has been described as Confucian Heritage Culture (CHC) in the Chinese context (Wong, 2008), where students expect their teachers to teach them everything they are expected to learn and have little aspiration to discover anything in this regard for themselves. This in itself suggests that, "They wish to be spoon-fed and, in turn, they are spoon-fed." (Phuong-Mai, Terlouw, & Pilot, 2006, p. 9) Rao (2006) also states that "traditional Chinese education values teacher- and textbook-centred approaches, as they highlight reviewing and repetition as well as rote learning. Such advocates may emphasise linguistics details and accuracy as well as specific syntactic constructions in language teaching" (Rao, 2002, cited in Rao, 2006, p. 5). Participant EFL teachers' description of their past experience of previous series of textbooks in relation to lived experience indicates a mismatch with contemporary social developments. That mismatch has not been anticipated as part of improved EFL teaching and learning implied by the new curriculum reform and it may not have been possible to have had such anticipation in the face of the enormous task of conceptualizing, resourcing and implementing the reform. Nonetheless, teachers' lived experience suggests that it is something which could be addressed at the present time.

10.2.3　Divergence and the "Directing Stick"

A directing stick (about one foot in length) is a stick used by police officers in China to direct traffic flow in the streets. Participant EFL teachers use the concept of a directing stick to represent various examinations conducted as part of Chinese teaching and learning, in particular the public examinations system. The examinations include the entrance examination to key senior high schools and examinations for university entrance. These examinations are represented by teachers as a "directing stick" which guides teachers and students to focus on various examinations' contents in their teaching and learning. As Chu, an EFL teacher, says, "Examinations guide us where to go and what to teach as well as how to teach. Examinations have been regarded as 'a teaching baton', suggesting a 'directing stick'." The research literature refers to the Chinese system as examination-oriented education, where teaching and learning in general focuses on what is being tested in examinations (Hu, 2003; Rao, 2006; Yang, 2002), something which has dominated Chinese education for thousands of years (Wang, 2008). In spite of this tradition, it is a feature which has been questioned by Chinese educators since implementing the current EFL curriculum reform in Chinese secondary schools (Wang, 2008), and I have taken this up for consideration in my examination of the intent and features of the new EFL curriculum. I have compared it with the 1993 EFL curriculum which also stressed summative assessment.

Participant EFL teachers' descriptions of their past experience of assessment indicate that the content of examinations focused so much on knowledge of the features of the English language that they ignored examining students' comprehensive language competence. Qing says:

In relation to CLOZE in the past, 10 or 20 questions would emphasize more

"Fix Up", "Grammatical Items" and "Choosing the Correct Verb Form" to "Fill in the Blank".

He states further, "In the past, four sentences were laid out for creating a composition. Students were only required to translate these sentences and that might be a composition." Chu says, "There was no Listening test in the examinations either", suggesting that this important skill was ignored in examinations. Qing and Chu describe the content of major public examinations in China in 1993 as having addressed grammar points rather than communicative points such as Listening and Speaking; they were more concerned with Reading and Writing than Listening and Speaking, and even then, they would focus on summative rather than formative assessment. Qing says, "[The exam] focused on summative assessment which means a focus on results." Ju, another EFL teacher, says, "In the past, students learned English in order to get certain marks." These two EFL teachers' experience, shows their attitudes to assessment in the previous reform and its focus on summative assessment, ignoring the possibilities of formative assessment altogether. Since participant EFL teachers regard various examinations as a directing stick in their EFL teaching and learning, the inclusion of formative assessment in current EFL teaching and learning practice suggests a divergence in the use, direction and function of the directing stick. It suggests a successful feature of the new EFL curriculum intent, a new emphasis on assessing teaching and learning protocols. Employing only one form to the exclusion of the other suggests that teaching and learning would lack balance, as has been the case with examination-oriented education. Kwok (2004) argues that examination-oriented education threatens ideals of quality education, inhibiting any shifts from teacher-centred to student-centred learning and teaching. This is a Western-informed perspective, one that has not been systematically tested in CHCs, as suggested by Biggs' (1996) discussion of Western misperceptions of CHCs. The examination system has, after all, served China well for thousands of years, and Chinese students still dominate the ranks of successful students at home and in educations institutions abroad (Zeegers & Zhang, 2005). To argue that the examination system in China is deficient in producing top level graduates is to apply Western attitudes to examinations to a context in which this may not be the case. A tension then emerges in relation to formative and summative assessment as these are played out in China. Participant EFL teachers do not suggest that the examination system be abolished; rather they suggest that it be modified and improved to incorporate specifically identified features and intent of the new EFL curriculum. Kwok's (2004) argument may hold for Western systems; it has yet to be shown to apply to China. Employing only one assessment may influence the quality of EFL teaching and learning as the past experience of Ju and Qing described above indicates. Given this, participant EFL teachers' past experience of assessment may be set against current perspectives on assessment for further examination of their present experience of the current EFL curriculum reform.

10.2.4　Teacher Education Programs

In the following section I will investigate participant EFL teachers' description of their past experience of teacher education programs with a focus on their pre-service teacher education programs in relation to exploring their relevant knowledge base. I have discussed their pre-service teacher education programs as having occurred mainly between the 1970s and 1990s. More than half of the participants graduated from two or three years of teachers' college. The other half graduated from four years of university programs with a Bachelor's Degree. Questionnaire data show that they all perceive that they have adequate knowledge of theoretical bases for language teaching and learning, which helps them to understand and implement the reform under study. My analysis of interview data presents a different picture, one in which some participant EFL teachers have an inadequate knowledge base, in spite of their own perceptions of their knowledge as EFL teachers, and this influences their understanding and implementing the EFL curriculum reform.

According to Hu (2005b), EFL teachers' theoretical base of language teaching in China needs to include linguistic and intercultural knowledge. More specifically, their theoretical base needs to include knowledge of Transformational Grammar and Vygotskian-based sociocultural perspectives, which play a significant role in implementing the reform in the Chinese context, as discussed in Chapter 3 in relation to language pedagogy. When they were asked about their awareness of Transformational Grammar and sociocultural perspectives, they indicated that they had little knowledge of these concepts, or had never heard of them. Qiang puts it this way, "I have never learned the linguistic knowledge that underlies language and language teaching." Hua also states, "No, never, and we had no such courses at school", when being a student in teachers' college. Qiang's and Hua's experience is one of never having been offered courses on knowledge of language acquisition such as Transformational Grammar and Vygotskian-based sociocultural perspectives as part of their pre-service teacher education programs. This suggests that two or three years of teachers' college was not enough to be able to include the range of knowledge that would constitute a comprehensive teacher education program. This is consistent with Hu's (2005b) evaluation of two or three years' Chinese teachers' college courses before 1993 as lacking relevant content for EFL pre-service teacher education programs. Chu, reflecting on the time of being a college student, confirms this view:

> **Foreign cultures or customs might refer to a course. The course has appeared in some universities recently. I didn't take this course when I studied at school because of the social conditions then.**

These three participant EFL teachers' description of their past experience indicates that they perceive that they lack adequate knowledge for teaching and learning, a shortcoming of their pre-service programs which would pose difficulties for them in understanding the EFL teaching and learning that forms part of the reform under study. I have included discussions of issues related to Transformational Grammar and Vygotskian-based sociocultural perspectives in Chapter 3 as providing significant insights to language acquisition, more specifically in second language acquisition. I have also considered this in relation to obtaining an understanding of EFL teaching and learning which these participant EFL teachers would have needed to have acquired as part of their teacher education programs, as the means by which to provide a sound theoretical basis of EFL teacher knowledge. As Fradd, Lee (1998) and Hu (2005b) argue, linguistic knowledge is the most important component to be developed in EFL teachers' knowledge bases.

Intercultural knowledge is an influential and central factor " in promoting effective cross-cultural communication and pragmatically appropriate language use" (Fradd & Lee, 1998, p. 767). The lack of such knowledge is similarly influential as this means that teachers lack an appreciation of intercultural features as part of developing language acquisition, an inhibiting factor when it comes to understanding EFL language teaching and learning in relation to the requirements of the current EFL curriculum reform. It is a point raised by Fradd and Lee (1998), who argue, "The value of knowledge base lies both in the conversion of information to understandings and the appropriate application of knowledge in a variety of contexts" (p. 764). Chu's experience described above has confirmed that he lacks such knowledge as it did not form part of the teacher education program that he experienced.

Those who have participated in my research have similarly found their pre-service education programs deficient in supporting what they have been required to be able to do to implement effective teaching and learning specified in the new EFL curriculum, and to obtain as complete an understanding as possible of the reform. A teacher's knowledge base plays a significant role in curriculum reform, especially in regard to their teaching practice. Freeman (2002) defines teachers' knowledge bases as "the hidden side" of teachers' work, one which is always ignored by educators, including teachers themselves (p. 1). Pre-service teacher education programs are designed to develop teachers' knowledge bases, which position teachers' past experience of their own professional learning as playing its own part as far as their future professional activities and further professional development are concerned (Freeman, 2002; Shulman, 1994; van Driel, Verloop, & de Vos, 1998). I have taken up this perspective to provide insights to participant EFL teachers' lived experience in relation to the present lived time and their expectations for professional development as part of the reform under study.

In the previous discussions, I have focused on exploring participant EFL teachers' past experience of previous EFL curriculum reforms through their teaching and learning experience as constituting part of lived time. Participants have picked up relevant problems that include issues that are encapsulated in concepts such as " a word class" and "passive listeners" as describing traditional teaching and learning methods that emphasize teachers' roles as central in classroom activities, issues which ignore students' roles as shaping their own learning and individual development, and "spoon-fed mode". They have described these as deficiencies in promoting the development of EFL teaching and learning. In relation to divergence and the "directing stick", I have highlighted these teachers' descriptions of their experience of examinations taken in schools, arguing that examination-oriented education has played an influential role in guiding teaching and learning as far as EFL is concerned (Hu, 2003; Rao, 2006).

These teachers' descriptions of their past experience indicate that they have been aware of the problems of the previous reform. I have considered that such past experience of problems suggests other issues in relation to teachers' self-awareness as playing a significant role in curriculum reform. Ferrari and Sternberg (1998) argue that self-awareness is a crucial part of consciousness, and according to Moustakas (1994), consciousness is intentionality associated with Phenomenological research. To take this a step further, self-awareness is part of intentionality that allows for exploration of participant EFL teachers' lived experience. This is particularly the case in relation to changes in participants' present experience, discussed in the following section. This is another significant point that has emerged from my research in relation to the theme of lived time. In the following section, I will discuss participant EFL teachers' present experience.

10.3   Present Experience

In the previous section I have discussed participant EFL teachers' descriptions of their past experience as part of lived time in relation to their lived experience. I have also previously investigated these teachers' descriptions of their present experience by analyzing their responses to the questionnaire. In the following section, I will examine their descriptions of present experience through their responses to interview questions. I have taken participant EFL teachers' descriptions as a reference point from which I have examined the meaning of their lived experience in ways suggested by Brough (2001). Brough represents the present as a certain privileged point from which to proceed, arguing that teachers have experienced a process of experience that has brought them to an arrival at a lived present time in relation to lived experience. A number of factors have brought them to that lived present.

In my overview of EFL teachers' experience developed out of their responses to the questionnaire, I have identified their own past experience as students as one of the factors that has brought them to their lived present. I have further identified concepts that have driven classroom EFL teaching and learning practices within that past experience, such as teacher-centred learning and students being constructed as passive listeners. I have teased these themes out further as part of my examination of participant EFL teachers' responses to interview questions. In the following sections, I will discuss a number of issues in relation to participant EFL teachers' descriptions of their present experience as these pertain to role shifts; changes in teaching;

modern, appropriate and relevant teaching content and adjustments to the "directing stick" with a new assessment system established as part of the reform. I have also approached issues of teachers' professional development. Exploring participant EFL teachers' descriptions of their present experience has guided me to examine ways in which they have achieved changes regarding philosophies and behaviours in relation to their professional practice in implementing the reform. I have also explored their descriptions of present experience as suggesting a certain measure of success of the new EFL curriculum intent and its features, and I will detail these below.

10.3.1 Role Shifts

Working with the new curriculum has meant that teachers have been required to focus on a different kind of knowledge of their students, a knowledge that aimed at improving their relationships with those students, and a shift from a dominating role in class to one of a friendly guide (Ministry of Education, 2001e). Participant EFL teachers are required to put such education ideas into effect in their teaching practice, as stipulated by the Ministry of Education (2001b). This has been evident not only in participant EFL teachers' responses to the questionnaire and interview questions, but also in my examination of the documents that pertain to the new EFL curriculum in relation to its intent and features. Data have further confirmed that participant EFL teachers' descriptions of their present experience involves having accepted students as an "active participant" (Hua) and "centre of teaching and learning" (Jun). Fang, too, expresses her awareness of this feature of change in her teaching practice, as she says:

> We didn't pay attention to this relationship in the past and we only focused on teaching and talking. Our students were passive listeners and there was no need to concern ourselves about their emotions and other aspects of their lives. Teachers didn't communicate with their students very often. However, the current students all have their strong personalities. The students like this new way of communication and also enjoy studying.

Qiang says:

Currently, teachers often communicate with their students in class and also exchange roles in question-and-answer exercises. The aim is to do more language practice which appeals to the students, inspiring them to participate actively.

Wei also describes the change as far as his EFL teaching is concerned, "Students feel more initiative and are more active in learning English while teachers only play the role of a director. "

These several EFL teachers are aware of changes they have had to make in relation to the shifts in the roles of teachers and students in their teaching and learning practice. As Huang (2004) argues, this reform stresses that teachers are expected to be organizers for and advisors of students, while students are to be able to manage their own learning. Wang (2007) also states that EFL teachers, in implementing the new EFL curriculum reform, are required to shift from a position of "a knowledge transmitter to a multi-role educator" (p. 101), highlighting a departure from traditional dominant roles to take up a supporting one. Such discussions indicate a new feature of the new curriculum, which I have discussed at the beginning of this chapter.

I have identified teachers' awareness of their role shift as an indication of a move towards significant educational change as part of the EFL curriculum reform. As Tabulawa (1998) argues, teachers' philosophies, including their views and beliefs, serve as premises to guide and understand their own classroom behaviours. Fullan (2007) argues that a significant education change includes a change in teachers in relation to "beliefs, teaching style, and materials, which can come about only through a process of personal development in a social context" (p. 139). Teachers' awareness of role shift, then, is part of this significant educational change as far as their own professional stance is concerned. It is one of the goals which the current EFL curriculum is expected to achieve in EFL teaching and learning (Wang, 2007).

Not every EFL teacher holds the same view on this issue. Jun, in Site A, expresses her awareness of what is happening in regard to the role shift:

Although the reform attempts to realize this goal, things still have not changed so much. As a matter of fact, the reform has been implemented to cope with exam-oriented education. In this sense, principles of teaching and learning may be seen to be contradictory to each other in relation to the relationship between teachers and students in the context of exam-oriented education.

This teacher expresses her awareness of role shift in the reform under study as part of her experience. She has pointed to problems in the current assessment system which has influenced teachers' role shifts in their teaching that are not acknowledged in the literature or in curriculum documents. She further suggests that teachers cannot easily realize role shifts if they are still directed by examination-oriented education. Her perspective is consistent with what I have explored in teachers' descriptions of their past experience, where they have focused on examinations as a "directing stick" which has guided their EFL teaching and learning. For Jun, the "directing stick" has dominated the role that she plays in classroom teaching, suggesting that a reconsideration of the assessment system of the new EFL curriculum reform is a key issue to be considered. The literature exhorts and promotes the sorts of changes away from those dimensions suggested by a "directing stick", but the reality of the teachers' experience in the classroom is such that they cannot implement the changes in teachers' and students' roles that are stated in the curriculum and policy documents as desirable. This is a tension, a feature of teachers' lived experience that is yet to be resolved.

Participant EFL teachers' stated desired and desirable role shifts indicate a significant change in relation to their past experience at the same time as it suggests a certain measure of success in implementing the new EFL curriculum reform. Teachers perceive that they are gradually realizing this shift in their EFL teaching and learning but some participant teachers' experience is affected by the influential factor of assessment as it is currently practised. The teachers suggest that while assessment maintains its examination orientation, it will be hard for them to achieve the sorts of comprehensive role shifts emerging as part of EFL teaching and learning in the Chinese context. I have identified this point as a significant issue that may be expected to play a significant role in relation to improving EFL curriculum reform in future.

10.3.2 Changes in Teaching

Questionnaire data have shown that almost all participant EFL teachers' experience include conscious implementation of relevant changes in their teaching practice as they have related to the reform under study. My interview data have further confirmed this. Qiang says:

I have always adjusted my teaching methods in my teaching practice and I found I had already changed myself, to a certain extent. I might not follow the traditional ones to repeat or translate sentences mechanically. I attempt to help my students actively to be involved in my teaching and also encourage them to synthesize their new and old knowledge. Further to this, I try to help them to apply their knowledge to their practice.

Qiang's perception and understanding of new sorts of teaching has required turning from traditional methods to those related to the new EFL curriculum. Fang's description of her experience also indicates her awareness of the changes in relation to her EFL teaching when implementing the reform. She says:

In relation to teaching, we only did in grammar in the past, in usage, sentences and examples. However, I found that we still needed to extend good students' knowledge as it was not good enough for them to have learnt these in class. We have to be concerned with those poor students who only have basic knowledge. All teaching of these students should be based on a special teaching strategy, one that is based on different levels of students. Every week, students are grouped and then separated [as part of teaching and learning strategies where students can be tutors so that they can help each other]. This kind of strategy is easier to adopt as students are quite different from their teachers and they have different perceptions regarding the same topic or question. Further, there is no gap between the ages of these students and they can communicate with and understand each other.

What this approach has given her is an experience of changes in teaching which highlight diverse students' needs that require her to explore new strategies of teaching. Qiang has been aware of the significance of changes in teaching practice which would influence students' development and has realized pedagogical changes in implementing the reform. These two teachers' descriptions of their experience indicate participant EFL teachers' responses to the new emphasis on students' individual development in the new EFL curriculum, another new feature of EFL curriculum which I have discussed in Chapter 6.

I have looked to the adoption of task-based learning as a key feature that presents in the current EFL curriculum reform, discussed in Chapter 6. I have also shown participant EFL teachers' descriptions of their experience through analyzing the questionnaire data discussed in Chapter 7. Interview data further show this. Yu, an EFL teacher speaking about her present experience in relation to changes in teaching, says, "The adoption of the *English Curriculum Standards* has encouraged us to adopt task-based teaching." Chu, referring to the new teaching methods adopted, says:

> The new teaching method has the potential to help students to relax or feel interested in [learning English language]. For example, I have in the past encouraged students to take up a role play as a lecturer in class and I got a good feedback about it.

Fang says:

> This new teaching method seems quite new to EFL teachers ... we completely discard our traditional teaching methods and try to incorporate ones with a focus on students' development.

These three EFL teachers have respectively shown their own awareness of task-based learning and reflections on using this approach in their EFL teaching in implementing the reform. Their statements on their experience of this teaching method indicate positive attitudes to the changes in teaching that are part of this reform. Hua, Xia and Qin's experience indicates that each of them has been engaged in an attempt to change their educational conceptualizations and their role as teachers by exploring a number of different ways to engage challenges that present as part of the reform under study. Hua says, "We have been guided by the current EFL curriculum reform to carry out our teaching practice, and this includes an emphasis on students as the main focus of our teaching, that is, student-centred teaching." Xia states, "As a teacher, I always use pair work or group work to help my students to communicate or to speak in English." Qin discusses her teaching approaches in some detail, as she states:

> When we do practice in dialogues in class, we ask our students to do their

preparation first. And then they listen to the relevant tape. After that, they try to answer the questions, which are tests of their listening skills... It is the same as our teaching on texts. After having a good preparation about a text, the students will communicate with their teachers and then have their questions dealt with.

These participant EFL teachers' descriptions of their practice show ways in which they have changed their teaching to cater for challenges presented by the reform under study. Their experience further reflects successful aspects of the new EFL curriculum intent and its features that present a focus on task-based learning. I have considered these teachers' awareness of teaching methods and their actual engagement of changes in teaching, particularly adopting task-based learning as a response to the reform under study, as indications of changes in teaching. These teachers' descriptions of their experience further indicate that task-based learning has had a measure of success in their schools, which is consistent with the claims of Carless (2007), that adopting task-based approaches need to be based on consideration of issues of culture, setting and teachers' existing beliefs, values and practices as these relate to and interact with task-based teaching methods. I have taken up such considerations in Chapter 3 with a focus on teaching methods, where I have scrutinized the prioritization of the adoption of task-based learning in EFL teaching in the Chinese context.

Achieving changes in teaching is one of the demands which the reform places on EFL teachers in their teaching, but making such demands by means of policy and curriculum statements does not necessarily lead to those changes being implemented. There are teachers who still hold to their own traditional conceptualizations of teaching and learning. As Wei says:

We still focus on explaining knowledge and grammatical points with traditional teaching methods because it is quite easy for these teachers to keep using the conventional teaching methods such as "a word class".

Lian says, "In relation to my own teaching practice, sometimes, I feel it quite easy to use traditional teaching methods in order to avoid trouble or to save time." The experience of Wei and Lian shows that although both of them have been involved in implementing the new EFL curriculum reform for some time, they still find it easier to use the traditional teaching methods which they have used for years in their teaching practice. This indicates that traditional ideas and approaches are not easily got rid of, for they have been persistently and insistently employed in teachers' practice to the extent that they have become ingrained. Both of these participant EFL teachers have a sense of convenience and safety in their resorting to traditional methods. In contrast, Xu has tended to adopt some changes in her teaching, but has a sense of disappointment and frustration after a number of attempts:

> As an English teacher, I usually try my best to teach students in English. But at times I have lost my confidence in using English, and in using the new teaching methods, as when I saw the students' results of examinations. This changed my mind.

Xu considers that it is important to teach students in English, to adjust her teaching in implementing the reform. However, she has felt an irresistible force which has held back her implementation of changes in teaching, suggesting that she turned back to traditional teaching methods when faced with the results of examinations. She cannot get rid of the influences of examination-oriented education; her experience reflects the problems in the present assessment system in her area, which I will discuss further in the following sections. As Cheng (1998) says, examinations play an important role in curriculum, teaching and learning as well as individual life, as with Xu's experience. Xu sees examinations as a pivotal factor that influences her, part of her lived experience in implementing the reform. This is another tension between traditional and new teaching methods required in the reform, one that reflects the examination-oriented education as still influencing these teachers' lived experience of implementing the reform, evidenced by Xu's experience. In Chapter 6, I have explored ways in which EFL teachers are encouraged to adopt new teaching methods to engage the new challenges of developing students' comprehensive language competence. The reality of teachers' experience of the restraints of traditional ideas associated with the results of examinations means that teachers are not effectively positioned to cope with the language acquisition and competence features of new curriculum and policy documents, and this needs to be resolved. This is particularly so in Site A. In this regard, it is understandable, as van Driel, et al. (2001) argue, that it is difficult for teachers to change their deep-rooted teaching ideas as they are disinclined to take risks as far as changes in their teaching practice, which has long been proved workable and satisfactory, are concerned.

I have highlighted participant EFL teachers' descriptions of their present experience of changes in teaching as such issues are part of the lived time which forms part of their lived experience. Some of these teachers have described their enthusiasm for making changes in classroom teaching. In their descriptions of their present experience, they have expressed a sense of enthusiasm for the reform under study, which is different from their descriptions of their past experience of EFL curriculum reform. Some participants have felt that task-based teaching conflicts with traditional methods of EFL teaching and learning with their focus on examination-oriented education, and it is a conflict that has not been resolved as far as they are concerned. As Carless (2007) argues, task-based learning in CHC contexts may yet prove to be an unresolvable source of contention with traditional education models. I have taken up the issue of changes in teaching in examining participant EFL teachers' descriptions of their present experience as it is one of three important components for effecting a significant education change. As Fullan (2001) argues, at least three dimensions need to be considered when implementing an education change: materials, teaching strategies, and beliefs. I will focus on these in the following section.

10.3.3   Modern, Relevant and Realistic

As part of my examination of the new EFL curriculum, I have explored the new series of textbooks which are based on content that are realistic, modern, rich and varied, closely related to students' life. This is consistent with Zeegers and Zhang's (2005) argument in relation to Chinese EFL textbooks, where they conclude that there is "a number of features that any ESL teacher in the world would use to promote active language engagement" (p. 256), indicating positive responses to the new Chinese EFL textbooks. Two of the biggest publishing houses in China have taken up the task of producing the textbooks and supplementary curriculum materials that are to be used in secondary schools in the implementation of the EFL curriculum reform. One series of textbooks is produced by Foreign Language Teaching and Research Press, and this is the series of textbooks used in Site B. The other series is produced by People's Education Press, and used in Site A. Both series are aimed at students at the same levels in both sites. My research focuses on participant EFL teachers' general perspectives on the textbooks that they use in their sites; I have not made a particular study of either of them, but have focused on teachers' opinion of them.

In analyzing questionnaire data, I have also found that the majority of the participant EFL teachers have a similar view of the new textbooks, and my interview data have further borne this out. Qin, for instance, says:

> These contents are helpful for teachers and students in relation to knowing more about the whole social contexts and the whole world. This has the potential to expand the children's vision of an English-speaking world.

She also says, "More and more new words and phrases relating to the 21st century have been added for study within the new curriculum"; that, "The new textbook has involved various aspects of knowledge including the economy, geography, and politics, and so on in the world". Ju, another EFL teacher, says:

> In terms of content, it is more related to real life. Every module has its own topic in relation to children's lives. This helps to stimulate students' interests and then apply it to practice, rather than only to address grammar, as in the old textbook. This is a salient change.

Qin and Ju's present experience has meant that they have felt the changes of the new textbooks as being modern and relevant to their teaching and learning contexts as they are specifically designed to be related to students' lives. They see that the textbooks that have been produced as part of the EFL curriculum reform are also linked to wider social, economic and political development as a Chinese education response to globalization. These are positive perceptions of the new teaching content as they focus on textbooks. Participant EFL teachers have also emphasized the improvements to be seen in the new textbooks regarding their designs, which include a reduction of what they considered as being excessive foci on grammar points in the textbooks of previous EFL programs. Qiang states:

> I think the content in relation to grammatical practice has been reduced in the new textbook and there are only a few relevant exercises with quite slow rhythms, for example. The textbook contents are easy to comprehend.

This is commonly experienced by participant EFL teachers, particularly by those teachers from Site B. They consider that there have been changes for the better in the new textbooks as far as their contents are concerned. These teachers have expressed positive attitudes to the new textbook designs and contents. Participant EFL teachers' descriptions of their experience further suggest that students have readily accepted these as part of the total experience provided by the new EFL curriculum. They consider that this would help students to achieve the sort of comprehensive language competence which is the stated goal of the reform.

I have considered participant EFL teachers' perspectives of their present experience on the new series of EFL textbooks as a certain measure of success in implementing the reform under study. I have also identified the extension of curriculum concerns to EFL teaching and learning for citizenship as a response to wider globalization issues, which I have discussed as part of the new EFL curriculum intent and its features. As Guan and Meng (2007) point out, the new curriculum has highlighted basic knowledge and skills, getting rid of difficult, outdated and irrelevant content, and developing new content that links to students' everyday lives within a modern society and the technological advances that are part of that. They also comment that such content is designed to assist students in obtaining knowledge of social, political and economic development on the world stage, which acts as a guide for their individual future development as EFL learners. Teachers' descriptions of their experience are similar to those given by Dello-Locovo (2009) in his study of curriculum reform in China: the new curriculum emphasizes "the links between the curriculum and society, science, technology and students' personal experience" (p. 244).

I have also considered the changes that I have outlined in relation to the new textbooks as constituting a response by EFL teaching and learning to issues of citizenship proposed in the new EFL curriculum, suggesting it as a progressive feature that was absent in previous reforms. New textbook content with modern features can also help students to acquire relevant knowledge and capacities to meet the challenges of globalization, for as Zeegers and Zhang (2005) say, language activities presented in the EFL textbooks that they have studied focus on language acquisition and language application born of the work of Vygotsky (1978), Chomsky (1957;1965) and other leading scholars in this field. This is consistent with my consideration of curriculum presented in Chapter 3 in relation to Transformational Grammar and sociocultural perspectives. McEneaney and Meyer (2000) argue that the content of language curriculum, especially when seen in the context of globalization, needs an emphasis on developing students' capacity for expression and understanding, as that of the EFL curriculum reform under study.

Again, not all teachers participating in this research agree on this point. Xu, an EFL teacher from Site A, says, "The textbook contents I think cannot be linked to students' actual English levels in my school."

Jun, another EFL teacher from Site A, says:

> The content embodied in the new textbook is not related to the children's or the students' actual life in rural, remote or poor areas. The children only use their imagination to comprehend the content and it might be the real life relating to cities.

Jiang, also an EFL teacher from Site A, has the same opinion:

> For example, the textbook content talks about popcorn and the children living in rural areas know nothing about it. My husband has grown up in a rural region and he has never seen such kind of machines [that would make popcorn]. Thus, it is hard for the children in rural regions to learn the current curriculum; they have to remember the content by rote learning ... As a consequence, I think the new textbook is designed for students or children in big cities, not for those in rural or poor regions. I would ask how many children have ever seen a microwave oven, for the children in these regions have no knowledge at all about this thing either.

She goes on to say:

> Even some teachers have never seen a microwave oven. If students are from wealthy families, perhaps they would know something about this. If not, they might not know how to cook a banana milk cake and what should be added.

These three teachers' descriptions of their experience from Site A show their negative perspectives on the new textbooks used in their areas, even as they have acknowledged the improvement of the new EFL textbook content as it involves words and expressions such as "a microwave oven", representing a feature of a modern appliance. They consider such textbook content, which is the same as that used in cities, as not being relevant to teachers and students in less developed regions, the remote mountainous or rural regions in particular. They consider that they need to have textbooks designed for those teachers and students in less developed areas of the country, the remote ones in particular, rather than using the same versions as those used in cities. Participant EFL teachers' descriptions of their experience in Site A have raised a problem that has emerged in relation to the choice of textbook in Site A. According to Marton (2006, cited in Dello-Locovo, 2009), China's State Education Commission has suggested that the national unified curriculum materials have since the late 1980s been required to cater for local conditions and contexts. To this end, that Commission has further called for local publishers and education departments to develop their own curriculum materials for use in schools in their regions. The *Outline* also clearly states its encouragement of various publishers producing a diverse range of textbooks on the basis of curriculum standards, rather than having all schools relying on only one series of textbooks (Ministry of Education, 2001c). Participant EFL teachers' descriptions of their experience in Site A suggest that they have not been provided textbooks designed for use in their regions, that is, the relevant requirements have not been acted upon. Schools in Site A, then, have not been able to engage the requirements stipulated in the *Outline* in relation to this feature of the reform, at least.

Participant EFL teachers' descriptions of their present experience of using textbooks are a salient aspect of their teaching, and of students' learning, specifically as part of their implementing the EFL curriculum reform. In the experience of participant EFL teachers from Site B, the new series of textbooks are modern and relevant, a feature of EFL teachers' experience which helps teachers and students to work towards the acquisition of required knowledge and to promote EFL development as part of a national concern to engage challenges of globalization. It is the experience of participant EFL teachers from Site A that the textbooks are modern but not relevant, an identified problem in relation to students' learning and understanding as the contents are not related to their lives and the realities of their existence. This may at the same time act as a barrier for teachers' implementation of the reform under study in such areas as Site A.

10.3.4 Continuity

In discussing the new EFL curriculum intent and its features, I have considered the feature of continuity in relation to English language learning starting from Grade 3 in primary schools and progressing into senior levels in secondary schools. Since my data were collected from participant EFL teachers who are from secondary schools in Northeast China, I have approached this issue through these teachers' perspectives as they have engaged with graduates from primary schools in their junior secondary schools, rather than through direct approaches to teachers and students in primary schools.

Several participant EFL teachers from Site B express their awareness of what is happening to EFL teaching and learning in primary schools through their interaction with students who have various backgrounds of EFL learning. They have seen the value of primary schools' English teaching. As Ying says:

> In primary schools in previous curriculum reforms, there were no opportunities for students to learn English, and they learned English when they came to junior secondary schools. They began to learn 26 letters first and then some sentences, such as, "How are you?" or "How do you do?" But now, students start learning in primary schools. It is quite different.

Qing, another EFL teacher, says, "The children now start to learn English when they are in kindergarten or in their primary schools, and some learn it even before the kindergarten." The experience of both Qing and Ying shows EFL teaching and learning has happened in their areas before the children come to their classrooms, so that their students have a certain background of EFL teaching and learning that may be built upon when they come to junior secondary schools, rather than learning from the beginning upon their arrival. This has given them a sense of support for their professional activities, one result of the priority of English as identified by Chinese education authorities, and not only in big cities. Hu (2007) states that teaching English in primary schools is part of an attempt to satisfy the increasing demand for English anticipated in future developments in the opening up of China to the rest of the world. It is also regarded as a strategy for upgrading citizens' competence in English, improving the linguistic capacities of Chinese citizens by expanding English teaching in Grade 3 in primary schools (Hu, 2007). Hu (2007) further considers it as part of China's continuing development in the context of accelerated globalization.

Participant EFL teachers' descriptions of their experience from Site A present different views in relation to this issue. Jiang says, "The new textbook is good for the students in cities as they have a good knowledge of English. They began to learn English when they were very young. " Xu, another EFL teacher, states, "English—this subject has not been emphasized in primary schools in our regions and as a result, the majority of children's English knowledge is quite poor. " She further says:

> For example, some of the students in Grade One in my school cannot recite the 26 letters of the alphabet or write them down. This phenomenon can be seen in almost all the rural regions. Thus, I think it is very hard for us, as EFL teachers, to teach such students in junior secondary schools.

For both Xu and Jiang, a problem has emerged in relation to policies for implementing EFL teaching and learning starting from Grade 3 in the rural areas, the remote and mountainous ones in particular. Their experience indicates the policies do not apply to their context as it has not been possible to implement them in primary schools in their regions. They have felt a sense of disappointment and frustration when they have been in a position of classroom interaction with students who have little knowledge of English. For them, it has not been enough to be able to draw on the new series of textbooks that have been designed with the idea of continuity from primary school EFL teaching and learning in mind. This has set up particular barriers for them as they struggle to find and choose the new series of textbooks with content that is relevant for their students. The demands on them as teachers required to implement the new EFL curriculum are undermined as policy is only partially implemented in their regions. This is consistent with Hu's (2005b) argument in relation to what he represents as necessary conditions for effective EFL teaching and learning in primary education:

> Suitable learning materials, appropriately trained teachers, a perceived need for English as a medium of instruction, a threshold level of learner proficiency in the medium language, a supportive language environment in the

larger social context (p. 19).

He further says that these conditions largely do not exist in the majority of Chinese regions, particularly the rural or less developed ones. Liu (2009) bears out this point, "Qualified teachers, suitable textbooks and teaching equipment are prerequisites required in carrying out EFL teaching and learning starting from primary schools in the Chinese context" (p. 37). Such discussions suggest that EFL teaching and learning starting from Grade 3 in primary schools need to be carried out in specified and appropriate contexts, not just any context in China. *ECS* has already stated that English needs to be offered to students in Grade 3 in primary schools nationwide, starting with cities and suburban areas in 2001 and extending to rural ones in 2002 (Ministry of Education, 2001a). Differences between rural areas and cities are in such ways identified, but appropriate strategies and programs to support such identification have not materialized to have the policy implemented successfully in remote and less developed areas. Site A is one such case; EFL teaching and learning is not appropriately supported in this area. Participant EFL teachers' descriptions of their experience in Site A shows their lived experience being affected by primary school graduates with a lack of EFL backgrounds being required to use the new series of textbooks designed for different contexts and conditions of teaching and learning. According to the Ministry of Education (2001a), teaching English starting from Grade 3 in primary schools needs to take into account the differences between rural and urban areas, and programs are expected to be implemented hierarchically, which I have discussed previously. Such issues have been overlooked by the local education department in Site A, and this is part of the lived experience of teachers here.

10.3.5 Adjusting the "Directing Stick"

I have discussed issues of participant EFL teachers' past experience in relation to a "directing stick" as referring to various examinations undertaken by Chinese secondary school students. I have also discussed teachers' identification of these examinations as a "directing stick" that drives teachers and students toward specific study of various examinations' contents in their classroom programs. Questionnaire responses have not raised this as a matter of concern, but it has emerged as one from interview data. Teachers' descriptions of their present experience of the changes in the content of examinations suggest a number of features in relation to success in implementing the reform. There are still examinations, part of a long and successful tradition in Chinese education, but these examinations have refocused teachers' and learners' efforts in relation to language acquisition and not just language learning. I have considered such changes as a response to the new EFL curriculum intent and its features, referring to the issue of adjusting the "directing stick". Qing, who comes from Site B, says:

> At present, examination content in the whole region has been greatly changed. For example, in terms of Multiple Choices, previously 18 or more among 20 questions were concerned with grammar, while now merely 2 or 3 among 20 do. The rest focuses on language function and language consistency in communication and word usage, which is related to choosing an appropriate word in the context.

He also states:

> In relation to CLOZE now, it emphasizes "right or wrong" which ought to show understanding of contexts. If you haven't read this passage or don't know about the contexts, perhaps you don't know which one to choose from the four. And this test might check students' comprehensive language competence in using the language... You can still see many changes in the examinations for high school entrance examination and for national college entrance examination. The examination content is in line with the curriculum standards as part of the examination system.

Qing has seen changes in the content of the major examinations in his area since the implementation of the reform. He considers that these changes aim to examine students' language competence, as with the use of CLOZE exercises, and are designed to test students' comprehensive reading competence in English, rather than placing an emphasis on grammar points. Such changes would guide him to focus on these aspects in his classroom teaching. Since examinations are a large part of the assessment system (Race, Brown, & Smith, 2005), Qing pinpoints a major feature of this new EFL curriculum. As Dello-Lacovo (2009) puts it:

There has been widespread discussion of reforming the examination content in line with the new curriculum goals and there have been some changes to the examination system with some regions now setting their own exams (p. 247).

Qing gives a further description:

Another tremendous change is the shift in assessment in the textbook. The previous one focused on Summative Assessment which means that it was concerned with the results. The curriculum now attempts to address Formative Assessment with a focus on learning processes embedded in each module.

Qing has given his insights to issues of assessments based on his experience of different versions of textbooks produced in two different times. His experience reflects a new feature of the new EFL curriculum with its focus on a new assessment system in its adoption of both summative and formative assessment, while summative assessment dominated the previous system. Qing's experience is further witness to the changes as they present in the reform under study.

Wei, who is from Site A, has given an account of his experience in relation to issues of assessment in implementing the reform as being different from that of teachers in Site B. As he puts it, "The exam content between the past and the present has not been changed a lot, and the old content or fashions are still shown in the current test papers." Wei's statements represent a general perspective of participant EFL teachers in Site A. Wei considers that examinations in his area are still in line with traditional content, and not a reform of it. This has influenced him to stress knowledge of these examinations' content in his teaching since implementing the reform. Public examinations are a key factor in the Chinese context, identified as one of the major barriers to curriculum reform implementation (Dello-Lacovo, 2009). This is the case in particular with examinations for high school entrance examination and national college entrance examination.

The two participants' descriptions of their experience in Site A and Site B present two different local responses to issues of assessment with regard to this reform. Qing's description of his experience in Site B shows a sense of forces which have driven him to implement the reform actively, based on the new assessment system as part of the new EFL curriculum. He says that this has helped him to turn to the goals of the new EFL curriculum in his teaching. In contrast, Wei, from Site A, has a sense of conflict between the new EFL curriculum intent in relation to reforming the assessment system and its presentation in examinations. He has felt such assessment as a barrier for him in teaching towards the goals of this reform. This is also a tension, representing a feature of EFL teachers' lived experience which is yet to be dealt with. Teachers' experience have offered different insights to the reform, part of the lived experience of curriculum implementation.

10.3.6 Emphasizing Teachers' Professional Development

I have discussed the new EFL curriculum intent and its features in Chapter 6, suggesting that it has stressed teachers' professional development. According to Fullan (2007), such features will never work by themselves as they need to "generate more and more people with the skills, knowledge, and dispositions" to implement education change (p. 264). I have argued that professional development programs need teachers to take them up in order to put reforms into practice, and that these teachers are expected to have certain capacities. The key players in any education change are teachers. This gives rise to issues of teachers' professional preparation before they take up their classroom roles as well as ongoing teachers' professional development as they work in their classrooms. It is an issue that has attracted increasing attention in the current curriculum reform in China, suggesting that teachers are expected to update knowledge constantly in order to cope with challenges of the new curriculum, EFL teachers in particular (Huang, 2004; Ministry of Education, 2001a; Zhang, 2008). Even though teachers' responses make it clear that they are enthusiastic for reform, or have confidence in implementing that reform, they also indicate that they still require relevant and appropriate training or, at the very least, guidelines to help them, of the kind suggested by Pintó (2004). I have explored issues of participant EFL teachers' professional development in relation to their pre-service teacher education programs in my discussions on their past experience above. As discussed in Chapter 8, teachers' professional development has emerged from my investigation as an issue to be resolved in the schools.

In Site A, EFL teachers' descriptions of their experience indicate that they have been given few opportunities and little time for professional preparation, particularly in relation to implementing the current EFL curriculum reform in their schools. If there is little opportunity, the training and preparation for the implementation of such a major curriculum reform is like the Chinese proverb: "In like a lion, out like a lamb", suggesting that it has not been emphasized in this region. In Site B, participant EFL teachers' descriptions of their experience indicate that teachers' professional development in relation to the EFL curriculum reform has been seriously addressed in their school. Fullan (2007) asks, "Why do even the best attempts fail?" and he answers, "It is a big problem primarily related to the fact that most societies do not treat teacher education as a serious endeavour" (p. 267). This indicates the important role of teachers' education in determining a significant education change. I have treated the schools in both sites in which the research has been conducted as a small society within a larger one, and these teachers' descriptions of their experience in Site A indicate that their school sits at odds with those of the sort that have informed Fullan's (2007) view. These EFL teachers' descriptions of their present experience provide a contrasting picture of teachers' professional development in relation to their in-service teacher education programs. Participant EFL teachers' descriptions of their experience in Site B reflect a certain measure of improvement in relation to their past experience with a focus on such issues. Teachers' descriptions of their experience in Site A indicate that they have experienced a less than complete commitment relating to teachers' professional development in relation to in-service teacher education programs, and preparation for the reform under study.

In the previous section, I have focused on participant EFL teachers' present experience in relation to examining the theme of lived time. I have used participant EFL teachers' present experience as a reference point to examine their experience of the past and of the future. It is in their present experience that they have experienced changes in their roles, teaching content and methods, assessment and professional development. Participant EFL teachers' descriptions of their experience of these changes are part of an attempt to engage the challenges of new EFL curriculum as they present in a globalization context, reflecting the substance of the new EFL curriculum intent and its features. This has particularly been borne out in participant EFL teachers' experience in Site B. Participant EFL teachers' descriptions of their present experience in Site B forms the horizons of their temporal landscape in relation to their lived experience. I have not considered their present experience in isolation, suggesting it has been linked with their past and their future. I have discussed their past and present experience in the foregoing; I will approach their future in the following.

An examination of EFL teachers' descriptions of their present experience in Site A and Site B has raised issues of glocalization in considering globalization. It has indicated that the influences of globalization on the reform under study are not uniform. Participant EFL teachers' present experience has been influenced by local and individual factors. Local factors include schools' responses to teachers' professional development, to issues of assessment, as well as to those of tailoring national textbooks to cater for local contexts. Individual factors include participant EFL teachers' individual teaching philosophies, attitudes and perspectives. Local and individual factors have influenced teachers' lived experience in relation to their implementation of this reform, and I have argued that these form the substance of a successful education change or otherwise in relation to the reform under study, more specifically in relation to those in Site B.

These teachers' descriptions of their present experience also reflects that they have experienced tensions between the requirements of the current EFL curriculum reform and the influences of previous reforms and traditions rooted in these teachers' minds, as well as in the traditions of China, particularly in Site A. They include tensions between teachers' role shifts in teaching and learning and the reality of examination-oriented education that is embraced in China; tensions between traditional teaching methods and task-based learning; tensions between modern, relevant textbook content and its inconsistency with students' real lives; tensions between formative and summative assessment as these are addressed in reality; and tensions between teachers' professional development and the lack of relevant support. These EFL teachers have described their experience of significant changes in implementing this reform; they have also experienced difficulties in implementing it. This is an aspect of the descriptions of their experience which I have explored in relation to their lived experience. In the following section, I will explore participant EFL teachers' expectations in relation to their lived experience and the future.

10.4   Expectations

A further temporal dimension in relation to issues of lived time is that of the future, with a focus on participant EFL teachers' descriptions of their expectations with regard to implementing the reform in coming years. I have taken up this issue as constituting part of the horizons of these teachers' temporal landscape, giving rise to issues of being "oriented to an open and beckoning future" (van Manen, 1990, p. 104). Brough (2001) draws on Husserl (1966, cited in Brough, 2001) in referring to a future included in time consciousness, "an intention directed toward what is to come" (p. 35). Participant EFL teachers have not approached issues of the future in their responses to the questionnaire, but it is an issue that has emerged from the interviews. I have teased out a number of issues which focus on their expectations for relevant teaching content, for sufficient resources and more opportunities for training, and for a reformed assessment system, which I will discuss in detail below.

10.4.1　Hoping for Relevant Textbooks

Participant EFL teachers' look to a new series of EFL textbooks that are modern and relevant, those teachers in Site B in particular. They expect them to be produced to suit diverse contexts. As Ju says:

> We wish textbook writers would come closer to us; that they would come to our classrooms, and help us to solve the problems in person. This might help textbook writers to produce more appropriate textbooks.

Hong says:

> I wish that textbook writers might come to our classrooms. It's better for them to observe our teaching. It would be much better for textbook writers to stay with teachers for a period of time so that they could produce more appropriate textbooks.

Hong comes from Site A while Ju comes from Site B, and both of them suggest that textbook writers need to involve themselves in teachers' classroom practice so that they may come to know about teachers' lives and students' reality. They feel that this would help textbook writers to produce more appropriate teaching content for teachers and students in less developed regions, and their areas in particular. Hong and Ju say that they expect to have more opportunities to participate in processes of curriculum reform, beyond that of practitioners. These teachers expect their role to be recognized and acknowledged further as part of the current reform, which they see as encouraging them to devote more time and energy to implementing it in their schools. This is a particular issue that participant EFL teachers are concerned about in relation to future directions.

The majority of EFL teachers across both sites also expect a number and variety of textbooks to be produced to cater for the needs of different regions and the diversity that this implies, anticipating that they may have multiple choices with regard to textbooks that might be used. Ju, recounting her experience of textbooks, says:

> I hope that when a new curriculum, a new syllabus or a new textbook is produced, it will be concerned with its being adopted in different contexts. If so, these new textbooks might get better, and would be more appropriate when applied to these different circumstances.

Wei says, "It is much better to produce various textbooks and relevant teaching materials for a diverse range of students in different regions." Both Wei and Ju have developed a sense of expectation in relation to various textbook versions being produced, textbooks which will engage the diverse needs for both developed and less developed areas in Northeast China. This is seen as part of an empowerment process for those participant EFL teachers who have complained about the outdated teaching content in the previous curriculum reform. This sort of anticipation has inspired anticipation of new versions of textbooks that will help them with curriculum implementation. It is something which has posed challenges for improving the current EFL curriculum reform in the coming years. The *Outline* (Ministry of Education, 2001d) states that the new curriculum reform intends to serve as an encouragement for various publishers to produce various EFL textbooks in China, to engage various needs from diverse regions of the sort discussed in the foregoing. Participant EFL teachers' expectations for teaching content have provided insights to possibilities for the improvement of teaching content in the coming years in relation to this reform. Their expectations have highlighted problems in relation to present teaching content as far as the textbooks used in the less developed regions are concerned.

10.4.2   Seeking Sufficient Sources and Opportunities for Training

In the following section I will examine participant EFL teachers' expectations in relation to issues about resources and opportunities for training in relation to implementing the EFL curriculum reform in the coming years. Participant EFL teachers from Site B consider that they have been provided with sufficient resources and training, but this does not mean that they have no expectations for the future. Their descriptions of their experience indicate that they still hope for more facilities and more opportunities for improving their EFL teaching and hence, student learning. As Qiang says, "EFL teachers should be provided with relevant facilities or professional training or supplementary materials in timely fashion". Qiang focuses on being provided with relevant facilities and training in a timely fashion, something which he considers would be helpful. He has regarded these as important factors which have needed to be highlighted for the purpose of improvement of the EFL curriculum reform in the coming years. Ying, another EFL teacher from Site B, has a similar expectation, "Set up more platforms for teachers' professional training, such as going out or inviting someone inside. This helps with expanding its relevant influences of the reform." Ying's expectations of professional development have made her more aware of the importance of training which she considers a main factor influencing her implementing the reform. Both Ying and Qiang look forward to even better facilities and better training than what they have had as part of their present experience.

In contrast, the experience of those from Site A indicates that they may entertain basic expectations as far as adequate resources, including teaching facilities and opportunities for learning, are concerned. As Hong says:

> I think it is better to provide opportunities for us to go out to learn and then invite some experts or scholars to come in and help us with teaching. Such support would help teachers to see or observe more as well as to learn more even as they stay in schools. Besides, it is much better to provide teachers adequate teaching facilities so that teachers may provide a good teaching environment for their students via multimedia.

Jun says:

> If possible, it is best to send us around and learn from others; otherwise we have no experience and don't know how to engage. Mentoring by other expert teachers may allow us to create our own better teaching environments as we

would have direction and know how to proceed.

Hong and Jun have had few opportunities to go beyond their schools to learn and exchange ideas; they are isolated from other EFL teachers because of their location, and they anticipate that this will be the case for them in the future as well. They would like to look forward to going beyond their schools to extend their own vision regarding EFL teaching and learning, expecting in such ways to generate their own knowledge of the reform they are to implement. As van Manen (1990) argues, "Through hopes and expectations we have a perspective on life to come or through desperation and lack of will to live we may have lost such perspective" (p. 104). I have considered such expectations as expressions of an ideal which underpins and spurs teachers to continue to implement the reform under study in order to make the reform meaningful for them and their students.

10.4.3　Looking Forward to a Thorough Reform on Assessment System

I have discussed issues of assessment in relation to the new EFL curriculum. I have also approached such issues in relation to participant EFL teachers' past, present and possible future experience. Part of teachers' concerns are their expectations for a thorough reform of the new assessment system, those teachers from Site A in particular. According to Xu, who is from Site A:

> Along with this curriculum reform, I think the examination system should also be reformed thoroughly. And there should be some changes in the examination system which will be in tune with the new teaching approaches.

Wei also gives his insights to his expectations for a thorough reform in the coming years:

> The contents of examinations should reflect the requirements of textbooks. You know, you teach the new knowledge appearing in the new curriculum, but the system checks your old knowledge in examinations, suggesting they cannot match each other. As a result, teachers gradually return to using traditional teaching methods. Thus, the directing stick should be in line with the new

curriculum. If we focus on Speaking, the paper tests should present relevant contents, and the same with Listening. Now Listening tests have been stressed in the examinations in some regions, but not so in others. It requires a gradual change.

Both Xu and Wei's descriptions of their experience show that they hope for a reform of the new assessment system, especially as this influences their classroom teaching, and affects their lived experience. In Wei's view, that content needs to be linked to the new EFL curriculum, rather than being out of joint as is presently the case. He indicates that this would help him to focus on implementing the new reform as part of his professional practice. Qing, who is from Site B, is also attracted to this perspective:

I think they should attempt to improve the assessment system further and make it align with the textbook content. This has the potential to stimulate teachers to implement the reform in line with *ECS*.

Three participant EFL teachers' have considered ways to improve the new assessment system, regarding content of examinations as affecting them as far as further improving teaching and learning is concerned. All participant EFL teachers indicate that their classroom practice is dictated by content. They express the hope of reform the assessment system. I have explored their expectations of more relevant textbook content, of adequate teaching facilities and more opportunities for training as well as of a thorough reform of assessment. I have regarded participant EFL teachers' expectations as another feature of the past and the present of the lived time of lived experience. As Brough (2001) argues, "A final achievement of time-consciousness is the sense we have our own continuity" (p. 36). I have drawn on their descriptions of their experience of expectations as implications for improving this reform.

10.5 Conclusion

In this chapter, I have focused on the theme of lived time that includes participant EFL teachers' past and present experience and their expectations. As I have discussed above, these three concepts have constituted their temporal way in relation to their lived experience. My examination of participant EFL teachers' descriptions of their past experience and their expectations for the future has highlighted their present experience as part of their lived experience. In examining their descriptions of their past and present experience, I have discussed problems that have emerged from previous curriculum reform as well as changes that have presented in the current one. In analyzing their descriptions of their expectations, I have discussed their hopes for improvement. These have provided a number of insights to the development of EFL curriculum reform in the Chinese context. I have also teased out some distinguishing aspects of the intent and features of the new EFL curriculum for discussion in relation to these. In the following chapter I will approach conclusions and implications of my research.

Chapter 11

Conclusions and Implications

11.1 Introduction

My research has focused on ways in which the current EFL curriculum reform in Chinese secondary schools is linked to globalization through an examination of EFL teachers' lived experience of it. I have investigated ways in which these teachers have thought about and worked towards the reform in the context of globalization on the basis of data collected and analyzed: interviews, a questionnaire and relevant documents. I have analyzed that data drawing on conceptual tools provided by Phenomenology and Reconstructionism, and in this final chapter I will position my discussion of the research that I have conducted in relation to a framework of ten elements for successful education change suggested by Fullan (2007). Drawing on this list, I have laid out some prominent issues related to this reform as it has been implemented in China, with a discussion of research outcomes and issues still to be faced, which I will outline below.

11.2 Fullan's Elements of Successful Change

Fullan's (2007) list of ten elements for successful education change is useful in considering ways in which to achieve success in education. There are overlaps across the various items, but his teasing out of these elements serve to inform my discussion of them. His list starts with the advice that educators who wish to implement successful change in their education system, " define the closing gap as the overarching goal" (p. 44). China's education authorities have stated that a major aim of the new EFL curriculum reform has been to close the gap between current levels of student English language competence that had been considered adequate in previous times and the higher levels demanded of a citizenry capable of operating on a world stage, engaging commerce and financial enterprise as part of global multinational corporations' activities, at the same time as they engage development of service industries demanded in such a context.

My research offers insights to new relationships between politics, economics, culture and education in a context of globalization as these relate to the current EFL curriculum reform, as represented in participant EFL teachers' experience. My focus has included China's entry into the WTO and successfully hosting the Beijing 2008 Olympic Games as part of China's public embracing of issues related to globalization. I have argued that such issues have informed participant EFL teachers' activities as they have had to cope with change and achieve pedagogical shifts in relation to the reform under study. In such ways have Reconstructionist-informed aims come to be realized as part of developing prosperity and well-being for all of China's citizens, based in large part on its EFL success.

In the late 20th and early 21st centuries, China has adopted an open system with its rapid economic development and which has enabled it to establish a significant role in a globalizing world. The current EFL curriculum reform was initiated on the basis of well-prepared, carefully detailed and considered projects and strategies, which I have detailed in Chapter 6. The current EFL curriculum reform that has been implemented in China has established a new set of goals for EFL teaching and learning as part of its reforming of teaching content and methods, reviewing assessment procedures, and highlighting teachers' professional development. I have considered these changes as responses to challenges of globalization posed for education in China as these have emerged from participant EFL teachers' descriptions of their experience, discussed in Chapters 7 to 10.

The next item for educators to attend to, according to Fullan (2007), is that of "attend[ing] initially to the three basics", which are "literacy, numeracy and well-being of students" (pp. 44-45). According to Fullan (2007), these three factors indicate students' comprehensive competence in comprehension, reasoning and solving problems as part of cognitive achievement. He also argues for the development of a healthy outlook with a focus on students' well-being, saying that these factors underpin education improvement (Fullan, 2007). My research has focused on EFL curriculum reform in Chinese secondary schools, where the sort of "literacy" and "well-being" that Fullan argues for is the focus. While I do acknowledge that numeracy is to be considered as one of the literacies taught in schools, I have not approached this as part of my research as it is not linked to mathematics, or mathematic language, my focus having been on English.

The current EFL curriculum reform that I have investigated aims to develop students' comprehensive language competence—their language skills, their language knowledge, their cultural understanding, their learning strategies—and develop appropriate stances in relation to their emotions and attitudes, in forms similar to those suggested by Fullan (2007). The people responsible for designing the current reform in EFL teaching and learning in China have devoted some considerable attention to students' all-round development, which in itself may be seen as a leap, especially as it compares with the EFL curriculum of 1993 discussed in Chapter 6. The current reform also addresses developing students with a healthy physique, building healthy outlooks on life and becoming successful 21st century citizens as it calls for EFL teaching and learning for citizenship, which brings to mind Fullan's (2007) argument of "well-being" as underpinning effective change in education.

An emphasis on "literacy" and "well-being", particularly in relation to citizenship in the new EFL curriculum, recalls the aims of Reconstructionism, which are to develop students' awareness of their individual responsibilities to reconstruct a better country. In China, the EFL learning engaged by students is to enable them to engage challenges brought about by globalization, and through this develop the whole country's capacity for such engagement. This is a concept that sits easily alongside China's socialist and collective socio-political system. I have considered this reform which focuses on developing students' comprehensive language competence and enhancing their awareness of citizenship in their EFL learning, as suggesting both well-being and literacy, and consistent with Fullan's (2007) "three basics" in relation to his list of elements of successful change.

Education reform being "driven by tapping into people's dignity and sense of respect" is the third element for successful change listed by Fullan (2007, p. 44). Teachers' descriptions of their involvement in the reform under study indicate that the central government has turned its attention to EFL teachers' roles regarding reform, treating this as something to be valued, and supported, as part of the implementation of the reform. An emphasis on teachers' professional development indicates that teachers' roles have been positioned as a priority concern in the curriculum reform that China has wanted to implement, and it is a concern that is couched in respectful terms in relation to the teachers charged with implementing reform. This in turn has sparked EFL teachers' enthusiasm for participating and implementing this reform, as I have discussed in Chapter 6.

This reform has also encouraged EFL teachers to realize changes in pedagogical perspectives and behaviours, such as a shift from teacher-centred to student-centred classrooms, from grammar-translation to task-based methods and strategies. As teachers have made such shifts they have taken up the notion of the central role of students in their EFL teaching. I have considered such shifts as part of providing the inspiration for students' enthusiasm for EFL learning. According to de Cremer (2002), being the object of concern by others is a form of being shown respect. Teachers' role shifts then indicates that students have been given a form of respect as part of the current EFL curriculum reform that has been absent in previous ones. It is a feature that Fullan (2007) has suggested, and it is one that has emerged from my investigations of the lived experience of the participants.

My research has made visible issues of students' enthusiasm as influencing teachers' enthusiasm for the reform as an unexpected research outcome discussed in Chapter 9, suggesting a sense of mutual respect as a feature of the current EFL curriculum reform. It is an issue that has received little attention from education scholars, suggesting a further feature of the significance of my research in its contribution to providing new knowledge to facilitate a further understanding of relationship between students and teachers in curriculum reform. I have identified student and teacher interaction as affecting teachers' lived experience, in particular as this relates to their professional development. This is an unexpected research outcome that has emerged from participant EFL teachers' descriptions of their lived experience.

The EFL curriculum as promoting both teachers' and students' enthusiasm suggests a sense of respect for each other that has emerged from the new approaches to EFL teaching and learning that forms part of the reform, a feature which is consistent with Fullan's (2007) description of the third of ten elements of successful change, which is "the key to people's feelings and thus to their motivation" (p. 48). The current EFL curriculum reform highlights teachers' and students' roles in teaching and learning in EFL, suggesting a leap that directs both teachers and students away from traditional teaching and learning approaches. Such moves have indicated a sense of disrespect of previous curriculum designers for teachers and students in teaching and learning, but at the same time this has also posed dilemmas for them as they have been required to take up new roles with the implementation of the new curriculum.

It is an issue which raises others in relation to Reconstructionism, which recognizes both teachers and students as the people who have significant roles to play in building a better, more equitable society. It is a perspective that is based on respect for both teachers and students as far as a Reconstructionist approach to education is concerned. The new EFL curriculum intent, then, is consistent with both Reconstructionist perspectives and Fullan's (2007) view of successful change as being based on respect. As I have described in Chapter 9, students' and teachers' enthusiasm is inspired by considerately designed, well-prepared and feasible strategies in EFL teaching and learning.

In relation to these three features alone, it is possible to identify a Reconstructionist feature of the reform, as the overarching goal itself is framed in relation to the good of the country as a whole emerging out of the good of individual cohorts of students, as part of China's positioning itself in a globalizing world. Major points of difference in the current EFL curriculum reform are the details that have been worked out by various education authorities, organizations and individuals that have drawn upon existing research and knowledge in the economic, political, cultural, and education fields.

Fullan's (2007) suggested elements for success in implementing education change takes several steps further. He argues that education change, to be successful, needs to "ensure that the best people are working on the problem" (p. 44). The enormousness of the task of implementing such a reform as the EFL curriculum one under study across China has required EFL teachers to assume new roles and to adopt new pedagogical practices in Chinese secondary schools. In such ways, EFL teachers can be seen as being "the best people" in relation to EFL teaching and learning. To this end, an emphasis on teachers' professional development as an important feature of the reform has been raised, having been identified a distinguishing feature of it, which I have discussed in Chapter 6.

I have examined participant EFL teachers' experience in both Site A and Site B.

Site B teachers say that they have been provided with various professional development programs and opportunities and adequate resources for implementing the reform in their area. This sort of working environment has been created by the local government, and their school allows them to develop as far as those of examples of "the best people" in implementing the current EFL curriculum reform in that site is concerned. This has not been the case with teachers in Site A. That is not to say that the participant EFL teachers in Site A are not "the best people"; it is to say that those teachers in Site A do not receive the same sort of amount and quality of support from the schools and relevant government departments, who are to develop them as being "the best people", as that provided for teachers in Site B. Their descriptions of their experience indicate that "the right combination of strategies and support provided" by governments and their school (Fullan, 2007, p. 51), is more completely realized at one site than another, part of strategies designed to attract "the best people" to the reform. Differences in the two sites highlight problems in relation to getting "the best people" for education change, an important aspect of the success or otherwise of the current EFL curriculum reform, for as Fullan (2007) argues, "Motivated people get better at their work" (p. 52).

Fullan's (2007) description of "the best people" is reminiscent of the ideals of Reconstructionist aims for the betterment of a society, which imply better people as well as better institutions and organizations. The current EFL curriculum reform is, then, consistent with both Fullan's (2007) perspective of this element of "best people" in relation to successful change as well as with the perspective of Reconstructionism in that respect. An emphasis on teachers' professional development aims to produce "the best people", not more people to implement this reform as another element for successful change.

Social considerations form Fullan's (2007) fifth element in his list of ten items, with educators wanting education change being advised to, "Recognize that all successful strategies are socially based and action oriented—change by doing rather than change by elaborate planning" (p. 44). The central government, and more specifically, Liaoning Provincial Government, commissioned a team of experts to travel the province and consult major stakeholders in the implementation of the EFL curriculum reform (see Chapter 9). "Elaborate planning" has been one the hallmarks of this reform, as shown by the very fact as such a team discussed in Chapter 9.

In spite of such planning, the desired results have not been achieved in relation to an even and equitable development of EFL competence in students across the province. Less developed areas, such as those in Site A, report that the policies are being implemented, but only with limited success because of the imbalance in resources available for them. Lack of adequate teaching facilities has emerged in my research as a salient issue which needs to be negotiated by participant EFL teachers in Site A as they implement this major reform. These teachers have found it difficult to achieve the goals of the reform while they lack modern teaching facilities, something which they consider to be an added burden to their professional lives. It is a problem to be taken up by political and bureaucratic stakeholders in EFL teaching and learning, this needs for implementing strategies to change this inequitable situation if there are to be the sorts of success required in further implementing the reform.

Participant EFL teachers' descriptions of their experience also suggest that they expect a specific series of EFL textbooks designed for teachers and students in regions such as their own, which may be described as less developed or remote. Teachers' descriptions of their lived experience in Site A stress that the current series of EFL textbooks are not applicable to the EFL teaching and learning needs of their students in their regions. They lack textbooks designed with the needs of their students in mind. Participant EFL teachers' descriptions of their experience reflect the sorts of Reconstructionists aims which highlight education as being linked with social systems, and where teachers as educators are encouraged to take up the role of improving their own education system through their interaction with this society (Ozmon & Craver, 2008). I have discussed this in some detail in Chapter 4 in relation to issues raised by teachers in Site A. These teachers' descriptions of their experience identify the lack of textbooks designed for their students as an integral of issue of "elaborate planning" in the new curriculum reform, but they have not had the benefit of "action oriented" support for that planning, recalling Fullan's (2007) view of acknowledging successful strategies as being "socially based", and "action oriented" in his list of elements of successful change (p. 44). EFL teachers have expressed their own attitudes to the reform implemented, making it clear that there are problems to be engaged, and doing so with no suggestion of any restraint or otherwise as they do this. It is not an issue for them. They are neither urged to nor discouraged from making their views known. What is more, these views may be drawn upon by governments to improve this reform further. Participant EFL teachers' descriptions of their experience show the significance of Fullan's (2007) item of "socially based" and "action oriented" strategies (p. 44) on the list of elements of successful change.

I have discussed teachers' concerns regarding a new assessment system as part of the reform under study in detail in Chapter 6. Participant EFL teachers' descriptions of their experience indicate that EFL teaching and learning in their areas is still predominantly influenced by examination-oriented education, particularly in Site A. Their experience suggests that a thorough reform of the assessment system has not occurred in their regions, something which EFL teachers have considered a key factor influencing their implementing the reform. It is an issue to be addressed by EFL teachers and other stakeholders in Northeast China, particularly in those regions such as Site A. These are issues raised mainly by teachers in Site A, and do not figure as prominently in Site B. Teachers in Site B suggest that "elaborate planning" for the reform under study has achieved its desired effect in their area by being supported by "action oriented" strategies, which is consistent with this item on Fullan's list of elements of successful change.

Participant EFL teachers' descriptions of their experience in both Sites A and B indicate an issue of concern in relation to a Reconstructionist issue of inequality being the very thing that is to be eradicated through an education system or program. This reform is consistent with Reconstructionist perspectives that focus on change as occurring socially and culturally, with reformers seeking solutions to existing social problems through education, which I have discussed in Chapter 4. This feature of a Reconstructionist view suggests that "action oriented" strategies occur within a social world, influenced by a social culture. This is consistent with Fullan's (2007) view of "socially based" and "action oriented" as one of the elements of successful change. EFL teachers and the other stakeholders are expected to take up such issues in their further implementing the reform under study, and I have considered these issues as having implications for further research.

The reform under study has been initiated and implemented on the basis of "elaborate planning" and "doing" (Fullan, 2007, p. 44). I have discussed "elaborate planning" in the new EFL curriculum intent and its features in Chapter 6, and "doing" in examining participant EFL teachers' descriptions of their experience of implementing the reform in subsequent chapters. I have considered that this reform suggests the substance of Fullan's (2007) fifth element of successful change, by "doing" as well as "elaborate planning" (p. 44).

I have examined some of the problems which participant EFL teachers say that they have faced in their implementation of the new EFL curriculum, and may continue to face as the reform is further rolled out across the country. I have considered that stakeholders have not yet given the sorts of fine and detailed consideration to such issues which teachers will be expected to engage further in implementing the reform. I have identified these issues as "initial problems" suggested by Fullan (2007), who argues that education reformers are to "assume that lack of capacity is the initial problem and then work on it continuously" (p. 44). My research has then suggested an area for further scholarly research regarding EFL curriculum reform and associated teaching and learning in China.

Participant EFL teachers' descriptions of their experience indicate that the professional development provided for them to implement the reform successfully has been overlooked in Site A. This is an issue that has presented in what they have described as being inadequate pre-service and professional development programs. Policy and curriculum documents have articulated a particular need for teachers' professional development training programs to strengthen particular groups of EFL teachers' grasp of the reform, especially in less developed or remote regions in China, such as in Northeast China. The programs have been described as being required to address EFL teachers' knowledge bases. This is the case particularly in relation to subject-matter knowledge in new approaches to EFL pedagogy, so that teachers may obtain a deeper understanding of the meaning of the reform they are to implement. Such professional development program delivery would tend towards the promotion of equity between rural and urban areas, assisting EFL teachers in successfully implementing the reform. This is part of participant EFL teachers' descriptions of their lived experience of being charged with implementing the reform, and this is still to be negotiated by them.

As far as a Reconstructionist perspective is concerned, a lack of focus on teachers' professional development has the potential to work in negative ways in relation to advancing the English language competencies of students. Policy statements and curriculum documents specify the skills to be developed in students, and the strategies to be employed by teachers, but the ways in which they have been grounded in their profession means that much still needs to be done, particularly in relation to teachers in Site A. In this case, ensuring that adequate professional development is implemented is "the initial problem" requiring attention and to be worked on constantly. Participant EFL teachers' descriptions of their experience suggest the importance of this sixth item on Fullan's (2007) list in determining the success or otherwise of the reform under study.

The current EFL curriculum reform has allowed a public acknowledgement of "lack of capacity" in implementing the reform. It has instigated a pilot set of processes which have been expected to identify and deal with issues in relation to "lack of capacity" which would be addressed as EFL curriculum implementation proceeded. I have discussed such issues in Chapter 6.

According to Fullan (2007), an emphasis on leadership is necessary when starting an education reform, particularly in response to poor engagement by students in education programs. He suggests that education leaders need to "stay the course through continuity of good direction by leverage leadership", arguing that they are to address "developing the leadership of others in the organization in the interests of continuity and deepening of good direction" (p. 59). This is Fullan's (2007) seventh element on the list.

The current EFL curriculum reform has given attention to principals' professional competence and expertise, which I have discussed in Chapter 9. Principals are expected to translate policy statements and curriculum documents into assisting EFL teachers in EFL curriculum implementation. Participant EFL teachers' descriptions of their experience in Site B exhibit a positive sense of the principal's role in that site. The negative feature of the lack of principals' expertise emerged from teachers' descriptions of their experience in Site A is an unexpected outcome of my research. This outcome suggests that it is an influential factor in need of address because it has had negative affects on participant EFL teachers' efforts on implementing the reform. My review of the literature has indicated scholars' foci on the role of competent principals in education reform in taking up challenges and complexities involved. The literature shows an inattention to aspects of negative influences that principals' lack of expertise may have on teachers' efforts in the implementing reform. I have then urged that such issues be highlighted and investigated further in the Chinese context, in Northeast China in particular.

A Reconstructionist focus on education reform emphasizes the role of schools in effecting wider social change. It is a perspective that is consistent with at least one strategy of the EFL curriculum reform, that of decentralization, where national, local and school level leadership is required to engage successfully in new curriculum implementation (Ministry of Education, 2001d). The new EFL curriculum reform engages not only the leadership of the central government, but also that of the leadership at provincial, local and school levels as part of a new focus on decentralization, discussed above and in Chapter 9. The EFL curriculum reform further suggests another insight of Fullan's (2007) seventh element in his list of successful change in relation to "leveraging leadership" (p. 44).

Fullan's (2007) eighth element in successful change is to "build internal accountability linked to external accountability" (p. 44), allowing public scrutiny of education change. My research has gone some way towards dealing with this aspect of Fullan's suggested elements of successful change. To begin with, I have taken up implications of issues of glocalization in relation to distinct local features in the context of globalization, as is the case with the different responses to policies in relation to the reform under study in China in general and in Northeast China in particular. My research confirms Hu's (2007) suggestion, "Given China's immense regional economic, social, and educational disparities, studies still need to be conducted on policy implementation in different provinces and regions" (p. 374). I have argued that it is with such public scrutiny and professional conversations between educators and education stakeholders, and public debates on such issues as they are played out in schools, that the EFL curriculum reform has an increased chance of success.

In the context of one child policy in today's China, parents' expectations and their efforts in relation to their children's EFL learning, which is tied to their concern about EFL teaching, stem from China's competitive learning contexts in China, expressed in its public examinations system. Parents' expectations for their children have given EFL teachers' indirect support but also pressure, which have played an influential role in teachers' implementation of the reform. These have emerged from teachers' descriptions of their experience, particularly from those in Site B. From a Reconstructionist perspective, parents' expectations for their children are manifested not in individual behaviors, but in community-oriented promotion of social benefit. EFL teachers' descriptions of their experience have included their responses to perceived expectations by parents. I have taken this up as an influential factor to be negotiated by teachers as it has emerged from participant EFL teachers' descriptions of their experience discussed in Chapter 9. I have considered that parents' expectations that have developed out of China's one child policy have generated tensions which EFL teachers have experienced and had to deal with as part of their professional lives, between support on one hand and pressure on the other, in implementing the reform under study.

Fullan (2007) suggests that education reformers need to "establish conditions for evolution for positive pressure" (p. 60) to ensure successful education change. Participant EFL teachers, particularly those in Site B, have described other stakeholders' support as being represented by their students' enthusiasm, parents' expectations, understanding and support, their principals' expertise, and governments' strategies. Such factors combined have created an appropriate environment for participant EFL teachers in Site B to implement the reform actively, "taking all the excuses off the table" as suggested by Fullan (2007, p. 61).

A number of participant EFL teachers in Site A report a different experience, represented in students' low achievement levels, a lack of adequate facilities, a lack of relevant textbooks, an examination-oriented education, and inadequate professional development. Such are the issues that EFL teachers in Site A have faced, and continue to face, in their implementing the reform, suggesting that governments in Site A have not been successful in establishing appropriate conditions for these teachers. I have, then, suggested that relevant governments take these issues into consideration for further curriculum implementation. It may be that if this is done, positive pressure "may be irresistible", as Fullan suggests (p. 61), as has already occurred in Site B, and may be anticipated to continue to occur, as discussed in Chapter 9. Such consideration is consistent with Reconstructionist perspectives of constant improvement and development in order to achieve growth and the best possible conditions for social improvement. Participant EFL teachers' descriptions of their experience indicate that they have felt a sense of positive pressure when being provided with an appropriate teaching and learning environment (see Chapter 9). The EFL curriculum reform has turned to concerns about individuals and individuals' personal development, something which has generated a positive pressure on teachers as they go about their professional duties. This in itself is consistent with the ninth item on Fullan's (2007) list which deals with this sort of positive pressure.

The implications of my research are consistent with Fullan's (2007) tenth element of successful change: "Use the previous nine strategies to build public confidence" (p. 44). My argument is that a successful reconstruction of EFL curriculum in China will be based on careful attention to fine-grained details such as those that have emerged from my research, where a detailed examination of two sites has highlighted differences between schools that emerge when such fine details are engaged. The broad brush strokes of central policy-making provide a general picture of issues dealt with in general ways. Details of implementation at classroom levels provide indicators of the strength of policy in generating reform, or not.

My research contributes to education research in general as I have undertaken an empirical study of salient issues in relation to the reform under study. I have arrived at the end of writing this book, at which point I would like to use a quote from one participant EFL teacher' description of her experience. Her comments on the reform under study further confirm my understanding of that reform:

> To be honest, in fact, as a classroom teacher, I think the new EFL curriculum reform can be recognized as a great leap and has achieved more and more substantial results (Ju).

Bibliography

Abdalla, A. -S. Y. (2005). The significance of incorporating language skills into EFL syllabus. Retrieved 6 April, 2009, from http://docs. ksu. edu. sa/KSU_AFCs/74597/Significance%20of%20Skills. pdf.

Adair-Hauck, B. , Willingham-McLain, L. , & Youngs, B. E. (1999). Evaluating the integration of technology and second language learning. CALICO Journal, 17(2): 269-306. https://72. 167. 96. 97/html/article_509. pdf.

Adamson, B. (1995). The "Four Modernizations" programme in China and English language teacher education: a case study. A Journal of Comparative Education, 25(3): 197-211. http://www. informaworld. com/smpp/content ~ content = a746395805 ~ db = all.

Adamson, B. (2001). English with Chinese characteristics: China's new curriculum. Asia Pacific Journal of Education, 21(2): 19-33. http://her. oxfordjournals. org/cgi/reprint/21/2/175.

Adamson, B. (2004). China's English: a history of English in Chinese education. Hong Kong: Hong Kong University Press.

Adamson, B. , Bolton, K. , Lam, A. , & Tong, Q. S. (2002). English in China: A preliminary bibliography. World Englishes, 21(2): 349. PDF Available http://content. epnet. com/ContentServer. asp? T = P&P = AN&K = 7122938&E bscoContent = dGJyMNHr7ESeqLQ4v% 2BvlOLCmrk% 2Bepq5Ss6u4TbC WxWXS& ContentCustomer = dGJyMPPk547g1% 2BqEuePfgeyx% 2BEu3 q64A&D = aph.

Adamson, B. , & Davison, C. (2003). Innovation in English language teaching in Hong Kong primary schools: one step forward, two steps sideways. Prospect, 18(1): 27-41.

Adamson, B. , & Morris, p. (1997). Focus on curriculum change in China and Hong Kong: the English curriculum in the People's Republic of China.

Comparative Education Review, 41(1): 3-26.

Adamson, B., & Morris, P. (2007). Comparing curricula. In B. Mark, A. Bob & M. Mark (Eds.), Comparative education research. Approaches and methods (pp. 263-282). Hong Kong: Comparative Education Research Centre and Springer.

Aguinaldo, J. P. (2004). Rethinking validity in qualitative research from a social constructionist perspective: from "Is this valid research?" to "What is this research valid for?" The Qualitative Report, 9(1): 127-136.

Ahern, K. J. (1999). Ten tips for reflexive bracketing. Qualitative Health Research, 9(3): 407-411. http://qhr. sagepub. com/cgi/reprint/9/3/407.

Altman, D. (1999). Globalization, political economy, and HIV/AIDS. Theory & Society, 28(4): 559.

Anfara, V. J., Brown, K., & Mangione, T. (2002). Qualitative analysis on stage: Making the research process more public. Educational Researcher, 31 (7): 28-38. http://edr. sagepub. com/cgi/reprint/31/7/28.

Angus, L. (2004). Globalization and educational change: bringing about the reshaping and re-norming of practice. Journal of Education Policy, 19(1): 23-41.

Ansari, W. E., & Weiss, E. S. (2006). Quality of research on community partnerships: Developing the evidence base. Health Education Research, 21(2): 175-180. http://her. oxfordjournals. org/cgi/reprint/21/2/175.

Anthony, T., & Kritsonis, W. (2006). National outlook: an epistemological approach to educational philosophy. Retrieved 2 March, 2008, from http:// dept. lamar. edu/lustudentjnl/EJSR% 20VOL. % 203% 20MANUSCRIP TS (PVAMU%20Cohort%20II)/National_Outlook_An_Epistemological_A pproach _to_Educational_Philosophy. pdf.

Antón, M. (2002). The discourse of a learner-centered classroom: sociocultural perspectives on teacher-learner interaction in the second-language classroom. The Modern Language Journal, 83(3): 303-318. http://www3. interscience. wiley. com/cgi-bin/fulltext/119072799/PDFSTA RT.

Appel, G., & Lantolf, J. (1994). Speaking as mediation: A study of L1 and L2 text recall tasks. The Modern Language Journal, 78(4): 437-452.

Armstrong, D. G. (2005). Teaching today: an introduction to education (7th ed.). New Jesey: Pearson Education, Inc.

Asia Society Business Roundtable Council of Chief State School Officers. (2005). Education in China: lessons for U. S. educators. Retrieved 7 October, 2007. from http://www. ecs. org/html/offsite. asp? document = http%3A%2F% 2Fwww%2 Einternationaled% 2Eorg% 2Fpublications% 2FChinaDelegation Report1201 05b%2Epdf.

Atkinson, D. (2002). Toward a sociocognitive approach to second language acquisition. The Modern Language Journal, 86(4): 525-545.

Auger, W. E., & Rich, S. J. (2007). Curriculum theory and methods: Perspectives on learning and teaching. Toronto: J. Wiley & Sons Canada.

Babbie, E. R. (2008). The basics of social research (4th ed.). Belmont, CA; Australia: Thomson/Wadsworth.

Baiasu, R. (2007). Being and time and the problem of space. Research in Phenomenology, 37(3): 324-356. http://web. ebscohost. com/ehost/pdf? vid = 2&hid = 17&sid = 741829b6-922b46e7-ac78-555829dd6a1e%40sessionmgr7.

Barkway, P. (2001). Michael Crotty and nursing phenomenology: Criticism or critique? Nursing Inquiry, 8(3): 191-195. http://www. blackwell-synergy. com/doi/pdf/10. 1046/j. 1320-7881. 2001. 00104. x.

Barnacle, R. (2004). Reflection on lived experience in education research. Educational Philosophy and Theory, 36(1): 57-67.

Bartelson, J. (2000). Three concepts of globalization. International Sociology, 15 (2): 180-196.

Bednall, J. (2006). Epoche and bracketing within the phenomenological paradigm. Issues in Educational Research, 16(2): 123-138. http://search. informit. com. au/fullText; dn = 155029; res = AEIPT.

Behar, L. S. (1994). The knowledge base of curriculum: an empirical analysis. Lanham [Md.]: University Press of America.

Bell, J. (1993). Doing your research project: a guide for first-time researchers in education and social science (2nd ed.). Buckingham: Open University Press.

Beneria, L. (1981). Conceptualizing the labor force: the underestimation of women's economic activities. Journal of Development Studies, 17(3): 10-28. http://web. ebscohost. com/ehost/detail? vid = 1&hid = 101&sid = 6fb802e2-5145-4d28-8845-9b99c86cb80b%40sessionmgr102&bdata =JnNpdGU9ZWhvc3Qtb Gl2ZQ%3d% 3d#db = aph&AN = 7140411#db = aph&AN = 7140411#db = aph&AN = 7140411.

Benner, P. (1994). The tradition and skill of interpretive phenomenology in studying health, illness, and caring practices. In P. Benner (Ed.), Interpretive phenomenology: embodiment, caring, and ethics in health and illness (pp. 99-128). Thousand Oaks, Calif: Sage Publications.

Berns, M. (1990). Contexts of competence: social and cultural considerations in communicative language teaching. New York: Plenum Press.

Biggs, J. B. (1996). Western misperceptions of the Confucian-heritage learning culture. In D. A. Watkins & J. B. Biggs (Eds.), The Chinese learner: cultural, psychological, and contextual influences (pp. 45-68). Hong Kong. CERC.

Blaikie, N. (1993). Approaches to social enquiry. Cambridge [England]: Polity Press in association with Blackwell.

Blaikie, N. (2000). Designing social research. Cambridge: polity Press/Blackwell.

Block, D. (2004). Globalization and language teaching. ELT Journal, 58(1): 75-77.

Block, D., & Cameron, D. (Eds.). (2002). Globalization and language teaching. London and New York: Routledge.

Bloom, B. (2007). The search for methods of instruction. In A. C. Ornstein, E. F. Pajak & S. B. Ornstein (Eds.), Contemporary issues in curriculum (4th ed., pp. 228-244). Sydney: Peason/AandB.

Boss, M., 1903-. (1983). Existential foundations of medicine and psychology. New York: J. Aronson.

Bottery, M. (2006). Education and globalization: redefining the role of the educational professional. Educational Review, 58(1): 95-113. http://web.ebscohost. com/ehost/pdf? vid = 2&hid = 2&sid = 00b38167-9fb0-4 359-bfbd-c77e53f7f8ec%40sessionmgr4.

Bourdieu, P. (1977). Outline of a theory of practice (N. Richard, Trans.). Cambridge; New York: Cambridge University Press.

Boyle, J. (2000). Education for teachers of English in China. Journal of Education for Teaching: International Research, 26(2): 147-155. http://dx. doi. org/10. 1080/02607470050127063.

Bradbury, I. (2007). China and globalization. Geography, 92(2): 162-175.

Bradley, J. (1990). China: A new revolution? London: Aladdin Books.

Brady, L. (1995). Curriculum development (5th ed.). Sydney: Prentice Hall.

Brameld, T. (1950). Education for the emerging age. New York: Praeger.

Brameld, T. (1956). Toward a reconstructed philosophy of education. New York: Praeger.

Brameld, T. (1971). Patterns of educational philosophy: diversity and convergence in culturological perspective. New York: Holt, Rinehart and Winston.

Brameld, T. (1977). Reconstructionism as radical philosophy of education: A reappraisal. The Educational Forum, 42(1): 67-76.

Brandt, R. S. (2007). Goals and objectives. In A. C. Ornstein, E. F. Pajak & S. B. Ornstein (Eds.), Contemporary issues in curriculum. Boston: Pearson/AandB.

Bresler, L. (1995). Ethnography, phenomenology and action research in music education. Retrieved 3 May, 2008, from http://www. rider. edu/ ~ vrme/v8n1/vision/Bresler_Article_VRME. pdf

Brislin, R. (1993). Understanding culture's influence on behaviour. Orlando, FL: Harcourt Brace.

Brookhart, S. (2001). Successful students' formative and summative uses of assessment information. Assessment in Education: Principles, Policy and Practice, 81 (2): 153-169.

Brough, J. B. (2001). Temporality and illness: a phenomenological perspective. In S. K. Toombs (Ed.), Handbook of Phenomenology and medicine (pp. 29-46). Dordrecht; London: Kluwer Academic.

Bruner, J. (1983). Child's talk. New York: Oxford University Press.

Bruner, J. S., & Garton, A. F. (Eds.). (1978). Human growth and development: Wolfson College lectures, 1976. Oxford: Clarendon Press.

Brush, T., & Saye, J. (2000). Implementation and evaluation of a student-centred learning unit: A case study. Educational Technology Research and Development, 48 (3): 79-100. http://www. springerlink. com/content/74727047515n547k/fulltext. pdf.

Bruton, A. (2005a). Task-based language teaching: For the state secondary FL classroom? Language Learning Journal, 31(1): 55-68.

Bruton, A. (2005b). Task-based language teching: For the state secondary FL classroom? Language Learning Journal, 31(1): 55-68.

Bryman, A. (2001). Social research methods. Oxford; New York: Oxford University Press.

Budd, J. M. (2005). Phenomenology and information studies. Journal of documentation, 61(1): 45-59.

Burbules, N. C., & Torres, C. A. (2003). Globalization and education: an introduction. In J. Gilbert (Ed.), The RoutledgeFalmer reader in science education (pp. 15-22). London: RoutledgeFalmer.

Burnaby, B., & Sun, Y. (1989). Chinese teachers' views of western language teaching: context informs paradigms. TESOL Quarterly, 23(2): 219-238. http://dzibanche. biblos. uqroo. mx/hemeroteca/tesol_quartely/1967_2002_f ulltext/Vol_23_2. pdf#page=28.

Burns, R., 1939-. (1994). Introduction to research methods. Melbourn: Longman Cheshire.

Busch, M. (1993). Using Likert scales in L2 research. TESOL Quarterly, 27(4): 733-736.

Bush, T., Coleman, M., & Xi, X. (1998). Managing secondary schools in China. Compare: a Journal of Comparative Education, 28(2): 182-195.

Bush, T., & Qiang, H. (2002). Leadership and culture in Chinese education. In A. Walker & C. A. J. Dimmock (Eds.), School leadership and administration: Adopting a cultural perspective (pp. 173-185). New York: RoutledgeFalmer.

Bygate, M., Skehan, P., & Swain, M. (2001). Researching pedagogic tasks: second language learning, teaching and testing. London: Longman.

Byram, M. (1997). Cultural studies and foreign language teaching. In S. Bassnett (Ed.), Studying British cultures (2nd ed., pp. 56-67): Routledge.

Camenson, B. (2007). Opportunities in teaching English to speakers of other Languages. New York: McGraw Hill. http://books. google. com. au/books? hl= en&lr=&id=BcQnXE46UxIC&oi=f nd&pg=PP8&dq=overseas+experiences+ and+EFL+teaching&ots=K_1Nr PXmNG&sig=0i2etcCPA7iF_ocDN5JALwvzs MI#PPA1,M1.

Carless, D. (2007). The suitability of task-based approaches for secondary schools: Perspectives from Hong Kong. System, 35(4): 595-608.

Carnoy, M. (1999). Globalization and educational reform: what planners need to know. Paris: UNESCO: International Institute for Educational Planning. http://unesdoc. unesco. org/images/0012/001202/120274e. pdf.

Carnoy, M. (2000). Globalization and educational reform. In N. P. Stromquist &

K. Monkman (Eds.), Globalization and education (pp. 43-60). Lanham, Md.; Oxford: Rowman & Littlefield.

Carnoy, M., & Rhoten, D. (2002). What does globalization mean for educational change? A Comparative approach. Comparative Education Review, 46(1): 1-9.

Castells, M. (1996). The rise of the network society. Cambridge, MA: Blackwell Publishers.

Chan, S. (1999). The Chinese learner: A question of style. Education and Training, 41 (6/7): 294-305. http://www. emeraldinsight. com/Insight/ viewContentItem. do; jsessionid = 08 37105202F584ECE3D462D59697989D? contentType = Article&contentId = 837607.

Chang, J. (2006). Globalization and English in Chinese higher education. World Englishes, 25(3/4): 513-525. http://web. ebscohost. com/ehost/pdf? vid = 2&hid = 103&sid = 70c51117-066d-4394-8cff-ddee1c57899d%40sessionmgr 103.

Chang, Y. F. (2008). Parents' attitudes toward the English education policy in Taiwan. Asia Pacific Education Review, 9(4): 423-435. http://brj. asu. edu/ vol30_no1/art8. pdf.

Chase-Dunn, C. (1999). Globalization: A world-systems perspective. Retrieved 2 January, 2009, from http://scholar. google. com/scholar? hl = en&lr = &q = globalization%3A+A+w orld-systems+perspective&btnG = Search.

Chase-Dunn, C. K., & Babones, S. J. (2006). Global social change: historical and comparative perspectives. Baltimore: Johns Hopkins University Press.

Chen, H. (2006). The relationship between curriculum standards and syllabus. Retrieved 8 October, 2008, from http://group. hexun. com/gxictnetblog/ discussion. aspx? articleid = 1808343.

Chen, L., Wang, Q., & Cheng, X. (Eds.). (2002). Explanation of English Curriculum Standards. Beijing: Beijing Normal University Publishing House.

Chen, Y. (2003). My province has not been chosen for experiments accompanying the new curriculum reform in senior secondary schools spreading. Retrieved 5 June, 2008, from http://www. qzwb. com/gb/content/2003-12/02/content _ 1069041. htm.

Cheng, K. -m. (1998). Can education values be borrowed? Looking into cultural differences. Peabody Journal of Education, 73(2): 11-30.

Cheng, L., & Wang, H. (2004). Understanding professional challenges faced by Chinese teachers of English. TESL-EJ, 7(4).

Cheng, Y. C. (2004). Fostering local knowledge and human development in globalization of education. International Journal of Educational Management, 18 (1): 7-24. http://www. emeraldinsight. com/Insight/viewContentItem. do; jsessionid = 85 D6A59C379C3071CD35694ABF810B0C? contentType = Article& contentI d = 1509119.

China Daily Online. (2007). Chinese economy remains in "good shape". Retrieved 28 August, 2008, from http://news. xinhuanet. com/english/2007-07/28/ content_6441444. htm.

China Travel Guide. (2007). Liaoning Province. Retrieved 28 October, 2007, from http://www. travelchinaguide. com/cityguides/liaoning.

Chomsky, N. (1957). Syntactic structures. The Hague: Mouton.

Chomsky, N. (1969). The current scene in linguistics: present directions. In D. A. Reibel & S. A. Schane (Eds.), Modern Studies in English (pp. 3-12). Englewood Cliffs, N. j. : Prentice-hall.

Chomsky, N. (1986). Knowledge of language: its nature, origin and use. New York: Praeger.

Chow, G. C. (1993). Capital formation and economic growth in China. The Quarterly Journal of Economic, 108(3): 809-842.

Chu, Z. , & Li, X. (2007). Balanced development of compulsory education: Cornerstone of education equity. Front. Educ. China, 2(4): 469-493.

Cichowski, R. A. (1998). Integrating the environment: the European Court and the construction of supranational policy. Journal of European Public Policy, 5(3): 387-405. http://pdfserve. informaworld. com/979692 _ 751313631 _ 713773672. pdf.

Clahsen, H. , & Muysken, P. (1986). The availability of universal grammar to adult and child learners—a study of the acquisition of German word order. Second Language Research, 2 (2): 93-119. http://slr. sagepub. com/cgi/ reprint/2/2/93.

Clark, A. M. (1998). The qualitative-quantitative debate: Moving from pisitivism and confrontation to post-positivism. Journal of Advanced Nursing, 27 (6): 1242-1249. http://www3. interscience. wiley. com/cgi-bin/fulltext/119123191/ PDFSTA RT.

Cogan, J. J. (1998). Citizenship education for the 21st century: setting the context. In J. J. Cogan & R. Derricott (Eds.), Citizenship for the 21st century: an international perspective on education (pp. 1-20). London: Kogan Page.

Cohen, L., Manion, L., & Morrison, K. (2000). Research methods in education (5th ed.). New York: Routledge.

Cohn, T. H. (2005). Global political economy: theory and practice (3rd ed.). New York: Pearson Education Inc.

Colaizzi, P. F. (1978). Psychological research as the phenomenologist views it. In R. S. Valle & M. King (Eds.), Existential-phenomenological alternatives for psychology (pp. 48-71). New York: Oxford University Press.

Counts, G. S. (1934). The social foundations of education. New York: Chaeles Scribner's Sons.

Counts, G. S. (1978). Dare the school build a new social order? Carbondale: Southern Illinois University Press.

Cowan, J. R., Light, R. L., Mathews, B. E., & Tucker, G. R. (1979). English teaching in China: A recent survey. TESOL Quarterly, 13(4): 465-482. http://links. jstor. org/sici? sici = 0039-8322% 28197912% 2913% 3A4%3C465 %3AETICAR%3E2. 0. CO%3B2-J.

Creswell, J. W. (1994). Research design: qualitative and quantitative approaches. Thousand Oaks, London and New Delhi: SAGE Publications,

Creswell, J. W. (1998). Qualitative inquiry and research design: choosing among five traditions. Thousand Oaks, London and New Delhi: SAGE Publications.

Creswell, J. W. (2002). Educational research: planning, conducting, and evaluating quantitative and qualitative research. Upper Saddle River, N. J.: Merrill.

Creswell, J. W. (2007). Qualitative inquiry and research design: choosing among five approaches. Thousand Oaks: Sage Publications.

Creswell, J. W., & Miller, D. L. (2000). Determining validity in qualitative inquiry. Theory into practice summer 2000, 39(3): 124-129. http:// pdfserve. informaworld. com/374292_751313631_789375383. pdf.

Crookes, G. (1997). What influences what and how second and foreign language teach? The Modern Language Journal, 81(1): 67-79.

Crossley, M. (2000). Bridging cultures and traditions in the reconceptualisation of comparative and international education. Comparative Education, 36(3): 319-332.

Crotty, M. (1996). Phenomenology and nursing research. South Melbourne: Churchill Livingstone.

Crotty, M. (1998). The foundation of social research: meaning and perspective in the research process. St Leonards: Allen and Unwin.

Crystal. (2003). English as a global language. Cambridge: Cambridge University Press.

Crystal, D. (1997). English as a global language. Cambridge: Cambridge University Press.

Cuffaro, H. K. (1995). Experimenting with the world: John Dewey and the early childhood classroom. New York: Teachers College Press, Teachers College, Columbia University.

Cui, Y. (2005, 2005-10-10). Liaoning sheng kecheng gaige yu jianfu qingkuang diaoyan zhongbaogao (Research reports on an investigation of curriculum reform and reducing overburden in Liaoning Province). Retrieved 9 Spetember, 2008, from http://ywjy. cersp. com/kgzt/yiwu/200510/311. html.

Cutcliffe, J. R. (2003). Reconsidering reflexivity: introducing the case for intellectual entrepreneurship. Qualitative health research, 13 (1): 136-148. http://qhr. sagepub. com/cgi/reprint/13/1/136.

Danaher, T. , & Briod, M. (2005). Phenomenological approach to research with children. In G. Sheila & H. Diane (Eds.), Researching children's experience: Methods and approaches (pp. 217-235). London. Thousand Oaks, Calif. : SAGE.

Davies, D. , & Dodd, J. (2002). Qualitative research and the question of rigor. Qualitative Health Research, 12(2): 279-291. http://qhr. sagepub. com/cgi/reprint/12/2/279.

Day, C. (2000). Effective leadership and reflective practice. Reflective practice, 1 (113-127).

Decrop, A. (2004). Trustworthiness in qualitative tourism research. In J. Phillimore & L. Goodson (Eds.), Qualitative research in tourism: ontologies, epistemologies and methodologies (pp. 156-169). New York: Routledge.

Dello-Lacovo, B. (2009). Curriculum reform and "quality education" in China: an overview. International Journal of Education Development, 29(3): 241-249.

Demidenko, E. S. (2007). The Prospects of education in a changing world. Russian Education & Society, 49 (6): 84. PDF Available http://content.

epnet. com/ContentServer. asp? T = P&P = AN&K = 25481910& EbscoContent = dGJyMNHr7ESep7c4v% 2BvlOLCmrk% 2BeprBSsq24Ta6 WxWXS&Content Customer = dGJyMPPk547g1% 2BqEuePfgeyx% 2BEu3 q64A&D = tfh.

Denzin, N. K. (2009). The research act: a theoretical introduction to sociological methods (3rd ed.). New Brunswick, NJ: AldineTransaction. http://books. google. com. au/books? hl = en&lr = &id = UjcpxFEOT4cC&oi = fn d&pg = PA1&dq = The + research + act: + A +theoretical + introduction + to + socio logical + methods&ots = ToNx2eV-wj&sig = H3z6rhWJN3mzAdhv5LNMg1 BEHCc # PPA304, M1.

Denzin, N. K., & Lincoln, Y. S. (2000). The discipline and practice of qualitative research. In N. K. Denzin & Y. S. Lincoln (Eds.), Handbook of qualitative research (2nd ed., pp. 1-29). Thousand Oaks, London, New Delhi: Sage Publications, Inc.

Dewen, W., Cai, F., & Gao, W. (2007). Globalization and the shortage of rural workers: A macroeconomic perspective. In R. S. Ingrid Nielsen, Marika Vicziany (Ed.), Globalization and labour mobility in China (pp. 19-38). Clayton, Vic.: Monash University.

Dietrich, C. (1986). People's China. New York and Oxford: Oxford University.

Donato, R., & McCormick, D. (1994). A sociocultural perspective on language learning strategies: the role of mediation. The Modern Language Journal, 78 (4): 453-464.

Donato, R., & Mccormick, D. (1994). A sociocultural perspective on language learning strategies: the role of mediation. Modern Language Journal, 78(4): 453-464. http://web. ebscohost. com/ehost/pdf? vid = 2&hid = 101&sid = 740e8a7e-c7b6-4e1d-9d69-752117f79dae% 40sessionmgr108.

Dossani, R., & Kenney, M. (2007). The next wave of globalization: relocating service provision to India. World Development, 35(5): 772-791.

Dunleavy, P. (1994). The globalization of public services production: Can government be "best in world"? Public Policy and Administration, 9(2): 36-64.

Dunne, M., Pryor, J., & Yates, P. (2005). Becoming a researcher: a research companion for the social sciences. Maidenhead: Open University Press.

Durkheim, E. (2006). Education: Its nature and its role. In H. Lauder, P. Brown, J.-A. Dillabough & A. H. Halsey (Eds.), Education, globalization, and social change (pp. 76-87). Oxford; New York: Oxford University Press.

Economy, E. (2005). China's rise in Southeast Asia: implications for the United States. Journal of Contemporary China, 14(44): 409-425. PDF Available http://content. epnet. com/ContentServer. asp? T=P&P=AN&K=17394949& EbscoContent=dGJyMNLr40SeqK84v% 2BvlOLCmrk% 2Bep7dSs6q4S7 GWxWXS& ContentCustomer=dGJyMPPk547g1%2BqEuePfgeyx%2BEu3q64 A&D=aph.

Edwards, R. , & Usher, R. (2008). Globalisation and pedagogy: space, place and identity. London; New York: Routledge.

Eggenberger, S. K. (2007). Being family: the family expereince when an audult member is hospitalized with a critical illness. Journal of Clinical Nursing, 16 (9): 1618-1628.

Egri, C. , & Ralston, D. (2004). Generation cohorts and personal values: a comparison of China and the United States. Organization Science, 15(2): 210- 220. http://faculty-staff. ou. edu/R/David. A. Ralston-1/2. pdf.

Ehrich, L. C. (1999). Untangling the treads and coils of the web of phenomenology. Educational Research and Perspectives, 26(2): 19-43.

Ehrich, L. C. (2003). Phenomenology: The quest for meaning. In T. O' Donoghue & K. Punch (Eds.), Qualitative educational research in action: doing and reflecting (pp. 42-69). London and New York: Routledge Falmer.

Ellis, R. (2000). Task-based research and language pedagogy. Language Teaching Research, 4(3): 193-220. http://ltr. sagepub. com/cgi/reprint/4/3/193.

Enderwick, P. (2006). Globalization and labor. Philadelphia: Chelsea House Publishers.

Erlandson, D. A. , Harris, E. L. , & Skipper, B. L. (1993). Doing naturalistic inquiry: a guide to methods. Newbury Park, Calif. : Sage.

Ezzy, D. (2006). The research process. In M. Walter (Ed.), Social research methods: an Australian perspective (pp. 29-52). South Melbourne: Oxford University Press.

Farmer, T. , Robinson, K. , Elliott, S. J. , & Eyles, J. (2006). Developing and implementing a triangulation protocol for qualitative health research. Qualitative health research, 16(3): 377-394. http://qhr. sagepub. com/cgi/reprint/16/ 3/377.

Fernández, M. , Wegerif, R. , Mercer, N. , & Rojas-Drummond, S. (2001). Re- conceptualizing "Scaffolding" and the Zone of Proximal Development in the context of yymmetrical collaborative learning. Journal of Classroom Interaction,

36(2): 40-54. http://www. dialogbox. org. uk/Rupert_Wegerif/rwpapers/JCI2_Fernandez. p df.

Ferrari, M. D. , & Sternberg, R. J. (1998). Self-awareness: its nature and developmentSelf-awareness. New York: Guilford Press. http://books. google. com. au/books? hl = en&lr = &id = JANokq-wOcsC&oi = fn d&pg = PA1&dq = self-awareness + in + education&ots = taQk1P3xl2&sig = LSXCgOtjSDA3SPrpcQ dcmxr4QV4#PPA13, M1.

Figueroa, P. (2004). Diversity and citizenship education in England. In J. A. Banks (Ed.), Diversity and citizenship education (pp. 219-244). San Francisco, Calif. : Jossey-Bass.

Finnegan, R. (2006). Using documents. In R. Sapsford & V. Jupp (Eds.), Data collection and analysis (pp. 138-153). London; Thousand Oaks, Calif: SAGE Publications in association with The Open University.

Fisherman, B. J. , Marx, R. W. , Stephen Best, & Tal, R. T. (2003). Linking teacher and student learning to improve professional development in systemic reform. Teaching and Teacher Education, 19 (6): 643-658. http://www. sciencedirect. com/science? _ob = MImg&_imagekey = B6VD8-4 983VRX-8-C&_cdi = 5976& _ user = 2307635& _ orig = search& _ coverDate = 0 8% 2F31% 2F2003& _ sk = 999809993&view = c&wchp = dGLbVlz-zSkWA& md5 = 8d82f85b3e0b5b122fa70e35a672a411&ie = /sdarticle. pdf.

Flyvbjerg, B. (2006). Five misunderstandings about case-study research. Qualitative Inquiry, 12(2): 219-245. http://qix. sagepub. com/cgi/reprint/12/2/219.

Fong, E. (2009). English in China: some thoughts after the Beijing Olympics. English Today, 25 (1): 44-49. http://journals. cambridge. org/action/displayFulltext? type = 1&fid = 4614528 &jid = ENG&volumeId = 25&issueId = 01&aid = 4614524.

Foster, J. (1999). Key concepts in ELT. ELT Journal, 53(1): 69-70. http://eltj. oxfordjournals. org//cgi/reprint/53/1/69.

Fotos, S. , & Ellis, R. (1991). Communicating about grammar: a task-based approach. TESOL Quarterly, 25(4): 605-628.

Fradd, S. H. , & Lee, O. (1998). Development of a knowledge base for ESOL teacher education. Teaching and Teacher Education, 14(7): 761-773.

Freeman, D. (2002). The hidden side of the work: teacher knowledge and learning to teach. A perspective from North American educational research on teacher education in English language teaching. Language Teaching, 35: 1-13.

Fullan, M. (2000). The Return of Large-Scale Reform. Journal of Educational Change, 1: 5-28. http://www. springerlink. com/content/hg346065u2031k70/fulltext. pdf.

Fullan, M. (2001). The new meaning of educational change. New York: Teachers College Press.

Fullan, M. (2003). The moral imperative of school leadership. Thousand Oaks, Calif. : Corwin Press. http://books. google. com. au/books? hl = en&lr = &id = f7LCIVDCFIUC&oi = f nd&pg = PR9&dq = the + role + of + principals + in + curriculum + reform + m-fulla n&ots = olSJ6fEv67&sig = y2H7RLHXgEQDModSVGRCDF6r9aQ#PPA5, M1.

Fullan, M. (2007). The new meaning of educational change (4th ed.). New York; London: Teachers College, Colubia University.

Fullan, M. , & Hargreaves, A. (1992). Teacher development and educational change. In M. Fullan & A. Hargreaves (Eds.), Teacher development and educational change (pp. 1-9). London; New York: Routledge.

Furlong, J. (2005). New Labour and teacher education: the end of an era. Oxford Review of Education, 31 (1): 119-134. http://web. ebscohost. com/ehost/pdf? vid = 2&hid = 103&sid = 896e4570-d50d-4ae4-a397-06d05eb970dd% 40 sessionmgr104.

Garrett, B. (2001). China face, debates, the contradictions of globalization. Asian Survey, 41(3): 409-427.

Gasson, S. (2004). Rigor in grounded theory research: an interpretive perspective on generating theory from qualitative field studies. In M. E. Whitman & A. B. Woszczynski (Eds.), The handbook of information systems research (pp. 79-102). Hershey, PA: Idea Group Pub. 4.

Gearing, R. E. (2004). Bracketing in research: a Typology. Qualitative Health Research, 14(10): 1429-1452. http://qhr. sagepub. com/cgi/reprint/14/10/1429.

George, A. L. (2006). Case studies and theory development in the social sciences. Cambridge, Mass. : MIT Press.

Giddens, A. (1990). The consequences of modernity. Stanford, Calif: Stanford University Press.

Gil, J. A. (2005). English in China: the impact of the global language on China's language situation. Griffith University, Griffith, Australia.

Giorgi, A. (2000). Concerning the application of phenomenology to caring research. Caring Science, 14(1): 11-15. ncbi. nlm. nih. gov.

Giulianotti, R., & Robertson, R. (2006). Glocalization, globalization and migration. International Sociology, 21(2): 171-198.

Giulianotti, R., & Robertson, R. (2007). Forms of glocalization. Sociology, 41(1): 133-152.

Glicksberg, C. I. (1944). Some considerations in postwar educational reconstruction. The School Review, 52(21): 299-306.

Golafshani, N. (2003). Understanding reliability and validity in qualitative. The Qualitative Report, 8(4): 597-607. http://www. nova. edu/ssss/QR/QR8-4/golafshani. pdf.

Goodman, Y. M., & Goodman, K. S. (1990). Vogosky in a whole-language perspective. In L. C. Moll (Ed.), Vygosky and education: instructional implications and applicatiopns of sociohistorical psychology. Cambridge; New York: Cambridge University Press, 1990.

Goodson, I. F., & Cole, A. L. (1994). Exploring the teacher's professional knowledge: Constructing identity and community. Teacher Education Quarterly, 21(1): 85-105.

Gordon, H. R. D., & Yocke, R. (1999). Relationship between personality characteristics and observable teaching effectiveness of selected beginning career and technical education teachers. Journal of Vocational and Technical Education, 16(1): 47-66.

Goulding, C. (2005). Grounded theory, ethnography and phenomenology: a comparative panalysus of three qualitative strategies for marketing reseach. European Journal of Marketing, 39(3/4): 294-308.

Grant, R. (2008). A phenomenological case study of a lecturer's understanding of himself as an assessor. Indo-Pacific Journal of Phenomenology, 8 (Spefical Edition), 1-10. http://www. ipjp. org/issues/sep2008special/Special_Edition _Education-01_Grant. pdf.

Graue, E. M., & Walsh, D. J. (1995). Children in context: interpreting here and now of children's lives. In J. A. Hatch (Ed.), Qualitative research in early childhood settings (pp. 135-154). Westport, Conn. : Praeger.

Grbich, C. (2007). Qualitative data analysis: an introduction. London: SAGE.

Green, A. (1999). Education and globalization in Europe and East Asia: Convergent and divergent trends. Journal of Education Policy, 14(1): 55-71. PDF Available http://content. epnet. com/ContentServer. asp? T = P&P = AN&K = 3818761&E bscoContent = dGJyMNHr7ESep7c4v% 2BvlOLCmrk% 2BeqK5Ssae4TK% 2BWxWXS&ContentCustomer = dGJyMPPk547g1% 2BqEue Pfgeyx% 2BE u3q64A&D = aph.

Green, B. (2003). Curriculum inquiry in Australia: toward a local genealogy of the curriculum field. In W. F. Pinar (Ed.), International handbook of curriculum research (pp. 123-142). Mahwah, N. J. : L. Erlbaum Associates.

Grin, F. (2003). English as economic value: facts and fallacies. World Englishes, 20(1): 65-78. http://www3. interscience. wiley. com/cgi-bin/fulltext/119023 984/PDFSTART.

Groenewald, T. (2004). A phenomenological research design illustrated. International Journal of Qualitative Methods, 3(1): 1-26.

Grove, C. (1999). Focusing on form in the communicative classroom: an output-centred model of instruction for oral skills development. Hispania, 82(4): 817-829.

Guan, J. , Ron. , M. , & Xiang, P. (2005). Chinese teachers' attitudes toward teaching physical activity and fitness. Asia Pacific Journal of Teacher Education, 33(2): 147-157.

Guan, Q. , & Meng, W. (2007). China's new national curriculum reform: innovation, challenges and strategies. Front. Educ. China, 2(4): 579-604.

Gwele, N. (2005a). Education philosophy and the curriculum. In L. R. Uys & N. S. Gwele (Eds.), Curriculum development in nursing: process and innovations (pp. 1-20). London, New York: Routledge.

Gwele, N. (2005b). Implementing a new curriculum. In L. R. Uys & N. S. Gwele (Eds.), Currculum development in nursing process and innovation (pp. 93-110). London; New York: Routledge.

Habibis. (2006). Ethics and social research. In M. Walter (Ed.), Social research methods: an Australian perspective (pp. 53-82). South Melbourne: Oxford University Press.

Hale, D. D. , & Hale, L. H. (2008). Reconsidering revaluation. Foreign Affairs, 87 (1): 57-66. http://web. ebscohost. com/ehost/detail? vid = 2&hid =

103&sid = ec42210a-64 d2-4ec5-947b-c631818ba796%40sessionmgr104&bdata = JnNpdGU9ZWh vc3QtbGl2ZQ%3d%3d.

Hall, S. (1986). Gramsci's relevance for the study of race and ethnicity. Journal of Communication Inquiry, 10: 5-27.

Hamel, J., Dufour, S., & Fortin, D. (1993). Case study methods. Newbury Park: Sage Publications.

Han, H. (2008). A study of Chinese college English teachers in China: Their beliefs and conceptual change. Unpublished PhD, Queen's University, Kinston, Ontario.

Hannum, E., & Part, A. (2002). Educating China's rural children in the 21st century, 05-05-09, from http://www. economics. ox. ac. uk/members/albert. park/papers/harvard. pdf.

Hanushek, E. A., & Kimko, D. D. (2000). Schooling, labor-force quality, and the growth of nations. The American Economic Review, 90(5): 1184-1208. http://veja. abril. com. br/gustavo_ioschpe/arquivos_270908/Hanushek%20a nd%20Kimko%202000%20-%20schooling,%20labor%20force%20quality %20and. pdf.

Hargreaves, A. (1997). Rethinking educational change. In M. Fullan (Ed.), The challenge of school change: a collection of articles (pp. 3-25). Melbourne: Hawker Brownlow.

Harris, J., & Chou, Y. -C. (2001). Globalization or glocalization? Community care in Taiwan and Britain. European Journal of Social Work, 4(2): 161-172.

Harris, R., Leung, C., & Rampton, B. (2002). Globalization, diaspora and language education in England. In D. Block & D. Cameron (Eds.), Globalization and language teaching (pp. 29-47). London and New York: Routledge.

Hartley, J. (2004). Case study research. In C. Cassell & G. Symon (Eds.), Essential guide to qualitative methods in organizational research (pp. 323-333). London; Thousans Oaks: SAGE Publications.

Hawkins, E. W. (1999). Foreign language study and language awareness. Language Awareness, 8(3&4): 124-142.

Hawkins, J. N. (2000). Centralization, decentralization, recentralization: Educational reform in China. Journal of Educational Administration, 38(5): 442-455. http://www. emeraldinsight. com/Insight/viewPDF. jsp? contentType = Article

&Filename = html/Output/Published/EmeraldFullTextArticle/Pdf/0740380503. pdf.

He, Q. (2002). English language education in China. Retrieved 3 March, 2008, from http://www. uwm. edu/People/noonan/402/He. China. pdf.

Heidegger, M. (1988). The basic problems of phenomenology. Bloomington: Indiana University Press.

Held, D. (1995). Democracy and the global order: from the modern state to cosmopolitan governance. Cambridge: Polity Press.

Held, D., Anthony, M., Goldblatt, D., & Jonathan, P. (1999). Global Transformations: Politics, Economics and Culture. Stanford, CA: Stanford University Press.

Held, D., & McGrew, A. (2002). Globalization/anti-globalization. Malden, MA: Blackwell Publishers.

Henry, M., Lingard, B., Rizvi, F., & Taylor, S. (1999). Working with/against globalization in education. Journal of Education Policy, 14(1): 85-97. PDF Available http://content. epnet. com/ContentServer. asp? T = P&P = AN&K = 3818759&E bscoContent = dGJyMMvl7ESeqK44v% 2BvlOLCmrk% 2Bep7 ZSsqa4TLSWxWXS&ContentCustomer = dGJyMPPk547g1% 2BqEuePfgeyx% 2BEu3 q64A&D = tfh.

Henson, K. T. (2001). Curriculum planning: integrating multiculturalism, constructivism, and education reform. Dubuque, IA: McGraw-Hill.

Herschensohn, J. (1990). Toward a theoretical basis for current language pedagogy. The Modern Language Journal, 74(4): 451-458. http://www. jstor. org/view/00267902/ap020537/02a00050/0.

Hewitt, T. W. (2006). Understanding and shaping curriculum: what we teach and why? Thousand Oaks, Calif. ; London: SAGE.

Higgs, J. (2003). Interpretive research to complement experiential practices in professional knowledge development. Paper presented at the Qualitative Research as Interpretive Practice Conference, Charles Sturt University.

Ho, S. -c., & Lo, W. -c. (1987). The service industry in China—problems and prospects. Business Horizons, 30(4): 29-37. http://web. ebscohost. com/ ehost/pdf? vid = 2&hid = 106&sid = 6e04d3b5-a86b-46a2-bf00-b23a210f0d 47% 40sessionmgr102.

Hoffer, A. (1989). Can there be translation without interpretation? "In other words…" International Review of Psycho-Analysis, 16: 207-212.

Holstein, J. A. , & Gubrium, J. F. (1998). Phenomenology, ethnomethodology, and interpretive practice. In N. K. Denzin & Y. S. Lincoln (Eds.), Strategies of qualitative inquiry (pp. 137-151). Thousand Oaks, California: SAGE Publications Ltd.

Horsburgh, D. (2003). Evaluation of qualitative research. Journal of Clinical Nursing, 12 (2): 307-312. http://web. ebscohost. com/ehost/pdf? vid = 2&hid = 7&sid = 4fa248d9-2046-45 f3-b031-cdcff00d3670% 40sessionmgr9.

Howard, R. M. (1994). Review: Reflectivity and agency in rhetoric and pedagogy. College English, 56(3): 348-355. http://www. jstor. org/stable/378526? seq=1.

Hu, G. (2002a). Potential cultural resistance to pedagogical imports: The case of communicative language teaching in China. Language, Culture and Curriculum, 15(2): 93-105. http://www. multilingual-matters. net/lcc/015/0093/lcc0150093. pdf.

Hu, G. (2002b). Recent important development in secondary English-language teaching in the People's Republic of China. Language, Cultural and Curriculum, 15(1): 30-49.

Hu, G. (2003). English language teaching in China: regional differences and contributing factors. Journal of Multilingual & Multicultural Development, 24 (4): 290-318.

Hu, G. (2005a). "CLT is best for China"—an untenable absolutist claim. ELT Journal: English Language Teachers Journal, 59(1): 65.

Hu, G. (2005b). English language education in China: Policies, progress, and problems. Language Policy (4): 5-24.

Hu, G. (2005c). Professional development of secondary EFL teachers: lessons from China. Teachers College Record, 107 (4): 654-705. http://web. ebscohost. com/ehost/pdf? vid = 2&hid = 5&sid = 6a3f96e0-8d4b-4b 29-b746-84837fbea 590% 40sessionmgr3.

Hu, Y. (2007). China's foreign language policy on primary English education: what's behind it? Language Policy, 6: 359-376.

Huang, F. (2004). Curriculum reform in contemporary China: seven goals and six strategies. Curriculum Studies, 36(1): 101-115.

Huang, Y. (1999). Inflation and investment controls in China: the political economy of central-local relations during the reform era. Cambridge: Cambridge

University Press. http://books. google. com/books? hl = zh-CN&lr = &id = 90DMDU_0N0wC&o i = fnd&pg = PR9&dq = decentralized + and + centralized + in + politics + in + 1950s + in + China&ots = Ry0UkIt _ TM&sig = 0On2CVSB1t1r OtpWUgV2cUhwj98.

Hubbard, P. L. (1994). Non-transformational theories of grammar: implications for language teaching. In T. Odlin (Ed.), Perspectives on pedagogical grammar (pp. 49-71). Cambridge; New York, NY, USA: Cambridge University Press.

Hui, W. (2006). Depoliticized politics, multiple components of hegemony, and the eclipse of the Sixties. Inter-Asia Cultural Studies, 7(4): 683.

Hunnum, E. (1999). Political change and the urban-rural gap in basic education in China, 1949-1990. Comparative Education Review, 43(2): 193-211.

Husserl, E. (1931). Ideas: General introduction to pure phenomenology (W. R. Boyce Gibson, Trans.). London: Allen & Unwin.

Husserl, E., 1859-1938. (1970). The crisis of European sciences and transcendental phenomenology: an introduction to phenomenological philosophy. Evanston: Northwestern University Press.

Hutschenreiter, G., & Zhang, G. (2007). China's quest for innovation-driven growth—The policy dimension. Journal of Industry, Competition and Trade, 7 (3-4): 245-254.

Hycner, R. H. (1999). Some guidelines for the phenomenological analysis of interview data. In A. Bryman & R. Burgess (Eds.), Qualitative research (Vol. 3, pp. 143-164). London: SAGE.

Ilon, L. (2000). Knowledge, labour and education. Compare, 30(3): 275-282. http://web. ebscohost. com/ehost/pdf? vid = 2&hid = 103&sid = 08ef6d0d-a5474399-9b17-b909cba669f7 % 40sessionmgr108.

Imam, S. R. (2005). English as a global language and the question of nation-building education in Bangladesh. Comparative Education, 41(4): 471-486. PDF Available http://content. epnet. com/ContentServer. asp? T = P&P = AN&K = 18622121& EbscoContent = dGJyMNHr7ESeqLQ4v% 2BvlOLCmrk% 2Bepq9SsK64Tb KWxWXS&ContentCustomer = dGJyMPPk547g1% 2BqEuePf geyx% 2BEu 3q64A&D = aph.

Jacobs, L., Guopei, G., & Herbig, P. (1996). The past 2,000 years of business in Europe and China: why Europe is Europe and China is China. European Business Review, 96 (1): 26-30. http://www. emeraldinsight. com/Insight/

viewContentItem. do; jsessionid = 21 26A931A7A49F915CCCA3A78F5A48CD? contentType = Article&content Id = 869065.

Jacobs, R. A., & Rosenbaum, P. S. (1968). English transformational grammar. Waltham, Mass: Blaisdell Pub. Co.

James, S. (2004). Language development in the young child. In T. Maynard & N. Thomas (Eds.), An introduction to early childhood studies (pp. 28-38): SAGE.

Jay, P. (2001). Beyond discipline? Globalization and the future of English. PMLA, 116 (1): 32-47. http://links. jstor. org/sici? sici = 0030-8129% 28200101%29116%3A1%3C32 %3ABDGATF%3E2. 0. CO%3B2-R.

Jin, L., & Cortazzi, M. (2002). English language teaching in China: a bridge to the future. Asia-Pacific Journal of Education, 22(2): 53-64.

Jones, G. (2006). Other research method. In M. Walter (Ed.), Social research methods. South Melbourne: Oxford University Press.

Jong, I. -J. (2006). EFL teachers' perceptions of task-based language teaching: with a focus on Korean secondary classroom practice. Asian EFL Journal, 8 (3): 192-206.

Jun, J. S., & Wright, D. S. (1996). Globalization and decentralization. In J. S. Jun & D. S. Wright (Eds.), Globalization and decentralization: institutional contexts, policy issues, and intergovernmental relations in Japan and the United States (pp. 1-18). Washington, D. C. : Georgetown University Press.

Kanbur, R., & Zhang, X. (2005). Fifty years of regional inequality in China: a journey through central planning, reform, and openness. Review of Development Economics, 9 (1): 87-106. http://web. ebscohost. com/ehost/ pdf? vid = 2&hid = 107&sid = 43f3a405-3aaa4fb9-a3fc-9ff822c43278% 40session mgr109.

Kang, J. (1999). English everywhere in China. English today, 15(2): 46-48.

Kato, F. (1998). Second language acquisition and pedagogic grammar, 2009/02/ 28, from http://www. cels. bham. ac. uk/resources/essays/fuyuko2. pdf.

Ke, J., Chermack, T. J., KLee, Y. -H., & Lin, J. (2006). National human resource development in transitioning societies in the developing world: the People's Republic of China. Advances in Developing Human Resources, 8 (28): 28-45. http://adh. sagepub. com/cgi/reprint/8/1/28.

Kellner, D. (2002). Theorizing Globalization. Sociological Theory, 20(3): 285-

305. http://links. jstor. org/sici? sici = 0735-2751% 28200211% 2920% 3A3%3C285 %3ATG%3E2. 0. CO%3B2-H.

Kelly, P. F. (1999). The geographies and politics of globalization. Progress in Human Geography, 23(3): 379-400. http://web. ebscohost. com/ehost/pdf? vid=2&hid=104&sid=3d83e332-a69a-4438-af18-fa0d5d290907% 40sessionm gr103.

Kettl, D. (2000). The transformation of governance: globalization, devolution, and the role of government. Public Administration Review, 2000, 60(6): 488-497. http://collections. europarchive. org/tna/20040722012352/http://www. numb er-10. gov. uk/su/future%20structuers/fs_kettlpaper2. pdf.

Khan, H. A. (2004). Globalization: Challenges and Opportunities. Retrieved 2 February, 2009, from http://hdl. handle. net/2261/2536.

Khondker, H. H. (2004). Glocalization as globalization: evolution of a sociological concept. Bangladesh e-Journal of Sociology, 1 (2): 12-21. http://www. bangladeshsociology. org/Habib%20-%20Glocalization. htm.

Kinginger, C. (2002). Defining the zone of proximal development in US foreign language education. Applied Linguistics, 23 (2): 240-261. http://applij. oxfordjournals. org//cgi/reprint/23/2/240.

Kininger, C. , & Belz, J. A. (2005). Socio-cultural perspectives on pragmatic development in foreign language learning: microgenetic case studies from telecollaboration and residence abroad. Intercultural Pragmatics, 2(4): 369-421.

Klein, M. F. (1994). Toll for curriculum reform. In George Peabody College for Teachers (Ed.), Peabody Journal of Education (Vol. 69, pp. 19-34). Nashville, Tenn: George Peabody College of Teachers.

Klein, P. , & Westcott, M. R. (1994). The changing character of phenomenological psychology. Canadian Psychology/Psychologie canadienne, 35(2): 133-158.

Knight, P. T. (2002). Small-scale research. London, Thousand Oaks and New Delhi: SAGE Publications.

Koch, T. (2006). Establishing rigour in qualitative research: the decision trail. Journal of Advanced Nursing, 53 (1): 91-100. http://www3. interscience. wiley. com/cgi-bin/fulltext/118563198/PDFSTA RT.

Krashen, S. D. (1985). The Input hypothesis: issues and implications. London; New York: Longman.

Krippendorff, K. (2004). Content analysis: an introduction to its methodology (2rd ed.). Thousand Oaks, Calif.: Sage. http://books. google. com. au/books? hl = en&lr = &id = q657o3M3C8cC&oi = fn d&pg = PR13&dq = content+analysis&ots = bJ9iwXMcEX&sig = 2YIRoaDA DCDGBmDauP0gHlxjB1c#PPA12,M1.

Krkgöz, Y. (2008). Globalization and English language policy in Turkey. Retrieved 3 January, 2008, from http://epx. sagepub. com/cgi/rapidpdf/089590480831 6319v1. pdf.

Kubota, R. (2002). The impact of globalization on language teaching in Japan. In D. Block & D. Cameron (Eds.), Globalization and language teaching (pp. 13-28). London and New York: Routledge.

Kuhn, T. S. (1970). The structure of scientific revolutions (2nd ed.). Chicago: The University of Chicago Press.

Kumar, R. (2005). Research methodology: A step-by-step guide for beginners (2nd ed.). Frenchs Forest, NSW: Pearson Education Australia.

Kwok, P. (2004). Examination-oriented knowledge and value transformation in East Asian cram schools. Asia Pacific Education Review, 5(1): 64-75. http://eri. snu. ac. kr/aper/pdf/Vol%205%20No%201%20July%202004%20 PDF/07. Kwok. pdf.

Ladkin, D. (2005). "The enigma of subjectivity". Action Research, 3(1): 108-126. http://arj. sagepub. com/cgi/reprint/3/1/108.

Lakoff, R. (1973). Transformational grammar and language teaching. In M. Lester (Ed.), Readings in applied transformational grammar (pp. 285-310). New York: Holt, Rinehart and Winston, Inc.

Lam, A. S. L. (2002). English in education in China: Policy changes and learners' experiences. World Englishes, 21(2): 245-256.

Lam, A. S. L. (2005). Language education in China: Policy and experience from 1949. Hong Kong: Hong Kong University Press.

Lamie, J. M. (2006). Teacher education and training in China: Evaluating change with Chinese lecturers of English. Journal of In-Service Education, 32(1): 63-84.

Lan, Y. (2006). Social development of 21st century and reform of China's elementary education. Frontiers of Education in China, 1(3): 350-369. http://www. springerlink. com/content/d1442p02571wg76l/fulltext. pdf.

Lantolf, J. (1996). SLA theory building: "Letting all the flowers bloom!" Language

Learning, 46(4): 713-749.

Lantolf, J., & Pavlenko, A. (1995). Socialcutural theory and second language acquisition. Annual Review of Applied Linguistics, 15: 108-124.

Lantolf, J., & Thorne, S. L. (2006). Sociocultural theory and second language learning. In B. VanPatten & J. Williams (Eds.), Theories in Second Language Acquisition: Routledge.

Lantolf, J. P. (1994). Sociocultural theory and second language learning. The Modern Language Journal, 78(4): 418-420.

Lantolf, J. P., & Thorne, S. L. (2007). Sociocultural theory and second language learning. In B. VanPatten & J. Williams (Eds.), Theories in second language acquisition (pp. 201-223). Mahwah, New Jersey: Lawrence Erlaum Associates, Publishers.

Larsen-Freeman, D. (2000). Second language acquisition and applied linguistics. Annal Review of Applied Linguistics, 20: 165-181.

Lather, P. (1986). Issues of validity in openly ideological research: between a rock and a hard place. Interchange, 17(4): 63-84.

Lather, P. (1993). Fertile obsession: Validity after poststructuralism. The Sociological Quarterly, 34(4): 673-693.

Law, W.-W., & Ng, H. M. (2009). Globalization and multileveled citizenship education: A tale of two Chinese cities, Hong Kong and Shanghai. Teacher College Record.

Lawton, D. (1980). The politics of the school curriculum. London; Boston: Routledge & Kegan Paul.

Lee, E. (1997). Globalization and labour standards: a review of issues. International Labour Review, 136(2): 173-189. http://scholar. google. com. au/scholar? hl = en&lr = &q = info: Ee5D6ILO9FYJ: scholar. google. com/ &output = viewport&pg = 1.

Lee, M. B. (2005a). Curriculum evaluation. In N. S. Gwele & L. R. Uys (Eds.), Curriculum development in nursing: process and innovation (pp. 111-126). London; New York: Routledge.

Lee, R. (2005b). Globalization, language, and culture. Philadelphia: Chelsea House.

Leech, A. J. H. (1989). Another look at phenomenology and religious education. British Journal of Educational Studies, 11(2): 70-75. http://dx. doi. org/10.

1080/0141620890110203.

Les, T. (2005). Clarifying the life-world: descriptive phenomenology. In I. Holloway (Ed.), Qualitative research in health care (pp. 104-124). England: Open University Press.

LeVasseur, J. J. (2003). The problem of bracketing in Phenomenology. Qualitative Health Research, 13(3): 408-420. http://qhr. sagepub. com/cgi/reprint/13/3/408.

Lewis, K. R. (1972). Transformational-generative grammar: A new consideration to teaching foreign languages. The Modern Language Journal, 56(1): 3-10. http://www. jstor. org/view/00267902/ap020444/02a00010/0.

Li, B. (2009). Processed-centred teaching and its implications in English teaching in China. English Language Teaching, 2(1): 24-31. http://ccsenet. org/journal/index. php/elt/article/view/359/287#page=26.

Li, E. (2005). A study on the development of Chomsky's linguistics. Unpublished Masters, Fujian Normal University, Fuzhou.

Li, M. (2007). Foreign language education in primary schools in the People's Republic of China. Current Issues In Language Planning, 8(2): 148-160.

Li, Q. (1999). Teachers' beliefs and gender differences in mathematics: a review. Retrieved 6 January, 2008, from http://www. ucalgary. ca/ ~ qinli/publication/Teachers_beliefs_and_gender_d ifferences_in% 20mathematics. doc.

Liao, X. Q. (2000). Communicative language teaching innovation in China: Difficulties and solutions. Retrieved 3 June, 2009, from http://eric. ed. gov/ERICWebPortal/custom/portlets/recordDetails/detailmini. jsp? _ nfpb = true& _ &ERICExtSearch_SearchValue_0 = ED443294&ERICE xtSearch_SearchType_0 = no&accno = ED443294.

Liaoning Education Department. (2002). Printing and Distributing Liaoning Province Compulsory Education Local Curriculum Implementing Project (For Experiments). Retrieved 8 May, 2009, from http://blog. sina. com. cn/s/blog_400c36c80100cc7p. html.

Liaoning Education Department. (2006). Education: overview. Retrieved 2 February, 2009, from http://www. lnen. cn/secpage. htm? actionType = viewjsp &id = 3547.

Lietz, C. A. , Langer, C. L. , & Furman, R. (2006). Establishing trustworthiness in qualitative research in social work: implications from a study regarding spirituality. Qualitative Social Work, 5(4): 441-458. http://qsw. sagepub. com/cgi/reprint/5/4/441.

Lim, L., & Renshaw, P. (2001). The relevance of sociocultural theory to culturally diverse partnerships and communities. Journal of Child and Family Studies, 1 (1): 9-21.

Lin, J. Y., Cai, F., & Li, Z. (2003). The China miracle: development strategy and economic reform. Hong Kong: Chinese University Press. http://books. google. com. au/books? hl = en&lr = &id = _OEwbLZ2vYwC&oi = fnd&pg = PR19 &dq = The + development + in + China&ots = 0ylB-50-_ W&sig = gy29CEc E52t8vwMK1x8g13_lNyg.

Lincoln, Y. S., & Guba, E. G. (1985). Naturalistic inquiry. Beverly Hills, Calif: Sage Publications.

Lincoln, Y. S., & Guba, E. G. (2000). Paradigmatic controversies, contradictions, and emerging confluences. In N. K. Denzin & Y. S. Lincoln (Eds.), Handbook of qualitative research (2nd ed., pp. 163-188). Thousand Oaks, London, New Delhi: Sage Publications, Inc.

Lingard, B. (2000). It is and it isn't: Vernacular globalization, education policy, and reconstructing. In N. C. Burbules & C. A. Torres (Eds.), Globalization and education: Critical perspectives (pp. 79-108). New York; London: Routledge.

Littlewood, W. (1981). Communicative language teaching. Cambridge: Cambridge University Press.

Liu, S., & Teddlie, C. (2003). The ongoing development of teacher evaluation and curriculum reform in the People's Republic of China. Journal of Personnel Evaluation in Education, 17(3): 243-261. http://www. springerlink. com/ content/n2664103429q1511/.

Liu, Z. (2009). Age effects in foreign language learning for children in China. English Language Teaching, 2(1): 37-45.

Lívia, N. F. (2006). From theoretical to pedagogical grammar: Reinterpreting the role of grammar in English language teaching. Unpublished PhD, Pannon University, Veszprém.

Lo Bianco, J. (2000). Multiliteracies and multilingualism. In B. Cope & M. Kalantzis (Eds.), Multiliteracies: literacy learning and the design of social futures (pp. 92-105). South Yarra [Vic.]: Macmillan.

Lock, S. (1986). Second-language learners in the classroom: Some considerations. Victoria: Curriculum Branch, Ministry of Education.

Love, P. (2003). Document analysis. In F. K. Stage & K. Manning (Eds.), Research in the college context: approaches and methods (pp. 83-96): Routledhe.

Luo, W. (2007). English language teaching in Chinese universities in the era of the World Trade Organization: a learner perspective. Unpublished PhD, RMIT University, Melbourne.

Lyotard, J. F. (1991). Phenomenology (B. Brian, Trans.). Albany: State University of New York Press.

Lyotard, J. -F. (2006). The field: Knowledge in computerized societies. In E. F. Jr, Provenzo. (Ed.), Critical issues in education (pp. 297-302). Thousands Oaks, London and New Delhi: Sage Publications.

MacFarquhar, R. (1983). The origins of the Culture Revolution (Vol. 2). New York: Columbia University Press.

Mak, B. S. -Y., & White, C. (1996). Communication apprehension of Chinese ESL students. Hong Kong Journals for Applied Linguistics, 2 (1): 81-95. http://sunzi1.lib.hku.hk/hkjo/view/5/500020.pdf.

Malhotra, N., Hall, J., Shaw, M., & Oppenheim, P. (Eds.). (2006). Marketing research: An applied orientation (3rd ed.). Frenchs Forest, N. S. W.: Pearson Education Australia.

Marsh, C. J. (1992). Key concepts for understanding curriculum. London; New York: Falmer Press.

Marsh, C. J. (2004). Key concepts for understanding curriculum (3rd ed.). London: RoutledgeFalmer.

Marsh, C. J., & Willis, G. (2007). Curriculum: Alternative approaches, ongoing issues. Columbus, Ohio: Pearson Merrill Prentice Hall.

Marshall, C. (2006). Designing qualitative research. Thousands Oaks, London and New Delhi: SAGE Publications.

Martin, T. (2005). Comprehensive readings on English curriculum standards for EFL teachers (Modified). Retrieved 3 April, 2009, from http://222.247.48.14/dtxkw/Soft/UploadSoft/200711/20071121181921679.doc.

Mathew, S. (2005). China's economic growth faces challenges. Retrieved 15 May, 2009, from http://www.ers.usda.gov/AmberWaves/February05/Findings/

ChinaEcono micGrowth. htm.

Mays, N. , & Catherine. , P. (2000). Assessing quality in qualitative research. Qualitative research in health care, 320: 50-52.

McEneaney, E. H. , & Meyer, J. W. (2000). The content of the curriculum: In institutionalist perspective. In M. T. Hallinan (Ed.), Handbooks of Sociology and Social Research (pp. 189-211). New York: Kluwer Academic/Plenum.

McKay, S. (2003). Teaching English as an international language: The Chilean context. ELT Journal: English Language Teachers Journal, 57(2): 139-148.

Mckernan, J. (2008). Curriculum and imagination: Process theory, pedagogy and action research. London; New York: Routledge.

McLaughlin, C. , & Fitzsimmons, J. (1996). Strategies for globalizing service operations. International Journal of Service Industry Management, 7(4): 43-57.

McLoughlin, C. , & Oliver, R. (1999). Instructional design for cultural difference: A case study of the indigenous online learning in a tertiary context. Retrieved 3 March, 2008, from http://www. ascilite. org. au/conferences/brisbane99/papers/mcloughlinolive r. pdf.

McMillan, J. H. , & Schumacher, A. (2001). Research in education. New York: Addison, Wesley Longman.

McTaggart, R. (1998). Is validity really an issue for participatory action research? Culture and Organization, 4 (2): 211-236. http://pdfserve. informaworld. com/263920_751313631_779784319. pdf.

Merleau-Ponty, M. , 1908-1961. (1962). Phenomenology of perception (C. Smith, Trans.). London: New York: Routledge.

Merriam, S. B. (1998). Qualitative research and case study applications in education: Revised and expanded from case study research in education. San Francisco: Jossey-Bass Publishers.

Metcalfe, A. , & Game, A. (2006). The teacher's enthusiasm. Australian Educational Researcher, 33 (3): 91-106. http://www. aare. edu. au/aer/online/0603f. pdf. http://search. informit. com. au/fullText; res = AEIPT; dn = 157902.

Ministry of Education. (1993). Quanrizhi zhongxue Yingyu Jiaoxue Dagang [English language syllabus for full-time junior secondary school]. Beijing: People's Education Press.

Ministry of Education. (1998). An action plan on resuscitating education for the 21st century. Retrieved 1 August, 2008, from http://news. xinhuanet. com/zhengfu/20010516/565908. htm.

Ministry of Education. (2000). Notice on teacher education of elites in basic education at national level. Retrieved 2 March, 2007, from http://www. 69law. com/Article/LAW_chl/18852. htm.

Ministry of Education. (2001a). English Curriculum Standards (X. Zhang, Trans.). Beijing: Beijing Normal University Press.

Ministry of Education. (2001b). Jiaoyubu bangongting guanyu yinfa<guanyu jiancha liaoningdeng qisheng (zizhiqu) shishi "zhongxiaoxue jiaoshi jixu jiaoyu gongcheng" qingkuang de tongbao> de tongzhi. Retrieved 9 February, 2009, from http://www. edu. cn/20041126/3122424. shtml.

Ministry of Education. (2001c). Jiaoyubu guanyu jiji tuijin xiaoxue kaishe yingyu kecheng de zhidao yijian (The Ministry of Education guidelines for vigorously promoting the teaching of English in primary schools). Retrieved 9 February, 2009, from http://www. edu. cn/20010907/3000637. shtml.

Ministry of Education. (2001d). Juchu jiaoyu kecheng gaige gangyao (shixing) [The outline of curriculum reform of basic education (For experiments)]. Retrieved 16 March, 2008, from http://www. edu. cn/20010926/3002911. shtml.

Ministry of Education. (2001e). A notice about expansion of teacher education on new curricula for basic education. Beijing. Ministry of Education announcement to schools. (Translator, Zhang, X.).

Mittelman, J. H. (2000). The globalization syndrome: Transformation and resistance. Princeton, N. J. : Princeton University Press.

Modiano, M. (2000). Rethinking ELT. English Today, 62(16): 28-34.

Modiano, M. (2001). Linguistic imperialism, cultural integrity, and EIL. ELT Journal, 55(4): 339-346.

Mok, J. K. H., & Lee, M. H. H. (2003). Globalization or glocalization? Higher education reforms in Singapore. Asia Pacific Journal of Education, 23(1): 15-42. http://dx. doi. org/10. 1080/0218879030230103.

Mok, K. (2003). Globalization and higher education restructuring in Hong Kong, Taiwan and Mainland China. Higher Education Research and Development. http://dx. doi. org/10. 1080/07294360304111.

Mok, K. -h. (2002). Policy of decentralization and changing governance of higher edcuation in post-Mao China. Public Administration and Development, 22(3): 261-273. http://www3. interscience. wiley. com/cgi-bin/fulltext/96015355/ PDFSTART.

Mondada, L., & Doehler, S. P. (2004). Second language acquisition as situated practice: Task accomplishment in the French second language cassroom. The Modern Language Journal, 88(4): 501-518.

Moon, B. (1994). The national curriculum: Origins, context and implementation. In B. Moon & A. S. Mayes (Eds.), Teaching and learning in the secondary school (pp. 245-260). London; New York: Routledge.

Moore, D. R. (2002). Competence, competency and competencies: Performance assessment in organisations. Work Study, 51 (6): 314-319. http://www. emeraldinsight. com/Insight/viewPDF. jsp? Filename = html/Outp ut/Published/ EmeraldFullTextArticle/Pdf/0790510605. pdf.

Morrow, S. L. (2005). Quality and trustworthiness in qualitative research in counseling psychology. Journal of Counseling Psychology, 52(2): 250-260.

Moustakas, C. E. (1994). Phenomenological research methods. Thousand Oaks, Calif. : Sage.

Moyles, J., & Hargreaves, L. (1998). The primary curriculum: Learning from international perspectives. London and New York: Routledge.

Murray, J. S. (1999). Methodological triangulation in a study of social support for siblings of children with cancer. Journal of Pediatric Oncology Nursing (4): 194-200. http://jpo. sagepub. com/cgi/reprint/16/4/194.

Myers, L. L. (2000, March 31-April, 2001). Task interpretation and task effectiveness: A Vygotskian analysis of a French L2 classroom task. Paper presented at the Texas Foreign Language Education conference 2000 (TexFLEC 2000), Austin, Texas.

National Council for the Social Studies. (1994). Expectations of excellence: Curriculum standards for social studies. Washington, D. C. : The Council.

National Education Committee. (1993). English Syllabus (X. Zhang, Trans.). Beijing: People's Education Press.

Neil, B. (1979). Phenomenology and Education. British Journal of Educational Studies, 27(3): 245-258.

Neuman, S. B., & Koskinen, P. (1991). Captioned television as "comprehensible input": effects of incidental word learning from context for language minority students. Retrieved 3 April, 2008, from http://eric. ed. gov/ERICDocs/data/ericdocs2sql/content_storage_01/000001 9b/80/22/f3/af. pdf.

Neuman, W. L. (1997). Social research methods: Qualitative and quantitative approaches. Boston: Allyn and Bacon.

Newton Suter, W. (2006). Introduction to educational research: A critical thinking approach. Thousand Oaks, London and New Delhi: SAGE Publications.

Ng, C., & Tang, E. (1997). Teachers' need in the process of EFL reform in China: a report from Shanghai. Retrieved 3 March, 2009, from http://sunzi1. lib. hku. hk/hkjo/view/10/1000116. pdf.

Ngok, K. -l. , & Kwong, J. (2003). Globalization and educational restructuring in China. In K. Mok & A. Welch (Eds.), Globalization and educational restructuring in the Asia Pacific region (pp. 160-188.). Houndmills UK and New York: Palgrave Macmillan.

Nida, E. A. (2001). Contexts in translating. Amsterdam; Philadelphia: J. Benjamins Pub. Co.

Nijman, J. (1999). Cultural globalization and the identity of place: The reconstruction of Amsterdam. Cultural Geographies, 6(2): 146-164. TEXT * PDF Available http://content. epnet. com/ContentServer. asp? T = P&P = AN&K = 1829501&E bscoContent = dGJyMNHX8kSep7Y4v% 2BvlOLCmrk% 2BeqK5Ssq% 2B4 SbOWxWXS&ContentCustomer = dGJyMPPk547gl% 2BqEueP fgeyx%2B Eu3q64A&D=aph.

Niss, M. (1993). Investigations into assessment in mathematics education. Dordrecht; Boston: Kluwer Academic.

Nunan, D. (2003). The impact of English as a global language on educational policies and practices in the Asia-Pacific region. TESOL Quarterly, 37(4): 589-613.

Nunan, D. (2004). Task-based language teaching. London: Cambridge University Press.

O' Leary, Z. (2004). The essential guide to doing research. London, Thousand Oaks and New Delhi: SAGE Publications.

O'Brien, E. A. (2003). Human values and their importance to the development of forestry policy in Britain: a literature review. Forestry, 76(1): 3-17.

Okano, K. (2006). Language in schools in Asia: Globalisation and local forces. Language & Education: an International Journal, 20(4): 263.

Olssen, M., Codd, J. A., & O'Neill, A.-M. (2004). Education policy: globalization, citizenship and democracy. London; Thousand Oaks, Calif: Sage Publications. http://www. loc. gov/catdir/enhancements/fy0657/2003106638-d. html.

Omaggio, A. C. (1993). Teaching language in context. Boston, Mass. : Heinle & Heinle.

Ornstein, A. C. (2007). Philosophy as a basis for curriculum decisions. In A. C. Ornstein, E. F. Pajak & S. B. Ornstein (Eds.), Contemporary issues in curriculum (4th ed. , pp. 5-21). Sydney: Pearson.

Ortega, L. (2007). Second language learning explained? SLA across nine contemporary theories. In B. VanPatten & J. Williams (Eds.), Theories in second language acquisition: an introduction (pp. 224-251). Mahwah, New Jersey: Lawrence Erlbaum Associates, Publishers.

Overholt, W. H. (2005). China and globalization. Retrieved 5 May, 2007, from http://www. rand. org/pubs/testimonies/2005/RAND_CT244. pdf.

Oxford, R. L. (2006). Task-based language teaching and learning: Overview. Asian EFL Journal, 8(3): 94-121.

Oyelade, A. F. (2002). Cultural reconstructionism and the Nigerian educational system. Retrieved 5 June, 2008, from http://www. ijeunilorin. net/dec2002/CULTURAL%20RECONSTRUCTIO NISM. pdf.

Ozmon, H. A., & Craver, S. M. (2008). Philosophical foundations of education (8th ed.). Upper Saddle River, New Jersey: Pearson/Merrill Prentice Hall.

Packer, M. J., & Goicoechea, J. (2000). Sociocultural and constructivist theories of learning: Ontology, not just epistemology. Educational Psychologist, 35(4): 227-241. http://pdfserve. informaworld. com/84987_751313631_784754679. pdf.

Paine, L. (1995). Teacher education in search of a metaphor: Defining the relationship between teachers, teaching and the state in China. In M. B. Ginsburg & B. Lindsay (Eds.), The political dimension in teacher education (pp. 76-98). London; Washington, DC: Falmer Press.

Pang, J., Zhou, X., & Fu, Z. (2002). English for international trade: China enters the WTO. World Englishes, 21 (2), 201. PDF Available http://content. epnet. com/ContentServer. asp? T = P&P = AN&K = 7122950&Ebsco Content = dGJyMNXb4kSep7c40dvuOLCmrk% 2BeqK5Sr624TLCWxWXS&Content

Customer = dGJyMPPk547g1%2BqEuePfgeyx%2BEu3q64 A&D = aph.

Parks, M. W. (2006). I am from a very small town: Social reconstructionism and multicultural education. Multicultural Perspectives, 8 (2): 46-50. PDF. Available http://content. epnet. com/ContentServer. asp? T = P&P = AN&K = 22172864& EbscoContent = dGJyMMTo50Sep644v%2BvlOLCmrk%2BeprFSrqe4 Sq%2BWxWXS&ContentCustomer = dGJyMPPk547g1%2BqEuePfgeyx%2BEu3q64 A&D = aph.

Patton, M. Q. (2002). Qualitative research and evaluation methods (3rd ed.). Thousand Oaks, Calif: Sage Publications.

Phillimore, J., & Goodson, L. (2004). Progress in qualitative research in tourism. In J. Phillimore & L. Goodson (Eds.), Qualitative research in tourism: ontologies, epistemologies and methodologies (pp. 3-29). New York: Routledge.

Phillipson, S. N. (2007). The regular Chinese classroom. In S. N. Phillipson (Ed.), Learning diversity in the Chinese classroom (pp. 3-34). Hong Kong: Hong Kong University Press.

Phuong-Mai, N., Terlouw, C., & Pilot, A. (2006). Culturally appropriate pedagogy: The case of group learning in a Confucian Heritage Culture context. Intercultural Education, 17 (1): 1-19. http://content. epnet. com/ ContentServer. asp? T = P& P = AN& K = 20189829& EbscoContent = dGJyMNLr40Sep7U4y9fwOLCmrlGep7ZSsqu4SK% 2BWxWXS&ContentCustomer = dGJyMPPk547g1%2BqEuePfgeyx%2BEu3q64A& D = aph.

Pintó, R. (2004). Introducing curriculum innovations in science: identifying teachers' transformations and the design of related teacher education. 89(1): 1-12. http://www3. interscience. wiley. com/cgi-bin/fulltext/109795422/PDFSTART.

Poon, S. K., Tang, C., & Reed, S. (1997). Problem-based learning in distance education. Paper presented at the 5th International Conference on Modern Industrial Training, Jinan, China.

Priestley, M. (2002). Global discourses and national reconstruction: The impact of globalization on curriculum policy. Curriculum Journal, 13(1): 121-138.

Pusack, J., & Otto, S. (1997). Taking control of multimedia. Technology-enhanced language learning.

Qi, W., & Tang, H. (2004). The social and cultural background of contemproary moral edcuation in China. Journal of Moral Education, 33(4): 465-480.

Qiang, N., & Woff, M. (2005). English as a foreign language: The modern day

Trojan horse? Retrieved 15 January, 2009, from http://www. usingenglish. com/esl-in-china/trojan-horse. pdf.

Qing, G. , & Meng, W. (2007). China's new national curriculum reform: Innovation, challenges and strategies. Front. Educ. China, 2(4): 579-604.

Race, P. , Brown, S. , & Smith, B. (2005). 500 tips on assessment (2nd ed.). London; New York. Routledge Falmer.

Ran, A. (2001). Travelling on parallel tracks: Chinese parents and English teachers. Educational Researcher, 43(3): 311-328. http://web. ebscohost. com/ehost/pdf? vid = 2&hid = 115&sid = d96b7742-4ceb-44ce-beaf-f2ce 29eaf7a2%40sessionmgr102.

Rao, Z. (2006). Understanding Chinese students' use of language learning strategies from cultural and educational perspectives. Journal of Multilingual & Multicultural Development, 27(6). http://web. ebscohost. com/ehost/pdf? vid = 2&hid = 2&sid = 95b4ae34-f1e4-41 eb-8886-35b44138b1a8%40sessionmgr2.

Rastall, P. (2006). Introduction: the Chinese learner in higher education—transition and quality issues. Language, Culture & Curriculum, 19(1): 1.

Reed, D. F. , & Davis, M. D. (1999). Social reconstructionism for urban students. Cleaning House, 72(5): 291-294. http://aaelinf. lib. latrobe. edu. au:8331/V/UB5GKAT3YQYB2JYTY881K5 RUU121T7JG.

Rees, G. , Fevre, R. , Furlong, J. , & Gorard, S. (2006). History, biography and place in the learning society: towards a sociology of life-long learning. In H. Lauder, P. Brown, J. -A. Dillabough & A. H. Halsey (Eds.), Education, globalization, and social change (pp. 926-935). Oxford; New York: Oxford University Press.

Rehorick, D. , & Taylor, G. (1995). Thoughtful incoherence: first encounters with the phenomenological-hermeneutic domain. Human Studies, 18: 389-414.

Reitz, R. R. (1999). Batterers' expereinces of being violent: A phenomenology study. Psychology of Women Quarterly, 23: 143-165. http://www3. interscience. wiley. com/cgi-bin/fulltext/119937033/PDFSTART.

Remillard, J. T. (1999). Curriculum materials in mathematics education reform: A framework for examing teachers' curriculum development. Curriculum Inquiry, 29(3): 315-342.

Ren, X. u. (2008). Architecture and nation building in the age of globalization: construction of the National Stadium of Beijing for the 2008 Olympics. Journal of

Urban Affairs, 30 (2): 175-190. http://faculty. washington. edu/stevehar/ Birdsnest. pdf.

Renou, J. (2001). An examination of the relationship between metalinguistic awareness and second-language proficiency of adult learners of French. Language Awareness, 10 (4): 248-267. http://multilingual-matters. net/la/ 010/0248/la0100248. pdf.

Richards, J. C. (2001). Curriculum development in language teaching. New York: Cambridge University Press.

Richards, J. C. (2002). Theories of teaching in language teaching. Retrieved 3 July, 2008, from http://sunzi1. lib. hku. hk/hkjo/view/10/1000037. pdf.

Richards, J. C. , & Rodgers, T. S. (2001). Approaches and methods in language teaching (2nd ed.). Cambridge; New York: Cambridge University Press.

Rie Konno Rn, B. , Mn. (2008). Lived experience of overseas-qualitified nurses from non-English-speaking backgrounds in Australia. Unpublished PhD, The university of Adelaide, Australia.

Rizvi, F. (2005). International education and the production of cosmopolitan identities. Retrieved 25 May, 2009, from http://www. cgs. uiuc. edu/ resources/conf_seminars_workshops/TSRizvi. pdf.

Rizvi, F. , & Walsh, L. (1998). Difference, globalisation and the internationalisation of curriculum. Australian University' Review, 41(2): 7-11.

Robert, H. (2005). Globalization. In A. Harrington (Ed.), Modern social theory (pp. 292-312). Oxford, New York: Oxford University Press.

Robertson, R. (1992). Globalization: social theory and global culture. London: Sage.

Robertson, R. (1995). Glocalization: Time-space and homogeneity-heterogeniety. In F. Mike, L. Scott & R. Robertson (Eds.), Global Modernities.

Robertson, R. , & Scholte, J. A. (Eds.). (2007). Encyclopedia of globalization. New York: Routledge.

Rogan, J. M. , & Grayson, D. J. (2003). Towards a theory of curriculum implementation with particular reference to science education in developing countries. International Journal of Science Education, 25 (10): 1171-1204. http:// pdfserve. informaworld. com/832892_731196568_716100207. pdf.

Rolls, L. , & Relf, M. (2006). Bracketing interviews: Addressing methodological challenges in qualitative interviewing in bereavement and palliative care.

Mortality, 11(3): 286-305. http://content. epnet. com/ContentServer. asp? T = P& P = AN&K = 21894418&EbscoContent = dGJyMMTo50 SeprI4yOvqOL CmrlCepq9Srqe4TLeWxWXS&ContentCustomer = dGJyMPPk547g1% 2BqEuePf geyx%2BEu3q64A& D=aph.

Rondinelli, D. A. (2007). Globalization and the Asian economic response. In D. A. Rondinelli & J. M. Heffron (Eds.), Globalization and change in Asia (pp. 39-64). Boulder, Colo: Lynne Rienner Publishers.

Rondinelli, D. A., & Heffron, J. M. (2007). Adjusting to globalization: Change and transformation in Asia. In D. A. Rondinelli & J. M. Heffron (Eds.), Globalization and change in Asia (pp. 1-14). Boulder, Colo.: Lynne Rienner Publishers.

Roseman, D. (2005). The WTO and telecommunications services in China: Three years on. info, 7(2): 25-48. http://www. emeraldinsight. com/Insight/view ContentItem. do; jsessionid = E D527FCE539B938B006CB8F3130625C0? contentType=Article&contentI d=1464969.

Salo, O. -P. (1998). Developing language in social context: On the relationship between dialogical theory and the study of language acquisition. In M. Lähteenmäki & H. Dufva (Eds.), Dialogues on Bakhtin: interdisciplinary readings (pp. 72-86). Jyväskylä: University Printing House, Jyväskylä.

Savignon, S. J., Savignon, S. J., & Wang, C. (2003). Communicative language teaching in EFL contexts: Learner attitudes and perceptions. IRAL: International Review of Applied Linguistics in Language Teaching, 41(3): 223. Scheurich, J. J., 1944-. (1997). The masks of validity: A deconstructive investigation. In J. J. Scheurich (Ed.), Research method in the postmodern. London; Washington, DC: Falmer Press.

Scholte, J. (2003). What Is Globalization? The Definitional Issue—Again. Paper presented at the The Symposium on Globalization: Past and Future, UK. http://www2. warwick. ac. uk/fac/soc/pais/staff/brassett/teaching/scholte-glo balization. pdf.

Schutz, A. (1963). Concept and theory formation in the social science. In M. A. Natanson (Ed.), Phylosophy of the social science (pp. 46-302). New York: Rondam House.

Schutz, A. (1973). Collected papers (Vol. 3). The Hague: Nijhoff.

Scott, D. (2003). Introduction. In D. Scott (Ed.), Curriculum studies: Major themes in education (pp. 1-6). London; New York: Routledge Falmer.

Scott, D. (2008). Critical essays on major curriculum theorists. London; New York: Routledge.

Scott, D. , & Morrison, M. (2005). Key ideas in educational research. London and New York: Continuum.

Sham, C. (2007). An exploratory study of corporate universities in China. Journal of Workplace Learning, 19(4): 257-264. http://www. emeraldinsight. com/ Insight/viewContentItem. do; jsessionid = 3 B89BB774AED128E3322082CCAD 28D01? contentType = Article&conten tId = 1603282.

Shao, X. (2004). Teachers' perceptions toward curriculum reform and in-service training programs in Chinese agricultural schools. Retrieved 26 June, 2009.

Sharma, C. K. (2008). Emerging dimensions of decentralization debate in the age of glocalization. Retrieved 05-05-09, 2009, from http://mpra. ub. uni-muenchen. de/6734/1/MPRA_paper_6734. pdf.

Shenton, A. K. (2004). Strategies for ensuring trustworthiness in qualitative research projects. Education for Information, 22 (2): 63-75. http://web. ebscohost. com/ehost/pdf? vid = 2&hid = 104&sid = ecdb489b-d0fe4679-b65f-d89a68268b4b%40sessionmgr104.

Shulman, L. S. (1994). Those who understand knowledge growth in teaching. In B. Moon & A. S. Mayes (Eds.), Teaching and learning in the secondary school (pp. 125-137). London; New York: Routledge.

Shulman, L. S. (2007). Knowledge and teaching: Foundations of the new reform. In A. C. Ornstein, E. F. Pajak & S. B. Ornstein (Eds.), Contemporary issues in curriculum (pp. 113-131). Boston: Pearson/AandB.

Silverman, D. (2000). Doing qualitative research: a practical handbook. London, Thousand Oaks and New Delhi: SAGE Publications.

Simmons, V. C. , & Robert-Weah, W. (2000). Service-learning and social reconstructionism: A critical opportunity for leardership. In C. R. O' Grady (Ed.), Integrating service learning and multicultural education in colleges and universities (pp. 189-207). Mahwah, N. J. : L. Erlbaum Associates.

Smith, C. A. , Vellenga, H. E. , Parker, M. , & Butler, N. L. (2006). Meeting the demands for TESL/TEFL teachers: An iterdisciplinary approach to increasing program accessibility and effectiveness. Retrieved 19 March, 2009, from http://forumonpublicpolicy. com/archivespring07/smith. rev. pdf.

Smith, D. G. (2003). Curriculum and teaching face globalization. In W. F. Pinar (Ed.), International handbook of curriculum research. Mahwah, New Jersey: Lawrence Erlbaum Associates, Inc.

Smith, J. L. (2007). The contribution of EFL programs to community development in China. Asian EFL Journal, 9(1): 177-194. http://asian-efl-journal.com/March_2007_EBook.pdf#page=177.

Smyth, J., & Shacklock, G. (1998). Behind the "cleansing" of socially critical research accounts. In J. Smyth & G. Shacklock (Eds.), Being reflexive in critical educational and social research (pp.1-13). London: Falmer Press.

Spiegelberg, H. (1982). The phenomenological movement: a historical introduction. The Hague: Nijhoff.

Stake, R. E. (1978). The case study method in social inquiry. Educational Researcher, 7(5-8).

Stake, R. E. (1995). The art of case study research. Thousand Oaks, London and New Delhi: Sage Publications.

Stake, R. E. (2000). Case studies (2nd ed.). Thousand Oaks, London and New Delhi: Sage Publication, Inc.

Stanley, W. B. (1992). Curriculum for Utopia: Social reconstructionism and critical pedagogy in the postmodern era. Albany: State University of New York Press.

Steinberg, L. D., Greenberger, E., Garduque, L., & McAuliffe, S. (1982). High school students in the labor force: some costs and benefits to schooling and learning. Educational evaluation and policy analysis, 4(3): 363-372. http://epa.sagepub.com/cgi/reprint/4/3/363.

Stern, B. S., & Riley, K. L. (2001). Reflecting on the common good: Harold Rugg and the social reconstructionism. Social Studies, 92(2): 56-59. http://www.questia.com/googleScholar.qst:jsessionid=Ls2d6Q31b19Jmkn yXW1b4Jb.

Stromquist, N. P. (2002). Education in a globalizedworld: the connectivity of economic power, technology, and knowledge. Lanbam, Boulder, New York and Oxford: Rowman and Littlefoeld Publishers, Inc.

Sturman, A. (1999). Case study methods. In J. P. Keeves (Ed.), Issues in educational research (pp.103-112). Kidlington, Oxford, UK; New York, NY: Pergamon.

Suárez-Orozco, M. M., & Qin-Hilliard, D. B. (2004). Globalization: culture and education in the new millennium. In M. M. Suárez-Orozco & D. B. Qin-Hilliard (Eds.) , Globalization: culture and education in the new millennium (pp. 1-28). Berkeley: University of California Press.

Sun, G. , & Cheng, L. (2000). From context to curriculum: a case study of communicative language teaching in China. Retrieved 6 April, 2009, from http://eric. ed. gov/ERICDocs/data/ericdocs2sql/content_storage_01/000001 9b/80/16/52/10. pdf.

Swales, J. (1987). Utilizing the literatures in teaching the research paper. TESOL Quarterly, 21 (1): 41-68. http://links. jstor. org/sici? sici = 0039-8322% 28198703%2921%3A1%3C41 %3AUTLITT%3E2. 0. CO%3B2-G.

Swanson, C. , & Stevenson, D. (2002). Standards-based reform in practice: evidence on state policy and classroom instruction from the NAEP state assessments. Educational evaluation and policy analysis, 24(1): 1-27. http:// epa. sagepub. com/cgi/reprint/24/1/1.

Tabulawa, R. (1998). Teachers' perspectives on classroom practice in Botswana: implications for pedagogical change. Qualitative studies in education, 11(2): 249-268. http://pdfserve. informaworld. com/166946_751313631_713848563. pdf.

Tan, S. S. (2007). Whither societas civilis in the Asia-Pacific after 11 September: Ideological absolutism and ethics in an age of terror. Australian Journal of International Affairs, 61 (2): 232-246. http://pdfserve. informaworld. com/ 934291_751313631_778944361. pdf.

Tanner, D. , & Tanner, L. (1995). Curriculum development: theory into practice. Englewood Cliffs, N. J. : Merrill.

Tanner, D. , & Tanner, L. (2007). Curriculum development: theory into practice (4th ed.). Upper Saddle River, N. J. : Pearson Merrill/Prentice Hall.

Tellis, W. (1997). Introduction to case study. The Qualitative Report, 3(2): 1-11. http://www. nova. edu/ssss/QR/QR3-2/tellis1. html.

Thomas, T. M. (1994). Multicultural education: reconstructionism coming of age. Retrieved 23 May, 2008, from http://teqjournal. org/backvols/1994/21_4/f94_ thomas. pdf.

Tobin, K. , & Dowson, G. (1992). Constraints to curriculum reform: teachers and the Myths of schooling. Educational Technology Research and Development, 40 (1): 21-92.

Toombs, S. K. (2001). Introduction: phenomenology and medicine. In S. K. Toombs (Ed.), Handbook of Phenomenology and Medicine (pp. 1-28). Dordrecht; London: Kluwer Academic.

Torres, C. A. (2002). Globalization, education, and citizenship: Solidarity versus markets? American Educational Research Journal, 39(2): 363-378. http:// aer. sagepub. com/cgi/reprint/39/2/363.

Tsang, M. C. (2000). Education and national development in China since 1949: Oscillating policies and enduring dilemmas. Retrieved 12 September, 2007, from http://www. teacherscollege. edu/centers/coce/pdf_files/d1. pdf.

Tsang, M. C. (2001). School choice in the People's Republic of China. Internet. http://www. teacherscollege. edu/centers/coce/pdf_files/b1. pdf.

Turner, B. S. (2000). Review essay: Citizenship and political globalization. Citizenship Studies, 4(1): 81. PDF Available http://content. epnet. com/ ContentServer. asp? T = P&P = AN&K = 3807721&E bscoContent = dGJyMNHX 8kSep684v% 2BvlOLCmrk% 2BeqLFSs6m4S7S WxWXS&Content Customer = dGJyMPPk547g1%2BqEuePfgeyx%2BEu3 q64A&D = aph.

Udvari-Solner, A. , & Thousand, J. S. (1996). Creating a responsive curriculum for inclusive schools. Remedial and Special Education, 17(3): 182-191. http://aarlinf. lib. latrobe. edu. au: 8331/V/9HV3HCA95GLG5YRMRESE1U CC4QK64XRF2AXFAEI5Y95AV9CSYB-06856? func = meta-3&short-for mat = 002&set_number = 000053&set_entry = 000001&format = 999.

Uys, L. R. (2005a). Developing a micro-curriculum. In L. R. Uys & N. S. Gwele (Eds.), Curriculum development in nursing: process and innovation (pp. 69-92). London; New York: Routledge.

Uys, L. R. (2005b). An overview of the process of curiculum development. In L. R. Uys & N. S. Gwele (Eds.), Curriculum development in nursing: process and innovation (pp. 21-32). London; New York: Routledge.

van Driel, J. H. , Verloop, N. , & Beijaard, D. (2001). Professional development and reform in science education: the role of teachers' practical knowledge. Journal of Research in Science Teaching, 38(2): 137-158. http://www3. interscience. wiley. com/cgi-bin/fulltext/76508802/PDFSTART.

van Driel, J. H. , Verloop, N. , & de Vos, W. (1998). Developing science teachers' pedagogical content knowledge. Journal of Research in Science Teaching, 35(6): 673-695. http://www3. interscience. wiley. com/cgi-bin/

fulltext/31871/PDFSTART.

van Manen, M. (1990). Researching lived experience: human science for an action sensitive pedagogy. London, Ont. : Althouse Press.

van Manen, M. (1997). From Meaning to Method. Qualitative Health Research, 7 (3): 345-369.

van Manen, M. (2003). On the meaning of pedagogy and its relation to curriculum and teaching. In S. David (Ed.), Curriculum studies: major themes in education (Vol. III, pp. 415-462). London and New York: RoutledgeFalmer.

Van Zanten, A. (2002). Educational change and new cleavages between head teachers, teachers and parents: global and local perspectives on the French case. Journal of Education Policy, 17(3): 289-304. javascript:open_window_ resource_name "http://aarlinf. lib. latrobe. edu. au: 8331/V/VFJDKAVTXVJ149 EJ6FC5FJ6TEQ9LCFMRSVXQBDHDUSE B6S8RX6-06532? func = full-external- exec&doc_number=031396757&line _number=0018&service_type=TAG".

VanPatten, B. , & Williams, J. (2006). Early theories in second language acquisition. In B. VanPatten & J. Williams (Eds.), Theories in second language acquisition (pp. 17-36): Routledge.

VanPatten, B. , & Williams, J. (2007). Early theories in second language acquisition. In B. VanPatten & J. Williams (Eds.), Theories in Second Language Acquisition. Mahwah, N. J. : Lawrence Erlbaum Associates Inc.

Vidovich, L. , Yang, R. , & Currie, J. (2007). Changing accountabilities in higher education as China "opens up" to globalization. Globalization, Societies & Education, 5(1): 89.

Vinson, K. D. (1998, 20-22, November, 1998). National curriculum standards and social studies education: Dewey, Freire, Foucault, and the construction of a radical citique. Paper presented at the 78th Annual Meeting of the National Council for the social Studies, Anaheim, CA. http://eric. ed. gov/ERICDocs/ data/ericdocs2sql/content_storage_01/000001 9b/80/16/0d/48. pdf.

Vygotskiy, L. S. (1978). Mind in society: the development of higher psychological processes. Cambridge: Harvard University Press.

Walker, D. F. , & Soltis, J. F. (1992). Curriculum and aims. New York: Teachers College Press.

Walter, M. (2006). The nature of social science research. In M. Walter (Ed.), Social research methods: an Australian perspective (pp. 1-28). South

Melbourne: Oxford University Press.

Wang, C., & Bergquist, M. (2003). Basic education development in China: From finance reform to World Bank projects. International Journal of Educational Management, 17 (7): 303-311. http://www. emeraldinsight. com/Insight/viewContentItem. do; jsessionid = D 3151A2ADD888A6B0B02EDDC515A4E50? contentType = Article&conte ntId = 838865.

Wang, M. (2004). Ethnic diversity and citizenship education in the People's Republic of China. In J. A. Banks (Ed.), Diversity and citizenship education: global perspectives (pp. 334-355). San Francisco, Calif: Jossey-Bass.

Wang, Q. (2007). The national curriculum changes and their effects on English language teaching in the People's Republic of China. In J. Cummins & C. Davison (Eds.), International Handbook of English Language Teaching (Vol. 15). Hong Kong: Springer.

Wang, W., & Lam, A. S. L. (2009). The English language curriculum for senior secondary school in China: Its evolution from 1949. RELC Journal, 40(1): 65-82. http://rel. sagepub. com/cgi/reprint/40/1/65.

Wang, X. (2008). Teachers' views on conducting formative assessment in the Chinese context. Engineering Letters, 16(2). http://www. engineeringletters. com/issues_v16/issue_2/EL_16_2_08. pdf.

Wang, Y., & Robertson, M. (2004). The influence of China's entry into the WTO on foreign language education in China. Retrieved 28 May, 2009, from http://www. aare. edu. au/04pap/rob04729. pdf.

Wardhaugh, R., Phillipson, R., & Crystal, D. (2003). Roles and impact of English as a global language. Retrieved 5 September, 2008, from http://www. cels. bham. ac. uk/resources/essays/Doms6. pdf.

Warschauer, M. (2000). The changing global economy and the future of English teaching. TESOL Quarterly, 34 (3): 511-535. http://links. jstor. org/sici? sici = 0039-8322% 28200023% 2934% 3A3% 3C511 % 3ATCGEAT% 3E2. 0. CO% 3B2-2.

Waters, M. (1995). Globalization. London and New York: Routledge.

Waylen, G. (2004). Putting governance into the gendered political economy of globalization. International Feminist Journal of Politics, 6 (4): 557. PDF Available http://content. epnet. com/ContentServer. asp? T = P&P = AN&K =

15328787& EbscoContent = dGJyMNXb4kSeqLc4v% 2BvlOLCmrk% 2BeqLFSsKi4Sre WxWXS&ContentCustomer = dGJyMPPk547g1% 2BqEuePfgeyx% 2BEu3q64A&D = aph.

Wei, B. , & Thomas, G. P. (2005). Rationale and approaches for embedding scientific literacy into the new junior secondary school chemistry curriculum in the People's Republic of China. International Journal of Science Education, 27 (12): 1477-1493. PDF Available http://content. epnet. com/ContentServer. asp? T = P&P = AN&K = 18685407& EbscoContent = dGJyMNHr7ESeqLQ4v% 2BvlOLCmrk% 2BeqK9Ss6a4SL CWxWXS&ContentCustomer = dGJyMPPk 547g1% 2BqEuePfgeyx% 2BEu 3q64A&D = aph.

Wei, H. (2008). The characteristics of China's compulsory education funding policy change, 1986-2006. Front. Educ. China, 3 (1): 115-122. http://www. springerlink. com/content/0521123484556742/fulltext. pdf.

Went, R. (2000). Globalization: neoliberal challenge, radical responses (P. Drucker, Trans.). London, Sterling, Virginia: Pluto Press.

Wertsch, J. V. , Del Rio, P. , & Alvarez, A. (1995). Sociocultural studies: history, action, and mediation. In J. V. Wertsch, P. Del Río & A. Alvarez (Eds.), Sociocultural Studies of Mind (pp. 1-34). Cambridge; New York: Cambridge University Press.

Wighting, M. J. , Nisbet, D. L. , & Tindall, E. R. (2005). Exploring a summer English language camp experience in China: a descriptive case study. Asian EFL Journal, 7 (4): 85-108. http://. asian-efl-journal. com/december_05_ mw&dn&et. php.

Wildy, H. , & Louden, W. (2000). School restructuring and the dilemmas of principals' work. Educational Management Administration and Leadership, 28 (2): 173-184.

Willis, K. (2006). Analysis qualitative data. In M. Walter (Ed.), Social research methods: an Australian perspective (pp. 257-281). South Melbourne: Oxford University Press.

Willis, P. (1999). Looking for what it's really like: Phenomenology in reflective practice. Studies in Continuing Education, 21 (1): 91-112. http://content. epnet. com/ContentServer. asp? T = P& P = AN& K = 6196976&EbscoContent = dGJyMNLr40SeqK44zOX0OLCmrk% 2Bep7dSr664TbSWxWXS&ContentCustomer = dGJyMPPk547g1% 2BqEuePfgeyx% 2BEu3q64A&D = aph.

Winter, G. (2000). A comparative discussion of the notion of "validity" in qualitative and quantitative research. The Qualitative Report, 4 (3 & 4). http://www. nova. edu/ssss/QR/QR4-3/winter. html.

Winter, S. (2001). Ontology: Buzzword or paradigm shift in GI science. International Journal of Geographical Information Science, 15 (7): 587-590. http://lab. geog. ntu. edu. tw/course/gislucc/GIS_Paper/ontology. pdf.

Wishart, J. (2008). Challenges faced by modern foreign language teacher trainees in using handheld pocket PCs (Personal Digital Assistants) to support their teaching and learning. ReCALL, 20 (3): 348-360. http://journals. cambridge. org/download. php? file =% 2FREC% 2FREC20 _ 03% 2FS0958344008000736 a. pdf&code = 5c328efc1 aad47551d84a553e6b9 2ef1.

Wong, L. (2004). Market reforms, globalization and social justice in China. Journal of Contemporary China, 13(38): 151-171. http://pdfserve. informaworld. com/782689_751313631_713622578. pdf.

Wong, N.-Y. (2008). Confucian heritage culture learner's phenomenon: From "exploring the middle zone" to "constructing a bridge". ZDM, 40(6): 973-981. http://www. springerlink. com/content/vjl13327p0q7v432/fulltext. pdf.

Wood, D., Bruner, J. S., & Ross, G. (1976). The role of tutoring in problem solving. Journal of Child Psychology and Psychiatry, 17(2): 89-100.

Woodward, R. (2003). An "ation" not a "nation": the globalization of world politics. In J. Michile (Ed.), The handbook of globalisation (pp. 309-317). Cheltenham and Northampton: Edward Elgar Publishing, Inc.

Wu, Y. A. (2001). English language teaching in China: trends and challenges. TESOL Quarterly, 35(1): 191-194.

Xu, F., & Warschauer, M. (2004). Technology and curricular reform in China: a case study. TESOL Quarterly, 38(2): 301-323.

Yang, F. (2002). Education in China. Educational Philosophy and Theory, 34 (2): 135-144. http://search. informit. com. au/fullText; res = APAFT; dn = 200202413.

Yang, T. (2005). A brief statement on educational principle of the People's Republic of China. US-China Review, 2(3): 26-29. http://eric. ed. gov/ ERICDocs/data/ericdocs2sql/content_storage_01/0000019b/80/27/f9/24. pdf.

Yin, R. K. (1994). Case study research: design and methods. Thousand Oaks, Calif: Sage.

Yin, R. K. (2003a). Application of case study research (2nd ed.). Thousand Oaks, London and New Delhi: SAGE Publications, Inc.

Yin, R. K. (2003b). Case study research: design and methods (3rd ed.). Thousand Oaks, Calif: Sage Publications Inc.

Yin, R. K. (2006). Case study methods. In G. Judith L, C. Gregory & E. Patricia B (Eds.), Handbook of complementary methods in education research (pp. 111-122).

Yonezawa, A. (2003). The impact of globalization on higher education governance in Japan. Higher Education Research & Development, 22(2): 145. PDF Available http://content. epnet. com/ContentServer. asp? T = P&P = AN&K = 9756008&EbscoContent = dGJyMNHX8kSeqLA40dvuOLCmrk% 2BeqK9Srqa4 TLKWxWXS&ContentCustomer=dGJyMPPk547g1%2BqEuePfgeyx%2BEu3q64 A&D=aph.

Yong, Y. (2006). Zhuanhuan shengcheng lilun dui yingyu jiaoxue de qishi (Inspiration of Transformational Grammar to English teaching in secondary schools). Basic Education: Foreign Language Research, 3.

Yu, L. (2001). Communicative language teaching in China: Progress and resistance. TESOL Quarterly, 35(1): 194-198.

Yueh, M. -C. M. (2007). Introducing a new subject: the case of environmental education in Taiwanese junior high schools. Unpublished PhD, University of Waikato, Waikato.

Zeegers, M. (2000). A Mercantilist Cinderella: Deakin University and the distance education student in the postmodern world. Geelong: Deakin University. http://adt. caul. edu. au/homesearch/find/? recordid = 132355&format = main.

Zeegers, M., & Zhang, X. (2005). China and secondary school textbooks: Surface and deep learning approaches. Paper presented at the Future of the Book, Beijing.

Zeng, T., Deng, Y., Yang, Y., Zou, X., & Chu, Z. (2007). Balanced development of compulsory education: Cornerstone of education equity. Front. Educ. China, 2(4): 469-493.

Zhan, S. (2008). Changes to a Chinese pre-service language teacher education program: Analysis, results and implications. Asia Pacific Journal of Teacher Education, 36(1): 53-70. http://dx. doi. org/10. 1080/13598660701793392.

Zhang, H., & Zhong, Q. (2003). Curriculum studies in China: retrospect and prospect. In W. F. Pinar (Ed.), International handbook of curriculum research. Mahwah, New Jersey: Lawrence Erlbaum Associates, Inc.

Zhang, X. (2006). Fiscal decentralization and political centralization in China: implications for growth and inequality. Journal of Comparative Economics, 34 (4): 1-16. http://www. wider. unu. edu/stc/repec/pdfs/rp2006/rp2006-93. pdf.

Zhang, X. (2008, 29-31/10/2008). The role of EFL teachers' knowledge in current EFL curriculum reform: an understanding from a Reconstructionist perspective. Paper presented at the Third International Language Learning Conference 2008, Malaysia.

Zhang, X. & Zeegers, M. (2010). Redefining the role of English as a foreign language in the curriculum in the global context. Changing English, 17 (2): 177-187.

Zhang, X. (2011). Interpreting China's changing status of English language education. Journal of Fujian University of Teachnology, 9 (5): 476-480.

Zhang, X. (2011). Construction of reliability in educational qualitative research. Journal of Liaoning Educational Administration Institute, 28 (4): 17-19.

Zhang, Y. , & Zhao, K. (2007). Impact of Beijing Olympic-related investments on regional economic growth of China: Interregional input-output approach. Asian Economic Journal, 21 (3): 261-282. http://www3. interscience. wiley. com/ cgi-bin/fulltext/118522770/PDFSTART.

Zhao, Y. , & Campbell, K. (1995). English in China. World Englishes, 14 (3): 377-390.

Zheng, D. -l. (2008). Krashen's input hypothesis and English classroom teaching. US-China Foreign Language, 6 (9): 53-56.

Zheng, X. , & Adamson, B. (2003). The pedagogy of a secondary school teacher o English in the People's Republic of China: challenging the stereotypes. RELC Journal, 34 (3): 323-337. PDF Available http://content. epnet. com/ ContentServer. asp? T = P&P = AN&K = 14658003&EbscoContent = dGJy MNXb4kSeqLc4v%2BvlOLCmrk%2BeprJSs664TbCWxWX S&ContentCustomer = dGJyMPPk547gl%2BqEuePfgeyx%2BEu3q64A&D = aph.

Zheng, X. -m. , & Davison, C. (2008). Changing pedagogy. London; New York: Continuum.

Zhong, Q. -q. (2006). Curriculum reform in China: challenges and reflections.

Frontiers of Education in China, 1(3): 370-382. http://www. springerlink. com/content/51q326m148lr706t/fulltext. pdf.

Zhong, Q. -q. , Cui, Y. , & Zhang, H. (2001). For renewal of the Chinese nation, for the development of every student (X. Zhang, Trans.). Shanghai: East China Normal University.

Zhou, H. (2002). Preface (X. Zhang, Trans.). In X. Zhang (Ed.), New curriculum teaching design. Dalian: Liaoning Normal University Press.

Zhou, W. (2008). Development in China: China-U. S. economic and trade relations (pp. 112-115). Ohio, the United States: Vital Speeches of the Day. Speech.

Zhu, C. , & Dowling, P. (1998). Performance appraisal in China. In J. Selmer (Ed.), International management in China: cross-cultural issues (pp. 115-136): Routledge.

Zhu, H. (2003). Globalization and new ELT challenges in China. English Today, 19(4): 36-41.

Zhu, M. (1999). The views and involvement of Chinese parents in their children's education. Prospects, XXIX (2): 233-238. http://www. springerlink. com/content/vl55658p21837xh1/fulltext. pdf.

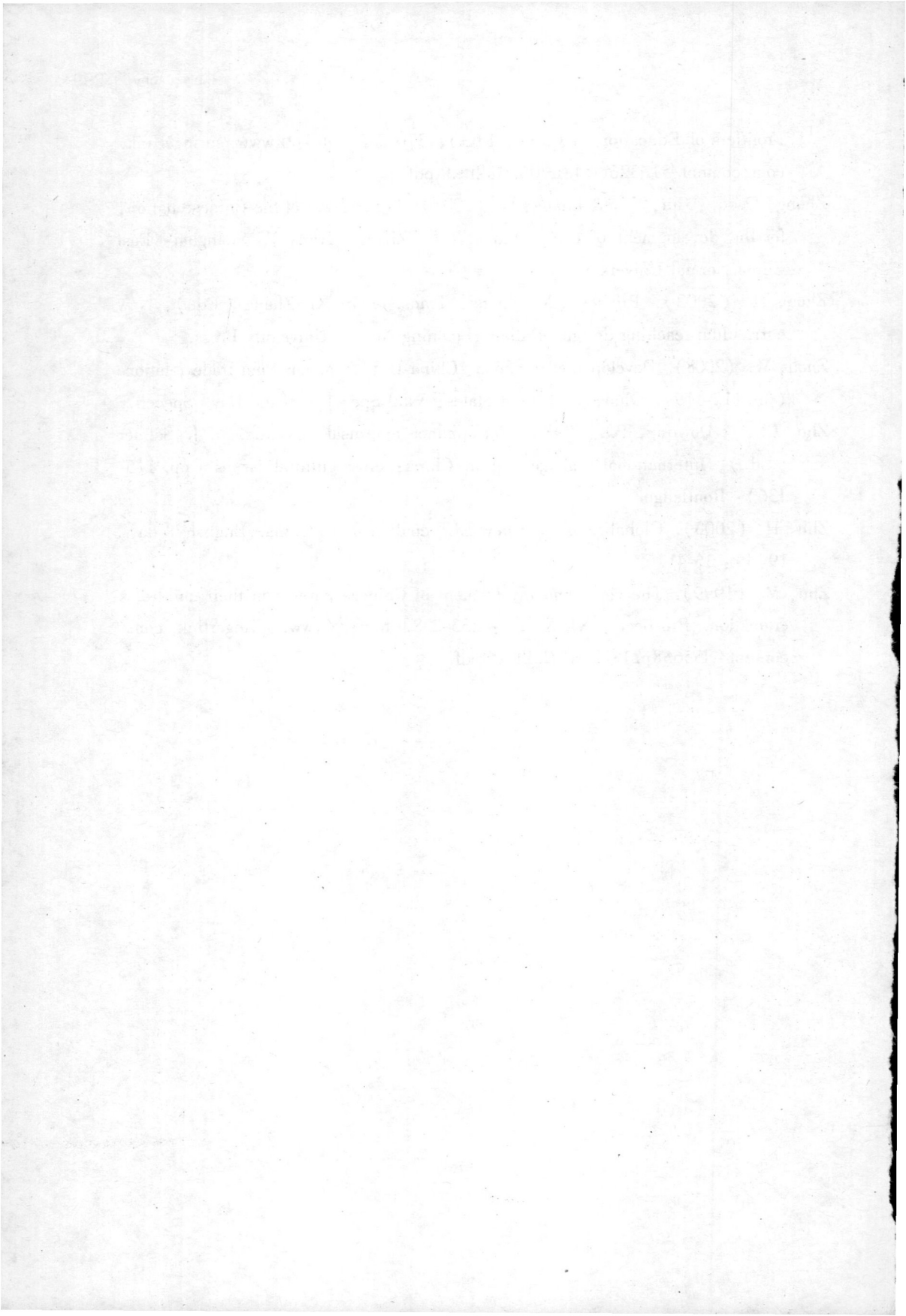